Human Rights and the Environment

Queen Mary Studies in International Law

Edited by

Malgosia Fitzmaurice, Panos Merkouris
and Phoebe Okowa

VOLUME 3

Human Rights and the Environment

Philosophical, Theoretical and Legal Perspectives

By

Linda Hajjar Leib

MARTINUS
NIJHOFF
PUBLISHERS

LEIDEN • BOSTON
2011

Library of Congress Cataloging-in-Publication Data

Leib, Linda Hajjar.
Human rights and the environment : philosophical, theoretical, and legal perspectives / by Linda Hajjar Leib.
p. cm. -- (Queen Mary studies in international law ; v. 3)
Includes bibliographical references.
ISBN 978-90-04-18864-8 (hardback : alk. paper) 1. Environmental law, International. 2. Human rights. I. Title.
K3585.L445 2011
344.04'6--dc22

2010042485

ISSN 1877-4822
ISBN 978 90 04 18864 8

Dedicated with love to Mark, Priscilla and Jackson

CONTENTS

LIST OF ACRONYMS AND ABBREVIATIONS

ACHR	American Convention on Human Rights
African Commission	African Commission on Human and Peoples' Rights
Banjul Charter	African Charter on Human and Peoples' Rights
CEDAW	Convention on the Elimination of All Forms of Discrimination against Women
CESCR	Committee on Economic, Social and Cultural Rights
DPSP	Directive Principles of State Policy
DRTD	Declaration on the Right to Development
ECHR	European Commission on Human Rights
ECtHR	European Court of Human Rights
ESCR	Economic, Social and Cultural Rights
European Convention	European Convention on Human Rights
IACHR	Inter-American Commission on Human Rights
ICCPR	International Covenant on Civil and Political Rights
ICESCR	International Covenant on Economic, Social and Cultural Rights
ICJ	International Court of Justice
ILA Declaration	International Law Association (ILA) New Delhi Declaration of Principles of International Law Relating to Sustainable Development
Inter-American Court	Inter-American Court of Human Rights
IPCC	Intergovernmental Panel on Climate Change
IUCN Draft Covenant	IUCN Draft International Covenant on Environment and Development
MNCs	Multinational Corporations
OHCHR	Office of the High Commissioner for Human Rights
OP-ICESCR	Optional Protocol to the International Covenant on Economic, Social and Cultural Rights
SERAC	Social and Economic Rights Action Centre
UDHR	Universal Declaration of Human Rights
UNCED	United Nations Conference on Environment and Development
UNEP	United Nations Environment Programme

UNFCCC	United Nations Framework Convention on Climate Change
UNHRC	United Nations Human Rights Committee
WSSD	World Summit on Sustainable Development
1994 Draft Declaration	1994 Draft Declaration of Principles on Human Rights and the Environment

INTRODUCTION

"We are not expendable. We are not flowers to be offered at the altar of profit and power. We are dancing flames committed to conquering darkness. We are challenging those who threaten the survival of the planet and the magic and mystery of life."[1]

Rachida Bee, Bhopal, India

Humankind all over the world is confronting tremendous environmental challenges in the form of global warming, pollution, loss of biodiversity, deforestation and desertification. The deepening ecological crisis our generation is witnessing is likely only to get worse. According to the 2006 Living Planet Report, "the Earth's regenerative capacity can no longer keep up with demand—people are turning resources into waste faster than nature can turn waste back into resources. Humanity is no longer living off nature's interest but drawing down its capital."[2] To date, global environmental issues have largely been dealt with through the machinery of international environmental law. However, even with a plethora of international environmental treaties and declarations as well as domestic environmental laws and policies,[3] one might ask what else can be done to reverse the destruction of natural ecosystems and to protect human beings, especially the most disadvantaged and vulnerable communities of the world, from the devastating effects of environmental despoliation.

Of course, there is no one way to deal with such a complex and global problem as environmental degradation. While the primary aim of environmental law is the regulation of environment-related activities, the human rights system carries the potential to address the effects of environmental degradation

[1] EarthRights International, "Bhopal Survivors Win 2004 Goldman Prize," http://www.earthrights.org/index2.php?option=com_content&do_pdf=1&id=80.

[2] World Wildlife Fund International (WWF) and Global Footprint Network, "Living Planet Report 2006," http://assets.panda.org/downloads/living_planet_report.pdf.

[3] In fact, international environmental law is the most rapidly evolving branch of international law. It is made up of "some 350 multilateral treaties, 1,000 bilateral treaties and a multitude of instruments of intergovernmental organisations that have been adopted in the form of declarations, programmes of action and resolutions." See *Final Report Prepared by the Special Rapporteur on Human Rights and the Environment*, Fatma Zohra Ksentini, Commission on Human Rights, UN Doc E/CN.4/Sub.2/1994/9. As of 2005, the UNEP's Register of International Treaties and other Agreements enumerated a total of 272 international treaties in the field of the environment and related instruments (such as amendments) on the basis of relevant information made available to the secretariat of UNEP. See *Register of International Treaties and Other Agreements in the Field of the Environment*, UN Doc UNEP/Env.Law/2005/3 (2005).

on human beings. The human rights system offers sophisticated legal and extra-legal mechanisms necessary to tackle both the severe impact of human activities on the environment and the human rights implications of ecological degradation. There are three main reasons for incorporating environmental concerns into the human rights sphere. First, the realm of human rights has unique mechanisms and methods that help promote environmental protection by empowering states, peoples and individuals to defend the interests of both human rights and ecosystems. Grounding environmental concerns in the human rights tradition is in response to the inability of international environmental law and policy as well as municipal administrative and legislative authorities to address these vital concerns alone. Second, environmental issues, until now considered the privilege of policy-makers, are increasingly becoming an important matter for human rights advocates, judges and other stakeholders. Environmental rights equip human rights activists, environmentalists and victims of environmental degradation with a powerful tool with which to overcome the 'sovereignty wall' often raised as a barrier to any form of state liability. International human rights law, unlike other forms of international law, deals with issues that arise between individuals or groups of individuals and an offending state, whether it is their state of citizenship, state of residence, or a foreign state. Third, human rights approaches to environmental issues are gaining currency in both international and domestic law. In 2008, the UN Human Rights Council formally declared climate change a human rights issue.[4] At the same time, many regional human rights instruments and national constitutions have explicitly recognised environmental human rights, albeit under different formulations, but these emerging statements of rights have stirred heated debate about their definition, scope, nature and enforcement.

This book seeks to achieve three main objectives. First, it examines the genesis and development of environmental rights (or the Right to Environment)[5] in international law and discusses their philosophical, theoretical and legal underpinnings. Second, it attempts to determine the scope and content of the 'Right to Environment' in the context of sustainable development and the notion of solidarity rights. Third, and most important, it explores the potential impact of emerging environmental rights on the international human rights system. In doing so, I consider two sets of concepts: first, the possibility of a rapprochement between environmental ethics and the human rights doctrine

[4] *Draft Resolution on Human Rights and Climate Change*, UNHRC, 7th sess, UN Doc A/HRC/7/L.21/Rev.1(2008).

[5] Because of the multiplicity of formulations used in connection with the human right to environment, I initially use environmental human rights and the right to environment interchangeably. In Chapter 4 below, I differentiate between both terms and propose the adoption of a 'Right to Environment' on the international level, similar to the right to development.

and, second, the theoretical and practical links among the concepts of development, democracy, environment and sustainable development. Accordingly, research questions that revolve around the book's objectives are explored through three levels of analysis (Figure 1):

- What are the philosophical and theoretical bases that underpin the interrelatedness between human rights and the environment?
- How does the conceptualisation of the 'Right to Environment', as a universal right, align with sustainable development rhetoric and third-generation rights?
- What are the nature and scope of the emerging right(s)? Do they refer to a 'Right to Environment' or to environmental rights?
- What is the purpose of a distinct 'Right to Environment' in the presence of the well-established human rights often invoked in an environmental context?

Several points help to provide conceptual clarification as this discussion proceeds:

1. Definition and the content of the 'Right to Environment'

The ambiguity and elasticity of the claims and rights ascribed to the environment and its living and non-living components are essential to the debate surrounding the potential links between human rights and the environment. For clarity, I adopt the term 'environmental human rights' as a broad conceptualisation that includes the many formulations used in the human rights approaches to environmental issues that are based on the sustainable use, maintenance and recovery of ecosystems. Throughout this book, many narrower formulations, such as the right to a clean environment or the right to a healthy environment, are referred to where cited by writers and scholars or in international and regional instruments and national constitutions. Moreover, I propose the adoption of a distinct 'Right to Environment' in international law, considered a solidarity right similar to the well-recognised right to development. The relationships among the 'Right to Environment' as a solidarity right, the right to development, environmental human rights and other human rights are elaborated in Chapter 4. However, this book does not attempt to provide a clear-cut definition of environmental rights, which would be an unrealistic target; rather, it highlights the potential frameworks that may be used to establish a clearer definition in the future.

2. Anthropocentrism versus ecocentrism

The anthropocentric-ecocentric dichotomy reflects two main strands of thought in environmental ethics. While anthropocentrism focuses on the centrality of human beings in environmental protection and conservation, ecocentrism advocates that non-human beings and entities be protected for their own worth, regardless of human interests. Drawing upon the concept of ecocentrism, I propose the inclusion of the rights of nature as the ecocentric dimension of environmental human rights. Despite the expected predominance of the human dimension in human rights discourse, environmental human rights have their own peculiarities. The inextricable connection between human beings and ecosystems makes these rights more ecocentric or (less exclusively anthropocentric) than other human rights.

3. The breadth of coverage

Environmental issues are often transnational because they reflect interdependencies based on natural, rather than political, geography. Global warming is a striking example of the scientific and socio-political complexities of global ecological threats. International law is one of the legal channels by which states can cooperate. The proliferation of multilateral international agreements after World War II reflects the commitment of the international community to deal with environmental issues. However, with some notable exceptions, such as ozone depletion, this trend in international lawmaking has had limited practical effect on the state of the environment.[6] Sovereignty and the global market are major hurdles to the advancement of international environmental law. In some respects, these obstacles validate the case for international environmental rights since human rights discourse has been historically conceived as able to permeate sovereign boundaries. Pollution, large-scale deforestation and illicit dumping of toxic waste have detrimental trans-boundary implications and should be addressed on the international stage. Nevertheless, this book presents environmental rights, not as a substitute for international environmental law, but as a complementary tool to existing instruments and principles. Similarly, a human rights approach to environmentalism cannot provide all of the elements essential to preserving and enhancing functioning ecosystems throughout the world, although it is an important strategy.

4. Third-generation rights or solidarity rights

Whether to fit the environment into traditional human rights or to expand the theory to include the third generation of human rights is a key question for the future recognition and implementation of environmental rights. The Czech-French jurist Karel Vasak, who coined the term 'third generation' of rights, defined the first generation of rights, a reflection of liberalism and individualism, as encompassing civil and political rights such as the right to life and the right to freedom of speech.[7] The second generation of rights,

---

[6] Rajendra Ramlogan, "The Environment and International Law: Rethinking the Traditional Approach," *Vermont Journal of Environmental Law* 3(2001-2002), http://www.vjel.org/journal/VJEL10008.html.

[7] Karel Vasak, "Pour Une Troisième Génération Des Droits De L'homme," in *ÉTudes Et Essais Sur Le Droit International Humanitaire Et Sur Les Principes De La Croix-Rouge En L'honneur De Jean Pictet* (Comité International de la Croix-Rouge 1984).

associated with Marxist theory and socialism, embodies social, economic and cultural rights such as the right to health and the right to education. Third-generation rights, known as solidarity or collective rights, constitute a new set of rights such as the right to development and the right to environment.[8] Because of the collective nature of this nascent set of rights and the breadth of issues they address, much more involvement from the international community is required to bring them into effect.[9] Accordingly, I differentiate between the international 'Right to Environment', considering it a solidarity right, and the set of substantive environmental rights, which can be adjudicated in the courts of law.

5. Sustainable development as a conceptual framework

Investigating the role that sustainable development plays as a facilitator or inhibitor of the recognition of international environmental rights is also useful in terms of conceptual clarification. Since the 1987 Brundtland Report of the World Commission on Environment and Development,[10] sustainable development rhetoric has swept the arena of environmental law but the flexibility of the concept has created a degree of ambiguity regarding its objectives. By focusing on sustainability, the Rio Declaration gave the impression that a new branch of international law was on its way to replace international environmental law. Throughout this book, the theme of sustainable development and the emerging legal principles related to it are considered a new paradigm for global, regional, national and local development. However, it is beyond the scope of this book to provide an in-depth analysis of the controversies and interpretations surrounding the new paradigm of sustainable development.

In order to construct the elements necessary to the conceptualisation of the Right to Environment and its sub-rights, I draw upon various disciplines and bodies of knowledge including the history of environmental philosophy, environmental ethics, human rights and sustainable development. The identification of synergies and/or incompatibilities among these concepts informs the three levels of analysis portrayed in Figure 1. Obviously, the interdisciplinary nature of this research stems from the examination of the above-mentioned disciplines. Through these levels of analysis, I attempt to develop a holistic understanding and a well-rounded vision of the philosophical, ethical and normative aspects of the emerging legal norms, identified herein as environmental rights.

---

[8] Prudence E. Taylor, "From Environmental to Ecological Human Rights: A New Dynamic in International Law?" *Georgetown International Environmental Law Review* 10(1998): 317-19.

[9] Ibid., 319.

[10] The World Commission on Environment and Development, *Our Common Future* (Oxford: Oxford University Press, 1987).

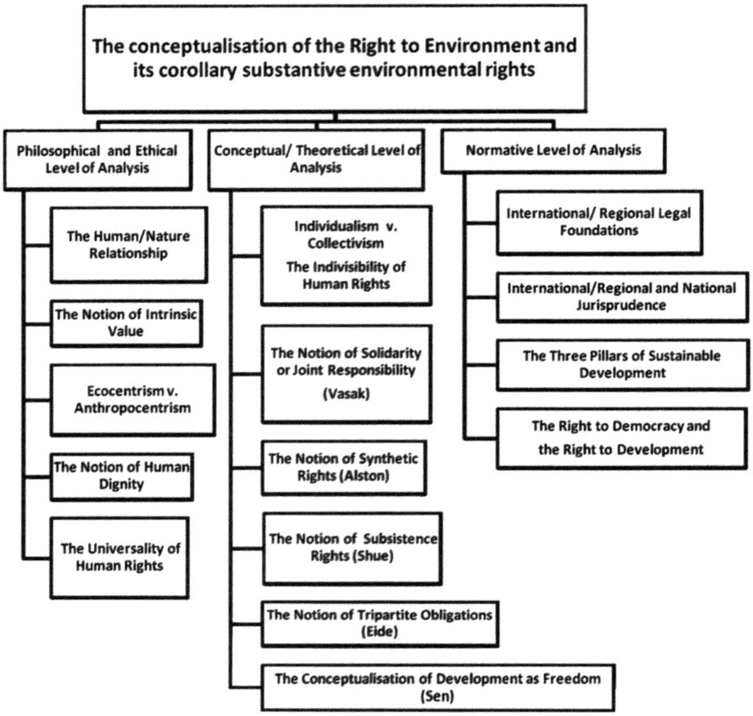

Fig.1. The Three Levels of Analysis.

As Figure 1 shows, the first level of analysis deals with the philosophical and ethical underpinnings of the links between human rights and the environment. To establish these links, I explore the human/nature relationship and the various ethical perspectives that emanate from philosophical debate. Of particular importance to this level of analysis are the notions of human dignity and the intrinsic worth of nature. The second level of analysis considers the various theories, notions and concepts that inform the two-level conceptualisation of environmental rights and the reconfiguration of human rights proposed in this book. This level of analysis surveys the theoretical foundations of human rights and draws upon notions of synthetic rights, basic rights and tripartite obligations. The interrelationships among the concepts of development, environment and democracy are examined in relation to sustainable development, the notion of solidarity and emerging environmental rights. The third level of analysis identifies the normative foundations of environmental rights in international/regional instruments, judicial decisions and the three pillars of sustainable development.

The book is divided into two parts, the first of which examines the two components of environmental rights: the environment and human rights. Chapter 1 delves into the roots of our ecological problems and the emergence of environmentalism and major concepts of environmental ethics, fleshing out the relationship problem between humankind and nature and underlining the philosophical and ethical foundations of the human rights-based approaches to environmental issues. Chapter 2 outlines the characteristics and controversies of the concept of human rights and highlights the criteria necessary to classify a claim as a human right. The second part of the book draws upon the theories, concepts and notions examined in the first part in order to establish and justify the theoretical and conceptual underpinnings of emerging environmental human rights. Chapter 3 presents a theoretical framework of the scholarly debate around the right to environment and tracks the evolution of environmental rights. Chapter 4 offers an innovative conceptualisation of environmental rights and a reconfiguration of the human rights system in light of sustainable development and solidarity rights. It stresses that contemporary approaches to human rights and the environment are now located in the sustainable development discourse; since the Johannesburg Summit and the Millennium Development Goals, the emphasis has been on poverty alleviation with clear ties to well-established political, civil, economic and social rights.

PART ONE

SETTING THE SCENE

CHAPTER ONE

HISTORICAL AND PHILOSOPHICAL UNDERPINNINGS OF THE ENVIRONMENTAL MOVEMENT

Introduction

In order to examine the subject of environmental human rights, it is necessary to locate it in its historical and philosophical contexts. A relevant environmental philosophy is a prerequisite for understanding our ecological problems and their potential solutions. Environmental philosophy was brought to prominence with the debate about the relationship between humans and nature and the possibility of extending the domain of ethics and rights to non-human beings or to nature as a whole.[1] As Lynn White Jr., an American historian, said, "what people do about their ecology depends on what they think about themselves in relation to things around them."[2]

This chapter consists of three sections. Section A explores the roots of our ecological crisis as depicted by philosophers and environmental writers. Section B sheds light on the emergence and development of environmentalism. By drawing upon the history of environmentalism and the development in environmental philosophy, Section C provides an overview of the ethical facets and philosophical trends of environmentalism.

A. *Roots of the Environmental Crisis*

The term 'environment' is derived from the French verb *environner*, meaning to surround or encircle. Thus, in an ecological and biological context, the environment can be defined as 'the complex of physical, chemical and biotic factors that surround and act upon an organism or ecosystem.'[3] This meaning implies that the environment is peripheral to the organisms or people that live within it.[4] The term 'ecosphere' provides a more precise and substantial substitute for the term 'environment'. The ecosphere is composed of four equally important constituents: atmosphere (air), hydrosphere (water), lithosphere

[1] Roderick Frazier Nash, *The Rights of Nature: A History of Environmental Ethics* (Wisconsin: University of Wisconsin Press, 1989), 4.

[2] Lynn White, Jr., "The Historical Roots of Our Ecologic Crisis," in *An Environmental Law Anthology*, ed. Robert L. Fishman, Maxine I. Lipeles, and Mark S. Squillace (Cincinnati, Ohio: Anderson Publishing Co., 1996), 5.

[3] Sirchin-The Free Encyclopaedia, "Environment: Definition," http://www.science.sirchin.com/?topic:environment.

[4] J. Stan Rowe, "What on Earth Is Environment?" *The Trumpeter* 6, no. 4 (1989). Available at http://www.ecospherics.net/pages/RoWhatEarth.html.

(soil) and biosphere (organisms).[5] Rowe concluded that 'ecosphere' is more meaningful to environmental protection because it gives intrinsic values equally to organic and non-organic parts of the environment and that, consequently, "the concept of Ecosphere as the prime reality can begin the cure of the disease of homocentrism by turning attention outward, ecocentrically" permitting the move from anthropocentrism to ecocentrism.[6] If anthropocentrism means that the whole universe revolves around the interests of humankind and that all human activities are human-centred, ecocentrism is a collection of views that is theoretically in contrast with anthropocentrism. This philosophical debate reflects the values and concepts that are at the heart of modern environmental ethics and politics.

1. *Religious Roots of the Ecocrisis*

Some ecological thinkers have accused the Judeo-Christian doctrine of Creation of engendering the roots of the ecocrisis by encouraging a domineering and arrogant human behaviour towards nature. Western Christianity represented by both Catholicism and Protestantism, has been labelled as 'the most anthropocentric religion', compared to other religions.[7] Anthropocentrism is a term used extensively in environmental ethics to indicate a human-centred attitude towards nature.

The American scholar Edward Payson Evans (1831–1971), the first to highlight the connection between anthropocentrism and Christianity, sharply criticised 'the anthropocentric character of Christianity', compared to holistic religions such as Buddhism and Brahmanism.[8] Seventy years later, in 1967, Lynn White reiterated the same criticism in an influential article, "The Historical Roots of our Ecologic Crisis".[9] According to White, the roots of our modern ecological crisis can be at least partially traced to the teachings of Judaism and Christianity, which tend to perceive human beings as masters, rather than a part of nature. White predicated his argument on Genesis 1:26, a controversial verse from the Old Testament that is often interpreted as permission for humankind to rule over nature: "And God said; Let us make man in our image, after our likeness: and let them have dominion over the fish of the sea, and over the fowl of the air, and over the cattle, and over all the earth, and over every creeping thing that creepeth upon the earth."[10] In White's opinion, this ingrained attitude of mastery and superiority over other creatures stems from the biblical statement that human beings are created in the likeness

[5] Ibid.
[6] Ibid.
[7] White, "Historical Roots," 5–6. White differentiated between Western Christianity and the orthodox traditions of Eastern Christianity, which were in greater harmony with nature.
[8] Nash, Roderick, *Rights of Nature*, 51.
[9] White, "Historical Roots."
[10] Gen. 1: 26 (King James Version).

of God. Thus, he concluded that this scriptural statement is at the root of the Judeo-Christian belief that God created the Earth and its bounties for human satisfaction and that nature is there to be exploited.[11] However, White singled out the doctrine of Saint Francis of Assisi, a highly critical view of the limitless power of humans over creation, as a revolutionary approach to nature in the Christian theology. He considered Assisi the 'patron saint for ecologists' because Assisi revered non-human living creatures and placed them on equal footing with humankind. With God as the mutual creator, Assisi refers to all living creatures as brothers and sisters.[12]

White argued that Christian theology, unlike paganism, removed the sanctity and spirituality of nature's components and phenomena. By freeing people from animism—the belief that elements of nature are inhabited by spirits—Christianity paved the way for science and technology to use nature without the moral restraints of older religions.[13] In this regard, the legitimate claims raised by Indigenous peoples concerning their cultural heritage provide a striking illustration of the spiritual aspect of humans' connection with nature.[14] Some writers have gone even further in their criticism of Christianity by depicting the 'Church' as an institution that annihilates the holiness of nature through the acquisition of lands and thereby transforms nature into commodities.[15] However, Christian theology is diverse and complex and able to embrace both extremes.[16] Advocates of the concept of stewardship view it as a better interpretation of the Book of Genesis than White's thesis and a step forward in the reconciliation between human beings and nature. Schaeffer, an evangelical theologian, denied White's characterisation of Christianity as anti-environmental, arguing that human dominion over nature was meant to be positive, not destructive, and that it was original sin, which entered the world with the 'Fall', that alienated the human-nature relationship.[17] Therefore, human beings have moral obligations towards nature because nature is God's gift to humankind. This guardianship vision implies that God nominated humans to take care of the non-human world.[18] Similarly, Dewitt maintained

---

[11] In contrast to this belief, John Passmore found that Stoicism, not passages from the Old Testament, is at the root of human despotism towards nature. See Robert Attfield, *Environmental Philosophy: Principles and Prospects* (Aldershot: Ashgate 1994), 16.

[12] White, "Historical Roots," 7–8.

[13] Ibid.

[14] See generally, *Final Working Paper Prepared by the Special Rapporteur on Indigenous Peoples and Their Relationship to Land*, Erica-Irene A. Daes, UN Doc E/CN.4/Sub.2/2001/21 (2001).

[15] David Pepper, *Modern Environmentalism* (New York: Routledge, 1996), 151.

[16] Broadly speaking, Protestantism was more straightforward than Catholicism in differentiating between creator and creation and in establishing that only God should be worshipped and there should be no guilt in using nature for human needs. See especially Peter Hay, *Main Currents in Western Environmental Thought* (Sydney: UNSW Press, 2002), 104.

[17] Michael S. Northcott, *The Environment and Christian Ethics* (Cambridge: Cambridge University Press, 1996), 126–27.

[18] It has been argued that the metaphor of stewardship is problematic because human beings do not have full control over natural forces. Other eco-theological alternatives have been

that the Bible is rich in ecologically friendly teachings and that the real problem lies in implementation of the doctrine, rather than in the doctrine itself. He calls for fruitful cooperation between ecologists and churches in order to save the natural world.[19]

Some writers have argued against White's thesis on the grounds that the anthropocentric attitude towards nature predated Christianity; they criticised White for overlooking the anthropocentric orientation of ancient Greek and Roman philosophies that were predicated on the exclusive moral standing of human beings and insisted that Christianity cannot be singled out as the only religion that embraces exploitative attitudes towards nature.[20] Other religious teachings, such as those of the Native Americans, authorise humans to despoil nature.[21] To a certain extent, most ancient civilizations and communities altered their natural surroundings.[22] According to Berry, an historian of cultures and a Catholic priest, even the Chinese's idyllic view of nature did not prevent Chinese people from wiping out most of their ancient forests.[23]

In a similar vein, Tomalin made a useful distinction between two religious approaches to nature: 'nature religion' and 'religious environmentalism'.[24] By 'nature religion', Tomalin referred to the traditional religious worship of some elements of nature, practised by many Eastern religions. This reverence emanates from the association of specific natural elements with gods

---

suggested. For instance, the 'priesthood metaphor' offers a better explanation of the Christian attitude to nature. According to Sherrard, human beings—as the sole mediators between God and nature—are entitled to offer nature to God as a sign of recognition and worship. See Northcott, *Christian Ethics*, 129–31. The metaphor of 'embodiment' is another theological alternative that offers a correction of the split between the spiritual and materialistic realms in Christian thinking. Some feminist theologians, such as Sally McFague, perceive the earth as the body of God, which results in greater reverence to and awe of nature. This eco-theological pantheism, defined as the identification of deity with nature, has been criticised for its desertion of the traditional Christian theism and for its ambiguity concerning the level of embodiment of God in different life forms. Northcott, *Christian Ethics*, 157–58.

[19] Calvin B. Dewitt, "Ecology and Ethics: Relation of Religious Belief to Ecological Practice in the Biblical Tradition," in *Ecologists and Ethical Judgements*, ed. N.S. Cooper and and R.C.J. Carling (London: Chapman & Hall, 1996), 55–65. Dewitt suggested seven biblical principles as practical tools to environmental disruption. While the 'Earth-keeping' and 'fruitfulness' principles imply that human beings bear the responsibility of keeping and preserving the elements of nature after using its resources, the 'Sabbath' and 'buffer' principles guarantee the restoration and integrity of the ecosystems. The 'contentment' and 'priority' principles oppose the spirit of modern consumerism and discourage people from abusing the environment. Finally, the 'praxis' principle calls for the correct practise of such principles.

[20] John Mizzoni, "St. Francis, Paul Taylor and Franciscan Biocentrism," *Environmental Ethics* 26(2004): 54.

[21] See Pepper, *Modern Environmentalism*, 154.

[22] Ibid.

[23] Paul Collins, *God's Earth: Religion as If Matter Really Mattered* (North Blackburn, Vic: Dove, 1995), 88.

[24] Emma Tomalin, "The Limitations of Religious Environmentalism for India," *Worldviews: Global Religions, Culture, and Ecology* 6, no. 1 (2002): 16.

and goddesses, rather than from an ethical concern for environmental protection.[25] In the Indian context, Tomalin pointed out that the Hindus' worship of sacred trees, groves and rivers does not necessarily stem from an awareness of the intrinsic value of nature per se but that Hindus may revere and respect certain species of trees for their linkage to deities. It is unlikely that such spiritual practices extend Hindus' worship to forests or the whole of nature.[26] On the other hand, 'religious environmentalism' is a contemporary environmental trend that emerged as a reaction to the growing capacity of humankind to exploit the natural environment on a large scale, leading to global environmental problems.[27] Religious environmentalists draw upon non-Western religious and cultural traditions in an attempt to anchor environmental activism in deeper spiritual foundations. However, the tendency to interpret Eastern religions as ecologically friendly does not genuinely reflect the core teachings of these religions.

Some view the influence of Eastern religions and new paganism on radical ecological movements as indicative of the inability of mainstream Christianity to offer a theological basis for an environmentally friendly society.[28] At the same time, it could be argued that the credibility of the environmental movement is compromised when it deliberately draws upon religious and spiritual beliefs in its quest for changes in social behaviour as it relates to the environment. For instance, through the metaphor 'Mother-Earth', eco-feminists have contended that the association between nature and the feminine has been used to justify the patriarchal, exploitative and domineering attitude towards both women and nature.[29] Bookchin, an eco-anarchist, regarded green spirituality as 'flaky' and not solid enough to be used in tough political battles.[30] In his opinion, the roots of the ecological catastrophe lie in 'capitalism and hierarchy' and that a great effort is needed to fight such deep-seated paradigms. Thus, Bookchin presented his social ecology as a rational alternative to the spiritualisation of the human-nature relationship.[31]

2. *The Agricultural Revolution*

Throughout most of human history, until the emergence of agriculture, hunting and gathering were the main methods of subsistence. While agriculture has traditionally been considered an indicator of human advancement and progress, some archaeological studies have shown that the shift to farming

[25] Ibid.
[26] Ibid.
[27] Ibid.,18.
[28] See especially Hay, *Main Currents*, 100.
[29] Ibid., 75.
[30] Ibid., 119.
[31] Ibid.

techniques was the first indicator of a significant human impact on the natural world.[32] Diamond maintained that human beings are still dealing with the dire consequences of our ancestors' unwise decision to favour agriculture and to abandon foraging as a lifestyle.[33] The quest for food supply by ancient civilizations exhausted and impoverished the land and opened the door for territorial conquest and trading. For example, the massive deforestation of China occurred as more food was required to meet the needs of its fast growing population. In modern history, European colonialism, driven by the rise of capitalist economies and competition among European nations, inflicted serious ecological degradation on non-European lands.[34] Similarly, the Dust Bowl of mid-1930s is a typical illustration of nature's limitations and its inability to cope with human greed without harmful side effects. Between 1934 and 1937, more than 200 dust storms blew away the soil covering the Great Plains, causing the destruction of crops and pasture and a deficiency in wheat production. This ecocrisis was attributed to unwise agricultural practices such as monoculture and the destruction of native vegetation.[35]

3. *The Scientific Revolution*

The scientific revolution of the 16th and 17th centuries originated with Copernicus' breakthrough heliocentric theory predicated on the centrality of the sun in the universe instead of the old belief that the Earth is the centre of the cosmos.[36] Descartes, Bacon and Newton revolutionised science by adopting new ways of conceiving the world: Descartes' and Bacon's theories contributed to the dissociation of the unity between society and nature, as conceived by pre-modern cosmology, and by emphasising the role of reason in acquiring knowledge, Newtonian science helped demystify the reliance on biblical scriptures and false science as sources of knowledge.[37]

The scientific revolution was accompanied by the 'mechanisation and mathematisation of nature', which contradicted medieval beliefs that were based on the intrinsic qualities and animistic aspects of nature.[38] The doctrine of mechanism, promoted by Descartes, influenced how human beings related to their environment by offering a dualistic view of nature: the corporeal substance and the mental substance. Natural things, including animals, were mere machines, the anatomy and function of which could be revealed through

---

[32] Northcott, *Christian Ethics*, 44.

[33] Jared Diamond, "The Worst Mistake in the History of the Human Race," *Discover Magazine* (1987).

[34] Northcott, *Christian Ethics*, 45.

[35] John McCormick, *The Global Environmental Movement: Reclaiming Paradise* (London: Belhaven Press, 1989), 22.

[36] Pepper, *Modern Environmentalism*, 136.

[37] Ibid., 146.

[38] Ibid., 138–39.

physics and chemistry, and eventually through mathematics. Mechanism is a reductionist view that differentiates between life and non-life based on the level of complexities of a substance, rather than on a 'vital principle.'[39] Descartes' mechanistic understanding of nature provided a justification for human abuse of animals for the sake of scientific progress. By separating mind from body, Descartes viewed humans as occupying a higher status in nature because of their mental capabilities, whereas animals, despite their biological resemblance to humans, are deprived of reason and, thus, cannot experience pain the same way humans do.[40] By transforming nature into a machine, classical science nurtured and facilitated the exploitative attitude of human beings towards their environment.[41] According to White, the Western science and technology developed in the Middle Ages are the main cause of environmental degradation.[42]

Another aspect of Cartesian dualism lies in its sharp distinction between mind and matter. Many radical ecologists believe that this distinction accentuated the separation between society and nature and led humans to regard themselves as superior and disconnected from their natural environment, which was reduced to the level of machine.[43] This separation was further developed by Francis Bacon, a leader of the Renaissance in England and among the first thinkers to link technology to science, who declared that nature exists solely for humans' use.[44] It follows that science cannot be pursued as an end in itself; instead, it is the means merely to promote technological advancement, which subordinates nature to the will of humankind.[45] In Bacon's view, nature is to be treated aggressively so it releases its secrets.[46] Both Cartesian and Baconian theories provided scientists with the moral permission to experiment on animals as well as human cadavers—viewed as 'unfeeling' machines—for the advancement of science, particularly medical science. When the practice of vivisection came under fire in the 17th century, scientists used the Cartesian 'objectification of nature' to justify the practice.[47]

Phenomenology, a school of philosophy, is an alternative to the Cartesian/positivist tradition. Phenomenology is the "study and description of phenomena in terms of their essential and particular qualities, as these reveal themselves through authentic human experiencing."[48] Phenomenology rejects all

[39] Ibid., 140.
[40] Hay, *Main Currents*, 125.
[41] See Pepper, *Modern Environmentalism*, 139.
[42] White, "Historical Roots," 8.
[43] See Pepper, *Modern Environmentalism*, 142.
[44] James Connelly and Graham Smith, *Politics and the Environment: From Theory to Practice*, 2nd ed. (London/New York: Routledge, 2003), 18.
[45] Hay, *Main Currents*, 123.
[46] Ibid., 140.
[47] See Nash, Ronald, "Radical Environmentalism."
[48] Hay, *Main Currents*, 143.

Cartesian dichotomies anchored in modern science and preaches a 'seamless unity between person and world'[49], a way of knowing the natural world without separating ourselves from it. Phenomenologists, such as Husserl, Merleau-Ponty and Heidegger[50] perceived the world differently from how science describes it.[51] Through phenomenological experience, humans are able to embrace the meaning, significance and value embedded in nature that are usually overlooked—and even masked—by science.[52]

4. *Capitalism*

Critics of capitalism, such as Hancock, have depicted 'economic rationality' as the leading cause of environmental destruction because it transforms natural assets into products for the purpose of accommodating consumers' lifestyles.[53] In this regard, environmental education plays a crucial role in making the public, especially younger generations, sensitive to the value of a shift in the economic paradigm in mitigating the capitalist tendency to favour profit maximisation over the environment. The preamble of the 1997 *Convention on Access to Information, Public Participation in Decision-Making and Access to Justice in Environmental Matters*,[54] known as the *Aarhus Convention*, reflects this shift to environmental awareness. The preamble pledges to "promote environmental education to further the understanding of the environment and sustainable development and to encourage widespread public awareness of, and participation in, decisions affecting the environment and sustainable development."[55]

Apart from the widespread capitalist economic paradigm, Shiva identified two other types of economies: 'nature's economy' and the 'sustenance economy'.[56] In her view, the ravaging nature of globalisation and its corollary, free market rules, undermine the flourishing of both nature and sustenance

---

[49] Ibid., 145.

[50] Heidegger is the first philosopher to have demonised technology and to have predicted its annihilating effect on all 'other modes of revealing.' In Heidegger's view, modernity represents the "struggle for the unlimited exploitation of the earth as a domain of raw materials, and for the illusion free deployment of human material in the service of an unconditional empowerment of the 'will to power'." See Stephen Schlosser, "Only a God Can Save Us: Disabling the Rational Subject in Heidegger's Reactionary Modernism," *Heythrop Journal* 36, no. 2 (1995): 191.

[51] Jane M. Howarth, "Ecology: Modern Hero or Post-Modern Villain? From Scientific Trees to Phenomenological Wood," in *Ecologists and Ethical Judgements*, ed. N.S. Cooper and R.C.J. Carling (London: Chapman & Hall, 1996), 8.

[52] Ibid., 9.

[53] Jan Hancock, *Environmental Human Rights: Power, Ethics and Law* (Aldershot: Ashgate 2003), 27.

[54] *Convention on Access to Information, Public Participation in Decision-Making and Access to Justice in Environmental Matters (Aarhus Convention)*, Opened for signature 25 June 1998, UNECE, 2161 UNTS 447 (Entered into force 30 Oct. 2001).

[55] Ibid., Preamble.

[56] Vandana Shiva, *Earth Democracy* (Cambridge: South End Press, 2005), 14.

economies. As a result, natural resources dwindle leaving local communities with tremendous crises of scarcity.[57] Shiva denounced the 'hypocritical' dichotomy between economy and ecology.[58] Etymologically speaking, both economy and ecology share the Latin *oikos* derivative—meaning 'home'. Nature's economy is the first and oldest form of economy on which the market economy is predicated, although this type of economy has been overlooked and destroyed over time. The reproductive and regenerative functions of nature are like a huge, organic factory able to produce living resources without the interference of humans. In contrast, sustenance economy requires a certain degree of friendly interaction with ecological processes to guarantee an appropriate extraction of basic resources, such as fresh water, food and other materials needed for the survival of rural communities.[59]

By shifting the debate from the possession or the 'have or have not' notion to the survival or the 'live or live not' notion, and by looking at the matter from an activist perspective, Shiva meant to create a sense of urgency or shock in the issues of development and environmental protection.[60] She contended that globalisation, fuelled by multinational corporations and international financial institutions, threatens the sustenance economy of two-thirds of the world's population in order to enrich and accommodate lavish Western lifestyles of the other third.[61] However, this concept of a paradigm shift in the philosophy of development does not provide satisfactory answers to old dilemmas related to the capacity of nature to sustain growing human populations, especially in the Third World, nor does it offer solid proof that the interaction of local communities with nature is necessarily positive and sustainable at all times.

5. *Population Growth*

Thomas Robert Malthus, an 18th-century English economist and clergyman, who linked the shortage in food supplies to an expanding population, was the first to depict overpopulation as a major source of famine and social unrest. Subsequently, Neo-Malthusians drew upon his hypothesis and added the environmental dimension to the problem of resource scarcity.[62] In his well-known article "The Tragedy of the Commons",[63] Hardin argued that environmental destruction can be attributed primarily to population growth and unlimited exploitation of the Earth's finite resources. As Hardin put it, "[f]reedom to

---

57 Ibid.
58 Ibid., 15–17.
59 Ibid.
60 Ibid., 14.
61 Ibid.
62 J. E. De Steiguer, *The Age of Environmentalism* (New York: McGraw-Hill, 1997), 5–6.
63 Garrett Hardin, "The Tragedy of the Commons," *Science* 162, no. 3859 (1968).

breed will bring ruin to all."[64] He refuted the social goal put forward by Bentham—'the greatest good for the greatest number'—on the basis that it is impossible to maximise human population without compromising human satisfaction.[65] He also criticised Smith's laissez-faire approach to economic growth, arguing that individuals' choices will not necessarily be in the public interest, especially as they apply to reproduction.[66]

In Hardin's opinion, there is no technical solution to the problem of human overpopulation, and the only way to "preserve and nurture other more precious freedoms is to relinquish the freedom to breed."[67] The core of the idea is that human beings have to restrict their freedom to reproduce in order to enjoy their 'right to the commons'.[68] However, these radical measures cannot be achieved without infringement on personal liberty.[69] In contrast to Hardin's stance, the Catholic Church has always been pro-natalist, prohibiting artificial contraception while emphasising the equitable distribution of goods between rich and poor countries.[70] Collins, a church historian and a specialist commentator on the papacy, argued against the anthropocentric approach adopted by the Catholic Church regarding the population issue.[71] Like Thomas Berry, Collins believed that human ethics should be viewed as part of the wider ecological spectrum and that the recognition of the rights of other species emanates from humans' moral responsibility for the natural world.[72] Collins went further in his argument by considering the restrictions on the human right to procreate as consistent with natural law, given that human beings are the main cause of ecological disturbance.[73]

6. *Extreme Poverty and Affluence*

Both extreme poverty and wealth have a detrimental impact on the well-being of the environment. People living in poor countries tend to rely directly on their natural surroundings to satisfy their basic needs, such as water and food. Consequently, environmental degradation infringes on people's basic rights to life and health, creating more poverty and despair. A vicious circle forms when poverty is at the same time both the result and the cause of environmental degradation. As Fabra noted, "[p]overty and environmental degradation are

---

[64] Ibid., 1248.
[65] De Steiguer, *The Age of Environmentalism*, 62.
[66] Hardin, "Tragedy of the Commons," 1243–44.
[67] Ibid., 1248.
[68] This entails the enclosure of commons such as farmland, pastures, hunting and fishing areas, as well as commons used for entertainment.
[69] Ibid.
[70] See Collins, *God's Earth*, 53.
[71] Ibid., 69–71.
[72] Ibid.
[73] Ibid.

often bound together in a mutually reinforcing vicious circle, and thus human rights abuses related to poverty can be both cause and effect of environmental problems."[74] For instance, the high demand for agricultural land by poor people led to the depletion of local forest resources in Mexico between 1980 and 1990.[75] Deforestation creates a chain of environmental disasters, including climate change, desertification and loss of biodiversity, and destructive logging practices disrupt the livelihoods of local communities. The dwindling of food supply and other local products, as well as the scarcity of clean water, adds extreme hardship and poverty to forest-dwelling people.[76] On the other extreme, industrialised countries promote consumption as a tool of economic growth and create highly sophisticated needs, leading to further strains on natural resources. However, wealth can also trigger increased environmental consumerism, such as ecotourism and demand for pollution-free recreational areas, e.g., forests, national parks and beaches. To a certain extent, then, both poverty and affluence lead to demands for environmental protection but for completely different reasons; while subsistence and sheer survival are the main concerns for the poor, maintaining a healthy lifestyle and aesthetics are of tremendous importance to wealthier societies.

In its quest for the theoretical and historical underpinnings to the current ecological ills, the environmental movement has pointed the finger to mainstream religious beliefs; the reductionist, mechanistic and instrumental characteristics of modern science; population growth; capitalism; and extreme poverty. Therefore, different trends of environmentalism have developed their own theories and offered alternative conceptions and interpretations of the relationship between humans and nature.

B. *Emergence and Development of Environmentalism*

The terms 'environmentalism' and 'global environmental movement' are often used interchangeably with 'green' or 'ecological movement'.[77] However it is named, this movement, developed in Europe and North America in the last two centuries, reflects growing concerns about the impact of human activities on the well-being of the environment. Initially, environmentalism emerged in

[74] Adriana Fabra, "The Intersection of Human Rights and Environmental Issues: A Review of Institutional Developments at the International Level" (paper presented at the Joint UNEP_OHCHR Expert Seminar on Human Rights and the Environment, Geneva, 14–16 Jan. 2002), 13.

[75] Anders Ekbom and Jan Bojo, "Poverty and Environment: Evidence of Links and Integration into the Country Assistance Strategy Process, Discussion Paper, No 4." (1999), 7.

[76] The logging industry is the major cause of deforestation in the world. Around 20% of tropical forests were cleared from the 1960s to the 1990s. See World Rainforest Movement, "The Future of Tropical Forests," http://www.flonnet.com/fl2012/stories/20030620000207100.htm.

[77] Hay, *Main Currents*, 1.

Europe after its long history of colonialism and natural resource exploitation before spreading to the United States.

1. *Founding Fathers of Environmentalism*

The flowering of natural history in England in the 18th century fuelled interest in the aesthetic value of nature and the preservation of wildlife. Private environmental groups such as the Commons, Open Spaces, and Footpaths Preservation Society, all established in Britain in 1865, were among the first organisations to campaign for the preservation of places for amenity.[78] Public wilderness preservation commenced for the first time in the US in 1864 when Congress granted the Yosemite Valley to the State of California for recreational purposes. In 1872, the world's first national park, Yellowstone, was established in a large area in Wyoming. The American invention of national parks mirrored the spread of ideas about the glorification of nature for its own beauty and values.[79] After spending two years in a cabin at Walden Pond in Massachusetts, Henry David Thoreau (1817–1862), an American writer, produced a rich literature reflecting the principles of transcendentalism, a philosophy based on intuition, rather than rationality.[80] He called for a simpler life represented by wilderness, as opposed to urbanism and its vices. Thoreau is considered the pioneer of ecocentric thinking.[81]

Albert Schweitzer (1875–1965) is another prominent intellect, whose 'Reverence for Life' philosophy is a forerunner of environmental ethics. Schweitzer's respect for life extends to all living beings and all matter.[82] The ethical person, according to Schweitzer, "shatters no ice crystal that sparkles in the sun, tears no leaf from its tree, breaks off no flower, and is careful not to crush any insect as he walks."[83] Consequently, people should use nature's resources when it is necessary and for practical reasons only. Aldo Leopold (1887–1948), a passionate conservationist, was more specific in his attempt to extend ethical values to the natural world.[84] His focus was on ecosystem integrity, which goes beyond living creatures "to include soils, waters, plants, and animals, or collectively: the land."[85] Leopold denounced the traditional view of land as property and urged people to maintain a harmonious relationship with

[78] McCormick, *Reclaiming Paradise*, 5.
[79] Ibid., 12.
[80] De Steiguer, *The Age of Environmentalism*, 9.
[81] Ibid.
[82] Nash, Roderick, *Rights of Nature*, 61.
[83] Ibid.
[84] Aldo Leopold, "The Land Ethic," in *An Environmental Law Anthology*, ed. Robert L. Fishman, Maxine I. Lipeles, and Mark S. Squillace (Cincinnati, Ohio: Anderson Publishing Co., 1996), 16.
[85] Ibid.

the land.[86] As early as 1864, George Perkins Marsh (1801–1882), an American diplomat and conservationist, observed in his book, *Man and Nature*, that human activities have had a destructive effect on the environment throughout history.[87] Marsh, called the first environmentalist, considered the human being to be a 'disturbing agent' and that "[w]herever he plants his foot, the harmonies of nature are turned to discords."[88] Thus, he urged humankind to adopt a constructive attitude towards nature and to rehabilitate destroyed landscapes.[89]

Environmental awareness culminated with the writings of visionaries like Thoreau and Muir. The naturalist John Muir (1838–1914) sought primarily to protect wildlife and ecosystems for recreational, educational and spiritual purposes.[90] His beliefs influenced President Theodore Roosevelt and led to the establishment of several national parks across the country.[91] In contrast to the protectionism and preservation preached by Muir, Gifford Pinchot (1865–1946), an American forestry expert, believed in a rational and efficient management of natural resources for 'human consumption'.[92] Pinchot and Muir's antagonism culminated in a debate over the construction of a dam and a reservoir in the Hetch Hetchy Valley in Yosemite National Park.[93] Muir's opposition to the project stemmed from his belief that the valley should be preserved for its own value; while Pinchot, whose view eventually prevailed, regarded natural assets as a means for public provision and welfare.[94] This conflict of views is still the essence of the debate between advocates of anthropocentrism and deep ecologists.[95]

Barrett v. State was a stark illustration of this debate. By outlawing the hunting, molestation or disturbance of beavers, New York State sought to protect the species from extinction.[96] The claimants, whose land was devalued by the damaging activities of the protected species, filed a suit against the State, claiming they had a right to compensation. Interestingly, the Court invoked the intrinsic value of the protected wild animals and the public interest to reject the petitioners' claim for damages caused by beavers stating that "the police power is not to be limited to guarding merely the physical or material

---

[86] See De Steiguer, *The Age of Environmentalism*, 16.
[87] Ibid., 9.
[88] Thinkexist.com, "George Perkins Quotes," http://en.thinkexist.com/quotes/george_perkins/.
[89] Ibid.
[90] Andres R. Edwards, *The Sustainability Revolution: Portrait of a Paradigm Shift* (New Society Publishers, 2005), 13.
[91] Ibid.
[92] Hay, *Main Currents*, 14.
[93] See De Steiguer, *The Age of Environmentalism*, 13.
[94] Ibid.
[95] See below Section C.
[96] *Barrett v. State*, 220 NY 423(1917). Available at http://www.animallaw.info/cases/causny220ny423.htm.

interests of the citizen. His moral, intellectual and spiritual needs may also be considered. The eagle is preserved, not for its use but for its beauty."[97]

Since *Barrett v. State*, an ideological division has existed between those who regard nature in terms of its economic benefits for humankind, and the advocates of nature conservation for its intrinsic values. Upon the creation of the 1907 Inland Waterways Commission to regulate American river systems, Roosevelt recommended some restraints on the use of water for such efforts as flood control and prevention of silting in order to guarantee its sustainability as a vital national resource.[98] These restraints can be likened to other familiar environmental principles, such as the polluter-pays principle, the principle of prevention and the precautionary principle.[99] Since then, conservation has been perceived as more practical than preservation. It continues to be at the top of the international environmental agenda.

2. *The Rise of Modern Environmentalism*

It is common to trace modern environmentalism to Rachel Carson's *Silent Spring* (1962), Paul Ehrlich's *The Population Bomb* (1968) and Garrett Hardin's essay, "Tragedy of the Commons" (1968), as well as to the writings of other scholars who have had great influence in raising public awareness of the gravity of environmental issues.[100] Carson's *Silent Spring* was hailed for its initiation of the 'Age of Environmentalism'[101] and its remarkable impact on public opinion. Through research findings and factual accounts, Carson, a marine biologist, revealed the devastating effects of chemical pollution on ecosystems and human health. In one story included in the chapter 'And No Bird Sing', Carson showed the danger of the accumulation of DDT, an agricultural insecticide, in the food chain.[102] Her writings challenged the interests of chemical and agricultural industries, who tried to discredit the book; however, her work was proven reliable following subsequent scientific approval from the United States Office of Science and Technology.[103] As a result of the heightened public and governmental awareness of threats posed by chemical toxins, the Environmental Protection Agency (EPA) banned the use of 50 of the most dangerous pesticides, including DDT.[104] By emphasising the direct responsibility of humans in contaminating their environment, Carson's work widened

---

[97] Ibid.
[98] McCormick, *Reclaiming Paradise*, 15.
[99] See generally Nicholas de Sadeleer, *Environmental Principles: From Political Slogans to Legal Rules* (New York: Oxford University Press, 2002).
[100] Rachel Carson, *Silent Spring* (Boston: Houghton Mifflin, 1962); Paul R. Ehrlich, *The Population Bomb* (New York: Ballantine Books, 1968); Hardin, "The Tragedy of the Commons."
[101] See De Steiguer, *The Age of Environmentalism*, 42.
[102] Ibid., 32.
[103] Ibid., 39.
[104] Ibid., 40.

the scope of environmental interests beyond wilderness preservation and isolated species of animals to include the health and well-being of humans and ecosystems alike.

Modern environmentalism was also a reactionary movement against modernism and major environmental incidents that occurred in many regions, especially in the United States. The first major incidents to raise public sensitivity to environmental issues were the Torrey Canyon and Santa Barbara spills,[105] as a result of which federal regulatory programs were enacted to protect the environment: the *Clean Air Act*, the *Clean Water Act* and the *Endangered Species Act*.[106] The implementation of these new statutes was assigned to newly established environmental agencies such as the Environmental Protection Agency and the Council on Environmental Quality. The influence of such a powerful movement even went beyond policies and legislation to reach some of the States' constitutions.

There is a discontinuity between the emergence of wilderness preservation—as conceived by Thoreau, Muir, and Leopold—and the subsequent resurgence of environmentalism in the 1960s, which was prompted by ecological issues such as pollution and population growth, as well as the warnings of doom-saying scientists. Interest in wilderness preservation was revived in North America and Australasia in the mid-1970s.[107] However, the emergence of the so-called third wave of environmentalism in the 1980s has challenged the idealism of earlier environmentalists. This new wave, which departs from the radical principles, focuses on solving ecological problems through negotiations and compromises with governments and corporations.[108] It is much more focused on economics and public policy than on ecocentric ideals such as exploration of the 'wild self' and social change.[109]

---

[105] In March 1967, the tanker *Torrey Canyon* wrecked on the south coast of England and spilled an estimated 117,000 tons of crude oil into the English Channel. As a result, the British government created the Royal Commission on Environmental Pollution in 1979. See McCormick, *Reclaiming Paradise*, 57–58. On January 28, 1969, a similarly devastating incident occurred in California when its pristine beaches on the Pacific Ocean were polluted by tens of thousands of crude oil spilled from a Union Oil Co. platform. This ecological nightmare galvanized the public as well as the Nixon administration to consider environmental issues seriously.

[106] Robert V. Percival, "“Greening” The Constitution-Harmonizing Environmental and Constitutional Values," *Environmental Law* 32(2002).

[107] Hay, *Main Currents*, 17–18.

[108] Ron Arnold, one of the staunchest adversaries of the environmental movement and the founding father of the Wise Use Movement, presents the latter as an alternative ideology to that underpinning environmentalism. In comparing the two 'competing paradigms', Arnold pointed out that "environmentalism by its very nature promotes feelings of guilt for existing … [while] wise use by its very nature promotes feelings of competence to live in the world." Ron Arnold, "Overcoming Ideology," in *A Wolf in the Garden: The Land Rights Movement and the New Environmental Debate*, ed. Philip D. Brick and R. McGreggor Cawley (Lanham, Maryland: Rowman & Littlefield Publishers, 1996).

[109] Greenpeace and Earth First! are illustrative manifestations of the radical environmental movement. While Greenpeace, the first radical environmental group, was initially formed to

C. *Major Concepts in Environmental Philosophy*

The rise of modern environmentalism fuelled a wealth of discussions and debates about the ethical relationship between human beings and their natural environment. This led to the emergence of environmental ethics, a subdivision of philosophy. Accordingly, different taxonomies and typologies have been proposed to depict the different trends in environmentalist thought.[110] While it is not the purpose of this section of the book to examine the nuances among these philosophical trends, it is appropriate at least to divide them into two environmental categories, anthropocentrism and ecocentrism, as central to the understanding of the concept of environmental human rights.

1. *Anthropocentrism*

Since the 16th century, anthropocentrism has been the dominant trend in Western societies. The philosophy of anthropocentrism regards human beings as the centre of the universe and the source of all value.[111] This philosophical perspective was nurtured by Western philosophical and theological predispositions as well as by the scientific and industrial revolutions discussed earlier in this chapter. However, the term 'anthropocentrism' itself came into common use only at the end of the 1970s.[112]

Norton distinguished between strong and weak anthropocentrism based on two different interpretations of human needs. The felt preference is human desire or need fulfilled through personal experience, while the considered preference is human desire or need attained through careful deliberations about, and in conformity with, established worldviews, such as scientific theories, aesthetic values and moral ideals.[113] Accordingly, strong anthropocentrism values non-human beings and objects for their ability to satisfy the felt preferences, while weak anthropocentrism values natural beings for their ability to satisfy both considered preferences and felt preferences.[114] Without acknowledging the inherent worth of non-human entities, weak anthropocentrism questions the value systems that underlie exploitative attitudes towards nature.

---

protect the atmosphere from nuclear testing and to defend whales, the main objectives of Earth First! revolved around the protection of the wilderness. See Bill Devall, "Deep Ecology and Radical Environmentalism," in *American Environmentalism: The US Environmental Movement 1970–1990*, ed. Riley E. Dunlap and Angela G. Mertig (New York: Taylor and Francis, 1992), 55–58.

[110] See Rodman's typology and Fox' taxonomy in Hay, *Main Currents*, 31.

[111] See generally Eccy De Jonge, *Spinoza and Deep Ecology: Challenging Traditional Approaches to Environmentalism* (Aldershot: Ashgate, 2004), 10.

[112] Klaus Bosselmann, *When Two Worlds Collide: Society and Ecology* (Auckland: RSVP Publishing, 1995), 4.

[113] See Susan J. Armstrong and Richard G. Botzler, eds., *Environmental Ethics: Divergence and Convergence*, 3rd ed. (New York: McGraw-Hill 2003), 314.

[114] Ibid., 309–10.

Advocates of anthropocentrism base their position on the Kantian idea that moral values should be restricted to human beings as the only beings able to use reason and language while decrying the extension of ethical considerations to non-humans, viewing such extension as irrational and unpractical.[115] However, advocates have argued that anthropocentrism is not necessarily synonymous with the greedy exploitation of natural resources or an unnecessary abuse of living creatures. As Murdy observed, "[t]he problem lies in our difficulty to distinguish between 'proper ends', which are progressive and promote human values, and 'improper ends', which are retrogressive and destructive of human values."[116] Still, anthropocentrism, rooted in the liberal tradition of individualism and rational thinking, is limited in its ability to extend compassion beyond animals.[117] Thus, "it seems 'unreasonable' to identify oneself compassionately with plants or even landscapes. Not only does reason struggle against this, but perhaps also feelings themselves."[118]

Most environmentalists view anthropocentrism as the philosophical driving force behind ecological crises. Bosselmann identified four objections to the anthropocentric paradigm.[119] The first is related to false anthropocentric assumptions, such as that of the superiority of humans over other living creatures and the centrality of humankind in the universe. Environmentalists claim that these assumptions are misleading because humans are neither at the centre of the universe nor the peak of evolution.[120] The second objection is that anthropocentric attitudes lead to ecological disasters and that ecological change through law and politics is ineffective without ecocentric change.[121] The third objection questions the validity of anthropocentric ethics since its reliance on criteria such as mental and communication abilities to exclude non-humans from moral consideration is illogical and unconvincing; the same criteria apply to different groups of humans, particularly infants and people with mental disabilities but does not exclude them from the ethical realm. The fourth objection is that anthropocentrism tends to lock people into its own orbit and makes the anthropocentric paradigm unavoidable.[122]

The distinction between anthropocentrism and ecocentrism is, in many respects, a distinction between instrumental and intrinsic values. The instrumental value of something ends with its use, so it follows that its value depends

---

115 Ibid., 310.
116 W. H. Murphy, "Anthropocentrism: A Modern View," in *Environmental Ethics: Divergence and Convergence*, ed. Susan J. Armstrong and Richard G. Botzler (London: McGraw-Hill, 1993), 303.
117 Bosselmann, *When Two Worlds Collide*, 176.
118 Ibid., 177.
119 Ibid., 139–41.
120 Ibid., 139.
121 Ibid., 140.
122 Ibid., 141.

on its connection to other entities or to functions it can accomplish in a specific system. However, the intrinsic value of a certain entity is the essence of any value system because it revolves around the worth of an entity independent of any other factor. In Callicott's words, "to value something intrinsically ... is to value something for itself, as an end-in-itself."[123]

2. *Ecocentrism*

a. *Definition*

Ecocentrism is not a unified theory or philosophy but a compilation of environmental trends wherein the spiritual, the scientific and the metaphysical intermingle to produce different forms of green or radical theories. In Bosselmann's words, "ecocentrism is developed out of criticism of anthropocentrism and is used today as a collective term for all systems of values that are not anthropocentric."[124] The intrinsic value of nature is the dominant concept in the philosophy of ecocentrism, and the core of the concept lies in removing humanity from the centre of the universe and replacing it with nature.[125] As Bosselmann explained, ecocentrism is the "shift of the centre of human thought from humans to the network of interrelations between humans and nature."[126]

In some instances, biocentrism has been regarded as synonymous with ecocentrism, but there are some philosophical differences between the two terms. While biocentrism assigns moral status to both sentient and non-sentient individual living organisms, ecocentrism stretches moral standing to include 'supra-individual wholes', such as species and ecosystems.[127] Rowe argued against the concept of biocentrism considering it a misleading and reductionist concept that restricts life to 'organisms', which implies that their surrounding environment is inorganic or deprived of life. This misconception opens the door to unrestricted exploitation of parts of the Earth that are perceived as 'dead', such as water, land and air. To subvert this 'biological fallacy', Rowe suggested the use of the term ecocentrism as more conducive to the

---

[123] J. Baird Callicott, "The Pragmatic Power and Promise of Theoretical Environmental Ethics: Forging a New Discourse," *Environmental Values* 11(2002): 16.

[124] Bosselmann, *When Two Worlds Collide*, 7.

[125] Multicentrism, a new paradigm in environmental philosophy, denounces the 'megacentrisms' of both anthropocentrism and biocentrism as too broad to be included in centres. According to Anthony Weston, "[m]ulticentrism envisions a world of irreducibly diverse and multiple centres of being and value—not one single circle, of whatever size or growth rate, but many circles, partly overlapping, each with its own centre." Multicentrism promotes a kind of 'communicative ethics' that stretches beyond the human sphere. Anthony Weston, "Multicentrism: A Manifesto," *Environmental Ethics* 26(2004): 38.

[126] Bosselmann, *When Two Worlds Collide*, 7.

[127] Espen Gamlund, "Who Has Moral Status in the Environment? A Spinozistic Answer," *The Trumpeter* 23, no. 1 (2007): 5.

"assignment of highest value to the ecosphere and to the ecosystems that it comprises."[128]

As an environmental concept, ecocentrism is not new but can be traced to the pre-modern era. Although under considerable fire, pre-modern perceptions of the relationship between society and nature did not vanish with the advent of scientific and technological advancement; some of these views, such as the Great Chain of Being, still permeate many modern ecological conceptions.[129] The Great Chain of Being conceives of the universe as an organic and orderly structure based on a succession of living and non-living creatures in a hierarchy that ranges from the most basic and sensible to the highest and most ideal.[130] In this chain, human beings are positioned between higher spiritual creatures, such as angels, and lower living and non-living entities, like animals, plants, water and air. Intimately interlinked, all these elements are equally necessary to the coherence of the hierarchical system, and it follows that the destruction of any link will jeopardise the viability of the whole chain.[131] Two important features characterise the Great Chain: animism and the humility of humans in their relationship to nature. First, the concept of the Great Chain of Being does not view humans as necessarily 'higher' than other beings 'below' them, which creates a sense of humility and reverence towards nature based on the animistic belief in the attribution of souls to animals, plants and natural objects such as mountains and rivers. Second, animism, which is practiced by many tribal communities and religious groups—infiltrated modern radical environmental concepts, such as deep ecology.[132] Deep ecology, transpersonal ecology and the Gaia hypothesis represent the modern forms of ecocentrism. Relatively older types of ecocentrism, such as animal liberation and holism, preceded these trends.

b. *Animal Liberation*

Jeremy Bentham (1748–1832) was the first philosopher to justify the assignment of moral values to some non-human life forms based on their ability to feel pleasure and to experience suffering. This criterion of sentience contradicts the rigidity of the Kantian morality, which limits moral consideration to beings able to reason and talk.[133] Drawing upon Bentham's utilitarianism,

---

[128] Stan Rowe, "From Shallow to Deep Ecological Philosophy," *The Trumpeter* 13, no. 1 (1996).

[129] See Pepper, *Modern Environmentalism*, 165.

[130] See generally Arthur O. Lovejoy, *The Great Chain of Being: A Study of the History of an Idea* (Cambridge, MA: Harvard University Press, 1936). Dictionary of the History of Ideas, "Chain of Being," http://etext.virginia.edu/cgi-local/DHI/dhi.cgi?id=dv1-45.

[131] Pepper, *Modern Environmentalism*, 131.

[132] Ibid., 133–34.

[133] See Andrew Brennan, "Ethics, Ecology and Economics," in *Ecologists and Ethical Judgements*, ed. N.S. Cooper and R.C.J. Carling (London: Chapman & Hall, 1996).

Singer maintained that all sentient creatures, whether human or non-human, have interests in avoiding pain and that these interests should be worthy of equal consideration.[134] Singer denounced discrimination against members of other species, which he called 'speciesism', arguing that excluding some animals from the moral realm is similar to sexism and racism.[135] He refuted the reliance on linguistic and rational capacities to exclude animals from moral consideration, drawing an analogy with groups of human beings, such as infants and people with mental illness or disability, who do not cease to be moral subjects.[136] Singer's philosophy inspired animal rights and animal liberation movements that have campaigned against animal experimentation and trading. Animal liberationists oppose the killing of animals for food or medical experimentation on the grounds that these creatures are capable of suffering, and that it is morally unacceptable to inflict pain upon sentient animals.[137]

While Singer, a utilitarian, opted not to confer moral rights to animals, Regan, a prominent advocate of animal rights, expounded on Singer's theory of animal liberation and suggested that animals, like human beings, are 'subjects of a life' and have equal inherent value. Individuals are considered 'subjects of a life' if they have "beliefs, desires, and preferences; if they are able to act intentionally in pursuit of their desires and goals; if they are sentient and have an emotional life …."[138] In Regan's view, animals endowed with inherent value are entitled to basic moral rights such as the right to respectful treatment and the right not to be harmed.[139] Apart from the criteria of reason and sentience used to justify the ascription of moral status to humans and some non-human beings, Spinoza's concept of 'conatus', or striving, has also been relied upon as a 'descriptive basis for a biocentric and ecocentric position on moral status.'[140] By 'conatus', Spinoza referred to "[e]ach thing, as far as it can by its own power [*quantum in se est*], strive to persevere in its being."[141] Based on this description, Gamlund argued that, if an entity possesses the power to strive and fight for its existence, whether it is aware of such power or not, it is entitled to moral status; otherwise it is not.[142] It follows that individual living

---

[134] See Peter Singer, *Animal Liberation*, 2nd ed. (London: Pimlico, 1995), 7.

[135] Peter Singer defined 'speciesism' as "a prejudice or attitude of bias in favour of the interests of members of one's own species and against those of members of other species." Ibid., 6–9.

[136] Ibid., 16–22.

[137] Mary Anne Warren, "The Rights of the Nonhuman World," in *Environmental Philosophy: A Collection of Readings*, ed. Robert Elliott and Arran Gare (St. Lucia, Brisbane: University of Queensland Press, 1983), 110.

[138] Ibid.

[139] Ibid., 327–29.

[140] See Gamlund, "A Spinozistic Answer," 7.

[141] Quoted in Jon Miller, "Spinoza and the Concept of a Law of Nature," *History of Philosophy Quarterly* 20, no. 2 (2003): 266.

[142] Gamlund, "A Spinozistic Answer," 7.

beings in a biotic community are endowed with moral status, which represents a philosophical foundation for the biocentric concept. Gamlund also suggested that it is possible to apply the same rationale to wholes, such as species, ecosystems or the biosphere, and that doing so provides the basis for an ecocentric concept.[143]

Many opponents of animal rights have refuted the idea on the basis that only humans are endowed with moral responsibility towards other humans and animals. Warren held that it is not plausible or morally compulsory to expand the scope of 'full and equal' rights to animals because animals lack the necessary moral autonomy that allows them to reciprocate moral rights to humans and other animals.[144] Other opponents of animal rights have based their argument on the fact that non-human predators rely on killing other animals for subsistence. Warren contended that "it is wrong to kill animals for trivial reasons, but not wrong to do so when there is no other way of achieving a vital goal, such as the preservation of threatened species."[145] Animal rights activists and advocates who adopt extreme misanthropic views have been criticised for prioritising the survival and well-being of animals over human beings.[146]

c. *Holism and the Gaia Hypothesis*

Holism argues that the respect for non-living natural features such as mountains, rivers and rocks can be compared to the respect for property rights in human societies. One cannot argue that it is possible to respect human beings in a specific society while disrespecting or spoiling their material belongings, such as houses or cars. The same principle applies to ecosystems that sustain all forms of life. Any unwise alteration to the system may disturb the life and well-being of the creatures belonging to that specific ecosystem, so the whole ecosystem, not only the species living in it, should be assigned value.[147] The Leopoldan philosophy, called the 'land ethic', is illustrative of this holistic view of the universe. In Leopold's words, "[a] thing is right when it tends to preserve the integrity, stability and beauty of the biotic community. It is wrong when it does otherwise."[148] This 'land ethic' is based on the notion of 'ecological conscience', which promotes an ethical relationship with the natural world.

---

143 Ibid., 10.

144 Warren, "Nonhuman World," 119.

145 Ibid., 164.

146 Newkirk, the co-founder of People for the Ethical Treatment of Animals (PETA), is a passionate advocate of the animal liberation movement. In her words, "[h]umans have grown like a cancer. We're the biggest blight on the face of the earth." Wikiquote, "Ingrid Newkirk," http://en.wikiquote.org/wiki/Ingrid_Newkirk.

147 See especially Holmes Rolston, *Environmental Ethics: Duties to and Values in the Natural World* (Philadelphia: Temple University Press, 1988), 18.

148 Leopold, "Land Ethic," 18.

In a similar vein, the Gaia hypothesis put forward by James Lovelock (1919) perceives the planet Earth as a 'super organism' worthy of respect and protection. The Gaia hypothesis originated as a scientific theory but its impact has radiated beyond science. Fascinated by this theory, many environmentalists, such as Goldsmith, have relied on Gaian science as a source of inspiration for social, ethical and spiritual principles.[149] The Gaia hypothesis claims that the Earth can regulate and renew itself and survive the destructive activities inflicted on its biophysical systems. However, this contradicts the fact that the environmental state of the Earth is worsening instead of coping with ecological threats.[150]

d. *Deep Ecology and Transpersonal Ecology*

'Deep ecology' and 'ecocentrism' are used interchangeably in referring to the philosophy concerned with granting intrinsic values to nature, but these concepts differ slightly. Ecocentrism is broader in its scope and encompasses a wider range of non-anthropocentric perspectives, while deep ecology is a specific philosophy with relatively well-defined principles. Arne Naess, a Norwegian philosopher, coined the term deep ecology in 1973 in opposition to what he considered shallow ecology.[151] By 'deep ecology', Naess referred to the thorough and deep questioning process related to human values and lifestyles that affect nature; by 'shallow ecology', Naess referred to the quick-fix environmental approaches and policies adopted to tackle ecological problems like pollution and shortages of natural resources.[152]

Naess promoted deep ecology as almost a messianic movement or 'a lifestyle-oriented theory', as Sylvan described it.[153] To achieve this ecocentric ideal, Naess urged human societies to adopt 'ecosophy', or ecological wisdom, which does not rely solely on ecological science but looks to other forms of knowledge, like intuition. The salient point in his 'Ecosophy T', as Naess

[149] Hay, *Main Currents*, 137.

[150] Ibid., 149.

[151] In 1984, an eight-point 'platform' prepared by Naess and George Sessions exhibited the definitive principles of deep ecology. The first two principles acknowledge the intrinsic value of non-human forms as well as the value emanating from their diversity and richness. According to principle three, the richness and diversity of life-forms should not be reduced except for vital human needs. Principle four notes that both human and non-human life requires a decrease in human population. While Principle five highlights the impact of human activities on the well-being of the natural world, Principle six urges a change in policies on the economic, technological and ideological levels. Principle seven clarifies the scope of the ideological change which emphasises life quality rather than higher standards of living. Principle eight obliges people who adhere to the other principles to try to fulfil the necessary changes. Abiding by these principles, as implicitly stipulated in the last principle, is a precondition to being accepted as a member of the deep ecology movement. See Bill Devall and George Sessions, *Deep Ecology: Living as If Nature Mattered* (Salt Lake City, Utah: Gibbs Smith, 1985), 70.

[152] Arne Naess, "The Shallow and the Deep, Long-Range Ecology Movement," *Inquiry* 16(1973).

[153] Pepper, *Modern Environmentalism*, 21.

labelled it, revolves around the recognition of an intrinsic worth of all life forms on Earth and the rejection of the deep-rooted instrumental approach to the environment. Ecosophy, or deep ecology, is a call for egalitarianism among all forms of life with the goal of bridging the gap between dichotomies such as subject-object, nature-human and civilisation-wilderness. Deep ecologists believe in the inherent value of nature and that human beings are a vital part of the planet. The biologist Lewis Thomas put it this way: "Earth is not a planet with life on it; rather it is a living planet."[154] Many deep ecologists maintain that the protection of the environment necessitates a paradigm shift in the Western mindset which currently overemphasises the role of material needs in achieving human satisfaction, instead of 'spiritual growth'. By creating unnecessary and false needs, such a hedonistic and consumption-oriented culture encourages the excessive production and supply of goods, which leads to detrimental ecological consequences.[155] On the practical level, supporters of the deep ecology philosophy put their beliefs into action by adopting ecologically friendly lifestyles based on the principle of 'least harm to living beings and ecocentric identity.'[156]

Mathews, a deep ecologist, views the world as a subject endowed with purposive and communicative abilities of its own.[157] Through an 'order of poetic revelation', the world, depicted as the 'One', reveals itself to the 'Many'. In light of this personification, it is not appropriate to recognise and approach the world only through conventional scientific paradigm; instead, it should be approached through the principle of letting-be.[158] Letting-be implies the adoption of the 'synergetic mode' of intervention in the world, rather than the usual manipulative and instrumental approach. In other words, human needs should be fulfilled in conformity with the 'patterns of energetic flow' that the world reveals to us; we should adjust to them, rather than ignoring them and thereby creating ecological disharmony. For instance, Mathews contended that, by switching to wind and solar power (renewable resources that require minimum intervention in the ecological equilibrium), human societies will help preserve the integrity of the planet, rather than exacerbating the destructive effect of extracting and using fossil fuels.[159]

Advocates of deep ecology regard it as an alternative or even an antithesis to anthropocentrism that leads to a radical shift in the human approach to nature. Deep ecology, unlike shallow ecology, attempts to create a social change by

---

154 Quoted in Rich Heffern, "The Fate of Nature Is Our Own," *National Catholic Reporter*, Oct. 8, 2004, Earth & Spirit section.

155 See especially Devall and Sessions, *Deep Ecology*, 68.

156 Devall, "Deep Ecology and Radical Environmentalism," 54.

157 Freya Mathews, "Beyond a Materialist Environmentalism," *Nanjing Forestry University* 2(2005), http://www.freyamathews.com/default.asp?p=CR&id=4.

158 Ibid.

159 Ibid.

fostering an 'ecological consciousness' among individuals, rather than working from already established social structures.[160] Self-realisation, as Naess described it, draws upon transpersonal psychology, which revolves around extending the human experience beyond the self.[161] Naess views self-realisation as "a question of community therapy, [rather] than community science: Healing our relations to the widest community, that of all living beings."[162]

Bosselmann identified three approaches to experiencing closeness and identification with nature: the intuitive, philosophical and scientific approaches.[163] Through intuition, humans can break the walls around the ego and identify with peoples and things around them; by extending love to all living beings and the natural world, a person experiences unity with nature.[164] This unity and closeness can be attained through the philosophical standpoints and religious beliefs that stress the ontological aspect of things.[165] Self-identification with nature is also facilitated by some scientific theories, mainly the Gaia hypothesis and the theory of evolution, which emphasise the ecological and historical processes whereby all living beings are connected. Awareness of this connection allows humans to identify with the 'one living planetary being'.[166]

In coining the term 'transpersonal ecology', Fox brought philosophy and psychology into the realm of ecology.[167] Fox opted for the term 'transpersonal', rather than 'deep', in describing ecology.[168] 'Transpersonal' is defined as "a sense of self that extends beyond one's egoic, biographical, or personal sense of self."[169] The self-awareness preached by transpersonal psychology, coupled with ecological values, generates 'transpersonal ecology'. As Fox explained it, "transpersonal ecology has as much to do with "ecologizing" transpersonal psychology as it has to do with "psychologizing" our ways of approaching ecophilosophical issues."[170]

3. *Criticism of Deep Ecology and Other Ecocentric Theories*

Opponents of deep ecology, the bedrock concept of radical environmentalism, have often criticised it for its radical and idealistic approach to the

---

[160] Pepper, *Modern Environmentalism*, 21.
[161] Arne Naess, "Self-Realization: An Ecological Approach to Being in the World," *The Trumpeter* 4(1987).
[162] Ibid., 40.
[163] Bosselmann, *When Two Worlds Collide*, 180.
[164] Ibid., 180.
[165] Ibid., 181.
[166] Ibid., 182.
[167] Warwick Fox, *Toward a Transpersonal Ecology: Developing New Foundations for Environmentalism*, 2nd ed. (New York: State University of New York Press, 1995).
[168] Ibid., 197.
[169] Ibid., 198.
[170] Ibid., 199.

environmental plight. Deep ecologists strongly believe that a fundamental change in people's values and lifestyles is central to rectifying the human exploitative attitude towards nature. Opponents of deep ecology have argued that this approach is 'politically naïve' and that it overlooks the ability of governmental institutions and big businesses to obstruct such social change.[171] Bookchin, the founder of social ecology, sharply criticised deep ecology for overlooking the social roots of the environmental crisis and for focusing on spiritualistic and mystical formulations. Bookchin's theory of social ecology draws upon Marxism and anarchism to see the domination of nature by humans as a reflection of the domination of humans by humans.[172] Social ecologists regard the empowerment of local communities through municipalities as the best way to redress ecological abuses because, unlike municipalities, the nation-state is perceived as an artificial and tyrannical institution that promotes primarily the interests of powerful classes in society. Social ecology presents the dissociation of hierarchies and classes as a solution for the ecocrisis. It also calls for 'ethics of complementarity', which stresses the link between the social and natural. In Bookchin's opinion, the teachings of deep ecology lead to what he termed 'deindividuation', implying the dissolution of the individual into a greater 'cosmic self'. This depersonalisation undermines human beings by putting nature at a higher level and worshipping it as a deity.[173]

Another point of contention with deep ecology has to do with its anti-human, misanthropic stance. Bookchin deplored Foreman's statement that we have to let 'nature [seek] its own balance' at the expense of Third World populations. For instance, starvation should be seen as a natural process with positive long-term effects on population control. Bookchin also criticised deep ecologists' reliance on the Malthusian explanation of the ecological crisis for being misleading and dangerous. However, many deep ecologists denounced the extreme views proposed by Foreman and others.[174]

Guha, an Indian historian, refuted deep ecology's differentiation between anthropocentrism and biocentrism as being ineffective in 'understanding the dynamics of environmental problems' and viewed it as the product of Western interpretation of Eastern religions.[175] In an attempt to universalise their beliefs, tenets of deep ecology indiscriminately depicted these religions as biocentric in their values, rather than acknowledging the complexity and diversity of Eastern spiritual traditions.[176] Guha also criticised the concept of eco- or

---

[171] Pepper, *Modern Environmentalism*, 29.

[172] See Murray Bookchin, *The Ecology of Freedom: The Emergence and Dissolution of Freedom* (California: Cheshire books, 1982).

[173] ———, "Social Ecology versus Deep Ecology: A Challenge for the Ecology Movement," *Green Perspectives*, no. 4–5 (Summer 1987).

[174] Ibid.

[175] Ramachandra Guha, "Radical American Environmentalism and Wilderness Preservation: A Third World Critique," *Environmental Ethics* 11(1989): 74.

[176] Ibid., 73–74.

biocentrism on the grounds that it prioritises non-human interests over those of human beings. For instance, tiger reserves in India, launched in 1973 to protect Royal Bengal tigers, were responsible for uprooting poor peasants from their villages.[177]

Advocates of deep ecology and similar concepts have often eulogised the spiritual heritage of Indigenous and tribal communities, arguing that their activities were environmentally sustainable, particularly in comparison to the exploitative Western cultures. Some have refuted this generalisation by pointing out that such beliefs are 'naïve and ill-informed' reminding us that primitive people may express reverence towards natural phenomena and creatures out of fear and lack of control, rather than out of a belief in the concept of intrinsic worth.[178] Moreover, Ronald Nash warned against hidden religious and political agendas that lie behind the teachings and philosophies of the greens, deep ecologists and animal rights activists. While the greens attack private property rights, deep ecologists and similar extremists instil new religions into society by promoting pantheism and egalitarianism.[179] The tendency of deep ecologists to embrace some of the ancient beliefs about nature and its relationship to humankind, such as the Great Chain of Being, is indicative of an express hostility to modernism. However, this does not imply that modern environmentalism is necessarily rooted in such pre-modern conceptions.[180]

D. *Internationalisation of Environmental Issues: From the Philosophical Arena to the Legal Arena*

The internationalisation process allows a global issue to be released from its local cocoon and to be exposed to wider international public opinion. The 1970s witnessed an evolution in national environmental policies and regulations and the internationalisation of environmental issues, which were reflected in the creation of international environmental treaties. The establishment of powerful environmental groups such as Greenpeace and Friends of the Earth has also facilitated such evolution.

The first UN global conference on the human environment was held in Stockholm in June 1972. This global gathering, known as the United Nations

---

177 Ibid., 75.

178 Pepper, *Modern Environmentalism*, 25.

179 Ronald Nash, "The Case against Radical Environmentalism," Christian Research Institute, http://www.equip.org/free/DE403.htm. A controversial book, *The Skeptical Environmentalist*, constitutes another blow in the face of environmentalism. The author, Bjørn Lomborg, a Dutch statistician and political scientist, attempts to demystify the claims of radical environmentalists by arguing that the state of the environment is not as alarming as it is portrayed worldwide and that environmental exaggerations, which he calls the 'Litany', are misleading public opinion and authorities. Bjørn Lomborg, *The Skeptical Environmentalist: Measuring the Real State of the World* (Cambridge: Cambridge University Press, 2001).

180 Pepper, *Modern Environmentalism*, 5.

Conference on Human Environment (UNCHE), was initiated by developed countries whose leaders were alarmed by the massive abuse that industrialisation had inflicted on the environment. The First Earth Day, a landmark event that took place in the United States on 22 April 1970, influenced the theme of the conference. The establishment of domestic environmental agencies and the creation of the United Nations Environment Programme (UNEP) were the direct outcomes of this global forum. In an attempt to bridge the gap between economic development and environmental protection, the UN General Assembly created the World Commission on Environment and Development in 1983. After four years, the Commission published its landmark report, Our Common Future.[181]

The United Nations Conference on Environment and Development (UNCED), also known as the Earth Summit or the Rio Summit, took place in Rio de Janeiro, Brazil, in June 1992. It brought together 172 countries with the participation of more than 100 heads of State or government. Apart from governmental representation, the Rio Summit was also host to 2400 non-governmental organisations (NGOs). It was praised for mobilising the UN system towards a new path away from confrontational issues, such as the North-South divide and the East-West antagonism.[182] Two international instruments on the environment and development were fashioned at this Summit: the Rio Declaration and Agenda 21. The Rio Declaration is a brief statement of 27 principles or objectives designed to be a source of inspiration and guidance for domestic legislators and policy-makers in issues relating to the environment and sustainability. Agenda 21 is a comprehensive plan of action that consists of a preamble and four sections: Social and Economic Dimensions, Conservation and Management of Resources for Development, Strengthening the Role of Major Groups, and Means of Implementation.[183] Two other major environmental treaties were also adopted: the *UN Convention on Biological Diversity* and the *UN Framework Convention on Climate Change* (UNFCCC).[184] On the institutional level, the UN Commission on Sustainable Development (CSD) was established in 1992 at the initiative of the Earth Summit. Its main mandate is to follow up the progress in the implementation of Agenda 21, the Rio Declaration and the Johannesburg Plan of Actions.[185]

---

[181] The World Commission on Environment and Development, *Our Common Future*, x.

[182] Nitin Desai, "Johannesburg: Achievements and Challenges," Carnegie Council Podcast, http://www.cceia.org/resources/transcripts/622.html#1.

[183] See UN Department of Economic and Social Affairs: Division for Sustainable Development, "Agenda 21," http://www.un.org/esa/dsd/agenda21/res_agenda21_23.shtml.

[184] *Convention on Biological Diversity*, Opened for signature 5 June 1992, 1760 UNTS 79 (Entered into force 29 Dec. 1993); *The UN Framework Convention on Climate Change*, Opened for signature 4 June 1992, 31 ILM 849 (Entered into force 21 Mar. 1994).

[185] UN Department of Economic and Social Affairs: Division for Sustainable Development, "Commission on Sustainable Development (CSD)," http://www.un.org/esa/sustdev/csd/aboutCsd.htm.

The World Summit on Sustainable Development (WSSD), known also as Earth Summit 2002, drew upon the outcomes of previous global conferences and agreements, mainly the Rio principles, Agenda 21 and the Millennium Development Goals.[186] The prime goal of the WSSD is to weigh the progress achieved since the 1992 Rio Conference and to draw up a plan of action to further the implementation of Agenda 21. The outcomes of the WSSD include the Johannesburg Declaration on Sustainable Development, The Johannesburg Plan of Implementation and WWSD Partnerships for Sustainable Development. The Johannesburg Declaration reiterates the commitment of 'representatives of peoples of the world' to sustainable development and highlights the role of the Johannesburg Summit "in bringing together a rich tapestry of peoples and views in a constructive search for a common path, towards a world that respects and implements the vision of sustainable development."[187] The Plan of Implementation establishes strong mechanisms for the realisation of sustainable development goals through specific targets and timetables.[188] The foundation of the Plan of Implementation stems from the adoption of a more balanced and integrated approach to the economic, social and environmental pillars of sustainable development. It focuses primarily on water and sanitation, energy, health, agriculture and biodiversity, known as the WEHAB issues.[189] The WWSD Partnerships are innovative ways of putting sustainable development goals into action through the participation of state and non-state actors, such as civil society groups and other stakeholders.

Conclusion

As societies become more technologically oriented, people tend to adopt lifestyles that are more sophisticated. When dependency on nature declines, so does the daily reliance on natural forces and natural resources. The innate and spiritual umbilical cord between Mother Earth and humans is severed and replaced by artificial chains of subsistence based on trade and economic transactions; for instance, in the quest for food and health, tribal communities had to rely directly on their natural surroundings to provide them with meat, grains, fruits, medicinal plants and other necessities. In contrast, modern societies rely on economic institutions, such as supermarkets and pharmacies to fulfil their basic needs. In the popular collective consciousness, nature is

[186] The WSSD was held in Johannesburg, South Africa, from 26 August to 4 September 2002.

[187] *Johannesburg Declaration on Sustainable Development*, UN Doc A/CONF.199/20 (2002).

[188] *Plan of Implementation of the World Summit on Sustainable Development*, UN Doc A/CONF.199/20 (2002).

[189] See Marie-Claire Cordonier Segger and Ashfaq Khalfan, *Sustainable Development Law: Principles, Practices and Prospects* (New York: Oxford University Press, 2004), 28.

reduced to a luxurious commodity, or, for some, a romantic shelter. In this regard, environmental ethics pledges to attenuate the modern human bias against nature by creating a paradigm shift in humankind's relationship with the natural environment.

In an attempt to fashion non-legal solutions to the ongoing debate over the ecological crisis, Environmentalists have increasingly relied on environmental ethics and philosophy. They drew upon metaphysical, ontological and religious interpretations to create social and cultural paradigm shifts in people's attitudes towards their environment and in a bid to bring a sense of reverence for and awe of the lost treasure called 'nature'. Although this line of thought may not be homogenous and coherent, its intent is to correct the imbalance between humans and nature in favour of the latter. However, anthropocentrism, even in its weakest form, is still the dominant philosophy in environmental legal systems and, despite the growing understanding and acceptance of the holistic approach to ecological issues, the ascription of inherent value to non-humans lacks the practicality of the anthropocentric approach. The belief that all species are endowed with intrinsic value independently of their worth to humans is a utopian concept. If this concept is put into action, it will logically threaten human biological survival. As Murdy observed, to acknowledge the intrinsic value of every animal and plant species will not prevent human beings from valuing their own survival above that of other species.[190]

By examining the philosophical and spiritual underpinnings of the ecological movements, this chapter revealed the role of environmental ethics in inducing a radical change in the way humankind perceives 'otherness'. In other words, it is an attempt to mend what many environmentalists perceive to be the distorted relationship between humankind and other non-human beings, ecosystems, land, the planet and the whole universe. These philosophical notions have found their way into many international instruments, such as the 1982 *UN World Charter for Nature*, which emphasises the relationship between the destiny of humanity and nature. The *World Charter* states in its preamble that "[m]ankind is a part of nature and life depends on the uninterrupted functioning of natural systems which ensure the supply of energy and nutrients."[191] This UN instrument has been hailed for its ecocentric approach to environmental protection and conservation and for stressing the rights of nature independently from those of human beings by acknowledging that "[e]very form of life is unique, warranting respect regardless of its worth to man [sic]."[192] This revolutionary approach to environmental thinking contradicts the anthropocentric statement of Principle 1 of the Rio Declaration,

---

[190] See Armstrong and Botzler, *Environmental Ethics*, 318.
[191] *UN World Charter for Nature*, GA Res 37/7, UN GAOR, 37th sess, 48th plen mtg, UN Doc A/Res/37/7 (1982).
[192] Ibid.

which places human beings at the centre of concerns for sustainable development.[193] More recently, the 2000 *Earth Charter*, the result of a decade of extensive international consultation, introduced a sense of solidarity and ethical dimension in dealing with environmental issues by proposing a "shared vision of basic values to provide an ethical foundation for the emerging world community."[194] The *Earth Charter* reiterates the principle of the inherent worth of nature provided in the *World Charter* by recognising "that all beings are interdependent and every form of life has value regardless of its worth to human beings."[195] Similarly, the *UN Convention on Biological Diversity* acknowledges the 'intrinsic value of biological diversity'.[196]

In the same vein, bringing the environment into the fascinating world of human rights is an evolutionary stage of both environmentalism and international human rights law. The philosophical debate over the relationship between humans and nature and the dichotomy between ecocentrism and anthropocentrism constitutes an integral part of the debate over the nature and scope of emerging environmental rights. This issue will be fully examined in Chapter 3, while Chapter 2 discusses the theoretical and legal foundations necessary to bridge the gap between the concept of human rights and environmentalism.

---

[193] *UN Conference on Environment and Development: Rio Declaration on Environment and Development*, UN Doc A/CONF.151/26 (Vol. I) (1992), Principle 1.

[194] *The Earth Charter*, Preamble.

[195] *The Earth Charter*, Principle 1.

[196] *Convention on Biological Diversity*, Preamble.

CHAPTER TWO

AN OVERVIEW OF THE CHARACTERISTICS AND CONTROVERSIES OF HUMAN RIGHTS

Introduction

In an examination of the nexus between the environment and human rights, Chapter 1 discussed the ethical and philosophical underpinnings of the concept of the environment. This chapter concentrates on the major controversies and issues in the conceptualisation and implementation of contemporary international human rights in order to determine the appropriateness and constraints of the human rights-based approach to environmental issues. The chapter is comprised of five sections. Section A examines the main theories that underlie the concept of human rights. Section B focuses on the issue of rights-holders and the expansion of human rights law beyond human beings. Section C considers the internationalisation and universalism of human rights. Section D presents the taxonomy of human rights and its corollary issues. Section E investigates the implementation mechanisms for human rights and the impediments to their enforcement at national and international levels.

A. *Theories of Human Rights: Philosophical and Legal Foundations*

While it is beyond the purpose of this chapter to examine thoroughly the philosophical underpinnings of the human rights concept, it is important to look at some of the main theoretical controversies that surround it in order to highlight the conceptual issues that accompany the transformation of a specific claim into a human right. Since its inception, the doctrine of human rights has oscillated between two theories of law: natural law and positive law. This oscillation reflects the unsettled debate in international human rights law over the source of human rights, that is, whether they emanate from the inherent dignity of the human person or from the will of the State.[1] Among the legal theorists and philosophers of the Enlightenment era who debated the legal aspect of human rights, Bentham represents the most extreme view against natural law. His stance was that positive law is the only accepted form of law and that

[1] See Philip Alston, "Making Space for New Human Rights: The Case of the Right to Development," *Harvard Human Rights Year Book* 1(1988): 31.

rights emanating from natural law are 'metaphysical' or even 'nonsense upon stilts'.[2]

Alternative concepts such as utilitarianism and socialism advanced to fill the gap created by the decline of natural rights at the end of the 18th century. The utilitarian principle, based on the quest for ultimate happiness, moved away from the 'metaphysical abstraction' of natural rights to be a channel for social reform.[3] Instead of liberal political philosophy, French social theorists such as Saint Simon proposed economic science as a remedy for what natural rights failed to achieve for the poor.[4] Similarly, Karl Marx expressed disdain for the 'rights of the man', describing them as bourgeois rights that overlooked the importance to human emancipation of socio-economic factors like labour, production and wealth.[5] Thus, the drift away from the emphasis on the natural rights of the individual that occurred in the 19th century opened the door to the development of socio-economic rights. Although individual rights did not vanish, they were viewed through utilitarian and socialist lenses as a channel of the public good instead of as part of the traditional concept of natural rights.[6]

Several contemporary human rights scholars have also reconsidered the validity of the philosophical underpinnings of the human rights concept. Gearty argued that the philosophical bases of human rights are fading and that there is a crucial need to look for an appropriate foundation to solidify the concept in the future.[7] If the term 'human rights' is neglected on the theoretical level, many might fill it with notions at odds with the essence of human rights.[8] To fill the gap, the term 'compassion' is suggested as a proper justification for human rights to replace both the religious and rational underpinnings of the past. Compassion, described by Davies as a 'virtuous disposition',[9] is a powerful channel through which human rights can be used to "frame and mobilise responses to suffering and to atrocities."[10]

On the other hand, some scholars have refuted the overemphasis on the notions of legality and justiciability to justify a new human right. Alston noted that notions of 'implementation' and 'supervision', rather than those of justiciabilty or enforceability are those that mainly govern international

---

[2] Jeremy Bentham, "Critique of the Doctrine of Inalienable, Natural Rights," *Anarchical Fallacies* 2(1843). Available at http://www.ditext.com/bentham/bentham.html.

[3] William A. Edmundson, *An Introduction to Rights*, Introductions to Philosophy and Law Series (Cambridge: Cambridge University Press, 2004), 28.

[4] Ibid., 29.

[5] Ibid.

[6] Ibid., 30.

[7] Conor Gearty, *Can Human Rights Survive?* (Cambridge: Cambridge University Press, 2006), 56.

[8] Ibid.

[9] Quoted in Gearty, 43.

[10] Ibid., 43.

human rights.[11] Thus, the enforcement of a human right is not necessarily tied to its judicial applicability. Contrary to the traditional legalist view that sees the legal component of a human right as the main factor in its recognition and implementation, Sen adopted the constructive view of human rights, which is predicated on social ethics and open public scrutiny.[12] Sen argued that the coercive force emanating from a legislated right does not necessarily lead to better enforcement of the desired claim; instead, the social and political awareness of human rights' abuses often create a tremendous public pressure that incites appropriate legislation or actions to address the violated right. In Sen's view, the moral realm of human rights is broader than their legal realm.[13]

Many philosophers differentiate between legal rights and moral rights. In Cranston's view, while legal rights are accompanied by *lawful* entitlements, moral rights are conducive to mere entitlements.[14] Accordingly, he considered human rights as moral rights with a universal dimension.[15] Edmundson equated human rights with natural rights, arguing that, despite the tendency towards the legal recognition of human rights, they are predominantly moral rights.[16] The distinction between legal and moral human rights is inextricably linked to the ambiguity inherent in the definition of human rights, so one can argue that a certain degree of osmosis has occurred between legal and moral rights over time. Human rights are rooted both in natural law and moral values and in positive law. The fact that not all moral rights can be transformed into legal rights indicates that society has already decided which rights are worthy of joining the legal realm in order to guarantee an appropriate level of protection and autonomy to the rights-bearers and that the chosen rights are perceived as urgent and important.[17]

B. *Human Beings as Rights-Holders*

Throughout history, the scope of human rights has expanded gradually to encompass all human beings, regardless of race, ethnicity, gender or social status.[18] Locke's perception of natural rights was exclusively confined to

---

[11] Alston, "Making Space," 35.

[12] Amartya Sen, "Human Rights and Development," in *Development as a Human Right: Legal, Political, and Economic Dimensions*, ed. Bård A. Andreassen and Stephen P. Marks (London: Harvard School of Public Health, 2006), 1–8.

[13] Ibid.

[14] Maurice Cranston, *What Are Human Rights?* (London: The Bodley Head, 1973), 19.

[15] Ibid., 23.

[16] See Edmundson, *Introduction to Rights*, 187.

[17] See especially Alice Erh-Soon Tay, "Human Rights Problems: Moral, Political, Philosophical," in *Rethinking Human Rights*, ed. Brian Galligan and Charles Sampford (Sydney: The Federation Press, 1997), 25.

[18] Jack Donnelly, *Universal Human Rights in Theory and Practice*, 2nd ed. (Ithaca, NY: Cornell University Press, 2003), 60.

property-owning Christian males. Slaves, oppressed minorities, women, children and homosexuals have been progressively added to the ever-expanding club of human rights-holders.[19] In conjunction with the expansion of the beneficiaries of human rights, their substance stretched tremendously from Locke's narrow list of the rights to life, property and liberty to a wide array of internationally recognised rights.[20]

In an attempt to extend the scope of human rights beyond human beings, some commentators have argued that the distinction between human rights and others' rights lies not so much in the 'human factor' as in the universality, inalienability and non-conditionality features of such rights.[21] This line of thought enables the human rights concept to spread out to non-human beings and entities. In order to find a justification for assigning the privileges of human rights to non-human beings or entities, some authors have suggested that the term 'human rights' is obsolete and must be superseded by another expression that reflects a more modern concept of the rights rhetoric. As Edmundson put it, "the expression "human rights" suggests that there is some deep conceptual connection between belonging to the human species and having rights; perhaps it should be retired–just as the phrase "the rights of *man*" has given way to gender-neutral equivalents."[22]

Legal philosophers such as Edmund Burke were deeply hostile to the idea of human equality that was asserted by the 'rights of man'. Burke based his objection on the fact that human beings are not equal in reality and concluded that human rights rhetoric is misleading and utopian.[23] However, his argument is untenable because the inequalities in people's physical abilities, mental abilities and their socio-economic status are not an impediment to the enjoyment of human rights. In contrast, the core function of human rights is, based on the inherent characteristic of human dignity, to rectify inequity among human beings. In other words, the emphasis is on what a person *is* rather than on what he or she *has*.[24]

---

[19] The atrocities and horrors inflicted on slaves in America and Europe triggered powerful anti-slavery movements in the 18th and 19th centuries. The abolition of slavery started in Great Britain with the Abolition Act of 1833. In contrast, the abolitionist movement in the United States stimulated domestic political turmoil and threatened the Union of the States. After a devastating civil war between US Southern and Northern States, the Thirteenth Amendment was incorporated into the American Constitution leading to the suppression of slavery in all States. By the end of the 19th century, abolitionism was successful in ending the slave trade and slavery practices all over the world. Women who were heavily involved in antislavery movements in Britain and the USA went on to form strong suffrage movements with a tremendous impact on women's rights in general. See generally Micheline R. Ishay, *The History of Human Rights: From Ancient Times to the Globalization Era* (Berkeley: University of California Press, 2004), 157.

[20] Ibid.

[21] See especially Edmundson, *Introduction to Rights*, 186.

[22] Ibid., 191.

[23] Cranston, *What Are Human Rights?* 15.

[24] In Cranston's words, human rights "belong to a man simply because he is a man [sic]". Ibid., 24.

The 'interest theory' of legal rights may be insightful to the justification of an emerging human right. The core of the theory is that rights are created to serve the interests of its addressees. In contrast, the 'choice theory' of legal rights limits the scope of rights to beings who are capable of making choices.[25] In that context, many groups of beings and non-beings who are not capable of making autonomous choices—such as infants, animals and even ecosystems—are automatically deprived of such rights.[26] By applying the 'interest theory', it is possible for the human rights doctrine to include nature, ecosystems and animals as rights-bearers based on their inherent worth, rather than the 'human' prerequisite mentioned by Cranston.

C. *Internationalisation and Universalism of Human Rights*

1. *Internationalisation of Human Rights*

Although sovereignty is the bedrock concept of international law, human rights have been the companion of this concept since WWII, when the internationalisation of human rights began.[27] There was a failed attempt to establish a human rights system in the aftermath of WWI. However, the atrocities caused by two consecutive global wars along with alarming fascist ideologies triggered the institutionalisation of human rights.[28] This ushered in a new era of rights wherein a state is no longer immune from international scrutiny in the case of egregious human rights violations, such as the Holocaust that shock the collective human consciousness. International scrutiny is promoted through the international standardisation of human rights norms that allow the international community to verify the commitment of a country to the protection of its citizens' rights.[29] According to Cranston, "human rights is the twentieth century name for what has been traditionally known as natural rights or … the rights of man."[30] In fact, our modern international human rights system can be traced to the earliest declarations and bills of rights of the 18th century: the 1776 United States Declaration of Independence, the 1789 French Declaration of the Rights of Man and of the Citizen, and the 1789 Bill of Rights of the United States Constitution.[31] These earliest rights, which were aimed principally at restricting the abusive power of rulers, laid the bases for democratic forms of government.

---

[25] Edmundson, *Introduction to Rights*, 120–21.
[26] Ibid., 127.
[27] Vesselin Popovski, "Sovereignty as Duty to Protect Human Rights," *UN Chronicle* 41, no. 4 (2004).
[28] George Kent, *Freedom from Want: The Human Right to Adequate Food* (Washington, D.C.: GeorgeTown University Press, 2005), 28.
[29] See Louis Henkin, *The Age of Rights* (New York: Columbia University Press, 1990), 17.
[30] Cranston, *What Are Human Rights?* 1.
[31] See Thomas Fleiner, *What Are Human Rights?* (Sydney: The Federation Press, 1999), 15.

Due to national and international pressure, human rights rhetoric made its way into the *United Nations Charter*, whose preamble affirms the organisation's "faith in fundamental human rights, in the dignity and worth of the human person, in the equal rights of men and women and of nations large and small."[32] Article 1 clarifies that one of the goals of the United Nations is to advance and foster the worldwide respect of human rights, regardless of 'race, sex, language and religion.'[33] While the Charter did not elaborate on the subject of human rights, its primary influence lies in the revolutionary idea that human rights can no longer be left to the discretion of public authorities and that the international community should respond to gross violations of human rights.[34] Thus, through Article 56, the Charter opened the door to a substantial codification of human rights that culminated in the proclamation of the 1948 Universal Declaration of Human Rights (UDHR).[35]

The UDHR[36] is a building block in the edifice of internationally recognised human rights. Szabo viewed it as "a success rarely encountered in the history of international law"[37] and Ignatieff described it as a 'fire-wall against barbarism.'[38] The UDHR, a non-binding document under international law, offers a conciliatory approach to human rights within the diverse cultural traditions of states that were not ready to comply or abide by the principles enshrined in the Declaration.[39] It took 18 years for the human rights embedded within the UDHR to materialise into treaties. In 1966, the *International Covenant on Civil and Political Rights* (ICCPR), its *First Optional Protocol*, and the *International Covenant on Economic, Social and Cultural Rights* (ICESCR) were adopted.[40] These Covenants, along with the UDHR, formed what is commonly known as the International Bill of Rights. Other international human rights treaties also focus on specific rights or rights-holders, such as the *UN Convention against Torture and Other Cruel, Inhuman or Degrading Treatment or Punishment,*

---

[32] *The United Nations Charter*, Preamble.

[33] Ibid., art. 1.

[34] See Thomas Buergenthal, "Centennial Essay: The Evolving International Human Rights System," *American Journal of International Law* 100(2006): 787.

[35] Ibid.

[36] *Universal Declaration of Human Rights*, GA Res 217A (III), UN GAOR, UN Doc A/810 (1948).

[37] Imre Szabo, "Historical Foundations of Human Rights and Subsequent Developments," in *The International Dimensions of Human Rights*, ed. Karel Vasak (Paris: Greenwood Press, 1982), 24.

[38] K. Anthony Appiah, "Grounding Human Rights," in *Human Rights as Politics and Idolatry*, ed. Amy Gutmann (Princeton: Princeton university Press, 2001), 5.

[39] Szabo, "Historical Foundations," 23.

[40] *International Covenant on Civil and Political Rights*, Opened for signature 16 Dec. 1966, 999 UNTS 171 (Entered into force 23 Mar. 1976); *Optional Protocol to the International Covenant on Civil and Political Rights*, GA Res 2200A (XXI), UN GAOR Supp, UN Doc A/6316 (1966), 999 UNTS 302 (Entered into force Mar. 23, 1976); *International Covenant on Economic, Social and Cultural Rights*, Opened for signature 16 Dec. 1966, 933 UNTS 3 (Entered into force 3 Jan. 1976).

UN Convention on the Elimination of All Forms of Discrimination against Women (CEDAW), and the *UN Convention on the Rights of the Child*.[41]

In addition to global agreements, many countries cooperate on a regional level. Europe, the Americas and Africa have fashioned their own human rights agreements with varying degrees of success. The *European Convention on Human Rights (European Convention)*, adopted in 1950, deals only with civil and political rights.[42] Under the terms of this agreement, states and individual persons from the Council of Europe are allowed to lodge complaints to the European Court of Human Rights (ECtHR). The *American Convention on Human Rights* (ACHR) excludes economic and social rights but includes them in a separate protocol.[43] Unlike the *European Convention* and the ACHR, the *African Charter on Human and Peoples' Rights (Banjul Charter)* adopted by the African Unity in 1981, encompasses all rights—civil, political, social, economic and cultural—in one document.[44] There is no regional human rights commitment among Asian States.

2. *Universalism versus Cultural Relativism*

The main characteristic of human rights, as opposed to particular rights, is their universality in that they stand for the equality of all human beings' fundamental rights.[45] Human rights are conceptualised as "something that pertains to all men at all times"[46] but, this universality is not accepted by all countries, cultures and ideologies. Broadly speaking, Asian nations, Islam and Western postmodernism question the validity of such a feature of human

[41] *Convention against Torture and Other Cruel, Inhuman or Degrading Treatment or Punishment*, Opened for signature 10 Dec. 1984, 1465 UNTS 85 (entered into force 26 June 1987); *Convention on the Elimination of All Forms of Discrimination against Women*, Opened for signature 18 Dec. 1979, 1249 UNTS 13 (Entered into force 3 Sept. 1981); *Convention on the Rights of the Child*, Opened for signature 20 Nov. 1989, UN Doc A/44/49 (Entered into force 2 Sept. 1990).

[42] *Convention for the Protection of Human Rights and Fundamental Freedoms (European Convention on Human Rights)*, Opened for signature 4 Nov. 1950, 213 UNTS 222 (Entered into force 3 Sept. 1953, as amended by Protocols Nos. 3, 5, 8 and 11, Entered into force 21 Sept. 1970, 20 Dec. 1971, 1 Jan. 1990, and 1 Nov. 1998 respectively).

[43] *American Convention on Human Rights*, Opened for signature 20 Nov. 1969, 1144 UNTS 123 (Entered into force 18 July 1978); *Additional Protocol to the American Convention on Human Rights in the Area of Economic, Social, and Cultural Rights (Protocol of San Salvador)*, Opened for signature 17 Nov. 1988, OAS Treaty Series No. 69 (Entered into force 29 Nov. 1999).

[44] *African Charter on Human and Peoples' Rights (Banjul Charter)*, Opened for signature 27 June 1981, OAU Doc CAB/LEG/67/3 rev 5, 21 ILM 58 (Entered into force 21 Oct. 1986).

[45] Mark Freeman and Gibran Van Ert, *International Human Rights Law* (Toronto: Irwin Law, 2004), 26. For different legal theories on the functions of fundamental rights, see Ernst Brandl and Hartwin Bungert, "Constitutional Entrenchment of Environmental Protection: A Comparative Analysis of Experiences Abroad," *Harvard Environmental Law Review* 16, no. 1 (1992): 9–15.

[46] Cranston, *What Are Human Rights?* 23.

rights based on cultural and practical considerations.[47] For instance, some Islamic nations argue against universalism on the grounds of religion and tend to view human rights through the teachings of the *Holy Quran*.[48]

A central objection against the universalism of human rights revolves around its alleged Western origin and 'cultural imperialism', as reflected in the Universal Declaration.[49] Many human rights scholars have rebutted these allegations, arguing that, throughout the half century of its existence, the UDHR has established itself as a reputable instrument of international law and politics. The UDHR was not drafted by a homogenous group of experts but was the outcome of the concerted efforts of eminent figures from all continents, who represented different religious, cultural and ideological backgrounds.[50] In addition, the wide ratification of human rights treaties is indicative of their universality and not a matter of moral or ethical preferences since desirable moral human rights often evolve into legal human rights.[51] The UDHR is itself a cultural instrument that transcends the cultural and ideological peculiarities underlying the inherent worth of human beings. To illustrate, societies that still deny equality between men and women should adjust to a higher value simply for the sake of individuals' well-being, rather than perceiving gender equality as a matter of acculturation or imperialism. The international human rights system is not concerned with cultural specificity unless it affects or degrades the individual for the sake of societal or political values.

The 1993 Vienna Declaration and Programme of Action clarified that, despite the cultural peculiarities of local or traditional groups, states are required to respect the universality of human rights.[52] The Declaration states that "[w]hile the significance of national and regional peculiarities and various historical, cultural and religious backgrounds must be borne in mind, it is the duty of states, regardless of their political, economic and cultural systems, to promote and protect all human rights and fundamental freedoms."[53] While it is true that cultural recognition is an essential component of human dignity, as Tully asserted, the aim of universal human rights is to transcend cultural differences that might jeopardise the *minimum standards* set by

---

[47] See generally Michael Ignatieff, "Human Rights as Politics and Idolatry," in *Human Rights as Politics and Idolatry*, ed. Amy Gutmann (Princeton: Princeton University Press, 2001), 58–63.

[48] Michael Freeman, *Human Rights: An Interdisciplinary Approach* (Cambridge: Polity Press, 2002), 112.

[49] Ibid., 107–08.

[50] Johannes Morsink, *The Universal Declaration of Human Rights: Origins, Drafting, and Intent* (Philadelphia: University of Pennsylvania, 2000), 21.

[51] Kent, *Freedom from Want*, 82.

[52] *Vienna Declaration and Programme of Action: Report of the World Conference on Human Rights*, UN Doc A/CONF.157/23 (1993).

[53] Ibid., par. 5.

international human rights norms.[54] For instance, some cultural practices, like child abuse, amputation of hands as punishment for theft, and female genital mutilation, are incompatible with the essence of international human rights law.

The accusation of 'cultural imperialism' is ill-founded because imperialism contradicts the egalitarian nature of universalism. Thus, the claim that cultural relativism protects the cultural specificities of local groups is suspicious, because, as long as these cultural claims are not revealed to the public, there is a risk that dominant elites will use the principle of cultural relativism to oppress minorities.[55] In this case, universalism is of paramount importance because it endows minorities with the ability to understand and claim their basic rights. As Fleiner pointed out, "we need human rights to protect minorities from discrimination by the majority."[56] Article 27 of the UDHR and Article 15 of the ICESCR acknowledge the right of everyone to participate in the cultural life of the community.[57] International human rights do not exclude cultural rights, and therefore the arguments in favour of cultural relativism are no more than pretexts to justify infringements on human dignity. As Ignatieff put it, "relativism is the invariable alibi of tyranny."[58] Cultural relativism is a convenient concept for undemocratic governments because it equips them with a 'legitimate' excuse to control and intimidate their citizens. For this reason, repressive regimes are often uneasy with the human rights doctrine, but this reluctance does not negate the universality of human rights and their purpose of protecting powerless people from authoritarian, theocratic or despotic regimes.

Rejecting human rights on the grounds of their Eurocentric origins is similar to refusing to travel by aeroplanes or to undergo certain medical procedures just because the West has invented them. Europeans had to go through two devastating global wars before they realised the necessity of universal human rights and adopted the UDHR. In Ignatieff's view, "human rights is not so much the declaration of the superiority of European civilisation as [it is] a warning by Europeans that the rest of the world should not seek to reproduce its mistakes."[59] In fact, the predominance of collectivism over individualism and the idolatry of the nation-state opened the door to Nazi and Stalinist oppression, which sacrificed individual rights on the altar of the nation-state.

---

[54] See Freeman, Michael, *Interdisciplinary Approach*, 118.
[55] Ibid., 110.
[56] Fleiner, *What Are Human Rights?* 21.
[57] *Universal Declaration of Human Rights*, art. 27; *International Covenant on Civil and Political Rights*, art. 15.
[58] Ignatieff, "Human Rights as Politics and Idolatry," 74.
[59] Ibid., 65.

Therefore, the emphasis on individualism in the UDHR aimed to empower the individual against an oppressive state.[60]

D. *Unity and Indivisibility of Human Rights: Taxonomy of Human Rights*

1. *Dichotomy of Human Rights*

Despite the different methods and theories adopted to classify human rights, many international instruments have reiterated and reaffirmed the principle of the unity and indivisibility of human rights. In a study of the history of the UDHR, Morsink found that the drafters perceived it as an 'organic unity' in which every right is interconnected with all other rights.[61] As early as 1968, the Proclamation of Teheran expressly acknowledged the 'indivisibility' of all human rights.[62] The categorisation of human rights is crucial for an emerging human right since how a nascent human right is classified is an important factor in its theoretical underpinnings, its justiciability and eventually its implementation. One of the most common classifications of international human rights is the one that emanates from the International Bill of Rights.[63] Initially, the two International Covenants were meant to be included in one covenant.[64] In 1950, the UN General Assembly issued a resolution regarding the drafting of an international covenant on human rights encompassing, on one hand, civil and political rights and, on the other, economic, social and cultural rights (ESCR). The resolution explicitly acknowledged the intimate links among all rights in stating that "the enjoyment of civic and political freedoms and economic, social and cultural rights are interconnected and interdependent."[65] However, in 1952, another resolution called upon the UN Commission on Human Rights to draft two separate covenants in order to distinguish between the two different types of rights and to give states the choice to adhere to either one.[66]

---

[60] Ibid., 65–66.

[61] Morsink, *Universal Declaration of Human Rights*, XIV.

[62] *Proclamation of Teheran*, Final Act of the International Conference on Human Rights, Teheran, UN Doc A/CONF. 32/41 (1968). Paragraph 13 of the Tehran Proclamation states that "[s]ince human rights and fundamental freedoms are indivisible, the full realisation of civil and political rights without the enjoyment of economic, social and cultural rights is impossible. The achievement of lasting progress in the implementation of human rights is dependent upon sound and effective national and international policies of economic and social development."

[63] The International Bill of Rights consists of the UDHR and the 1966 Covenants: ICCPR and ICESCR.

[64] Szabo, "Historical Foundations," 29.

[65] *Resolution on Draft International Covenant on Human Rights and Measures of Implementation: Future Work of the Commission on Human Rights*, GA Res 421, UN GAOR, 5th sess, 317th plen mtg, UN Doc A/Res/421 (1950).

[66] *Resolution on the Preparation of Two Draft International Covenants on Human Rights*, GA Res 543, UN GAOR, 6th sess, 375th plen mtg, UN doc A/Res/543 (1952).

Some commentators have not regarded these reasons as sufficiently well-founded to justify such a dichotomy in rights.[67] Typical of this view is that of Jhabvala who refuted the validity of the division of rights, as well as their corresponding monitoring mechanisms, describing it as an 'artificial, even unhelpful, formulation.'[68] This earliest division in human rights mirrored the ideological divide that hovered over the Cold War era.[69] It was a reflection of the fierce struggle between the Soviet camp and the Western camp, each of which hailed and prioritised one aspect of the UDHR while accusing the other of human rights violations.[70] The Soviet Union and its European allies were persistently inimical to civil and political rights, considering them 'bourgeois' values of little benefit to most nations.[71]

The idea of positive freedoms was not always appealing to Western powers because of the ingrained liberal conception that prohibited the state from interfering in the individual realm of its citizens.[72] Many American political and business figures viewed socio-economic rights as an obstacle to private enterprise. For instance, there was a tendency in the US Supreme Court to interpret the Constitution in terms of negative rights and to deny the positive duty of the government to grant socio-economic rights like medical assistance.[73] Not surprisingly, the United States has refrained from ratifying the ICESCR on the grounds that these rights represent aspirational goals, rather than rights. From a political perspective, some US Congressmen were particularly suspicious about the adoption of economic and social rights during the Cold War era because they associated the enthusiastic espousal of socialism by some nations with communism.[74] However, not all Western countries adopt the same stance concerning socio-economic rights. Many European constitutions, such as those of Germany and Sweden, explicitly incorporated provisions compelling the government to provide a certain degree of social and economic protection.[75] As Gordon noted, ethical problems arise from the

---

[67] Szabo, "Historical Foundations," 30.

[68] Quoted in W. Paul Gormley, "The Legal Obligation of the International Community to Guarantee a Pure and Decent Environment: The Expansion of Human Rights Norms," *Georgetown International Environmental Law Review* 3(1990): 113.

[69] Edmundson, *Introduction to Rights*, 173.

[70] Paul Gordon Lauren, *The Evolution of International Human Rights: Visions Seen* (Philadelphia: University of Pennsylvania Press, 2003), 236–38.

[71] Ibid., 237.

[72] Justice Michael Kirby, "Human Rights: An Agenda for the Future," in *Rethinking Human Rights*, ed. Brian Galligan and Charles Sampford (Sydney: The Federation Press, 1997), 2–3.

[73] *Deshaney v. Winnebago County Department of Social Services*, 489 U.S. 189(1989); *Webster v. Reproductive Health Services*, 492 U.S. 490 (1989).

[74] David P. Forsythe, *Human Rights in International Relations* (Cambridge: Cambridge University Press, 2000), 41.

[75] Ziyad Motala, "Socio-Economic Rights, Federalism and the Courts: Comparative Lessons for South Africa," *South African Law Journal* 112(1995): 71–72.

exclusion of socio-economic rights from the human rights philosophy.[76] For instance, economic sanctions imposed on a country that does not respect the civil and political rights of its citizens have the unintended consequence of depriving the most vulnerable from means of survival, like food, water and medical treatment.[77]

A sense of integration between both sets of rights is noticeable in international human rights instruments.[78] The *UN Convention on the Rights of the Child* is the first international human rights instrument to include all rights embedded in both the ICCPR and the ICESCR.[79] The *UN Convention on the Elimination of All Forms of Racial Discrimination* and the CEDAW also stressed the need for both types of rights.[80] The division between the two types of rights often coincides with the distinction between negative rights and positive rights. Negative rights or 'rights of abstention' such as the right to freedom of expression and the right to privacy require the non-intervention of the state. In contrast, positive rights such as the right to health and the right to education necessitate a proactive approach by the state in order to be fulfilled.[81] Realistically, both types of rights require a certain degree of state involvement or abstention, depending on the right involved.[82] For instance, in its General Comment on Article 2 of the ICCPR, the UN Human Rights Committee (UNHRC) asserted that the duty of states is not restricted to the respect of human rights but "calls for specific activities by the States Parties to enable individuals to enjoy their rights."[83]

Shue rejected the differentiation between positive and negative rights and replaced it with the notion of basic human rights, which encompass the security rights and subsistence rights, considered essential to human survival and, therefore, indispensable to the enjoyment of all other rights.[84] Shue argued that the real distinction lies in the correlative duties required to fulfil these basic rights and suggested three types of duties for each basic right: avoidance, protection and aid.[85] For example, the right to physical security requires the

---

[76] Joy Gordon, "The Concept of Human Rights: The History and Meaning of Its Politicization," *Brooklyn Journal of International Law* 23(1997–1998): 725–26.

[77] Ibid.

[78] Eide Asbjørn, "Economic, Social and Cultural Rights as Human Rights," in *Economic, Social and Cultural Rights*, ed. Allan Rosas, Eide Asbjørn, and Catarina Krause (Dordrecht/Boston/London: Martinus Nijhoff Publishers, 1995), 23.

[79] *Convention on the Rights of the Child*, arts. 4–17.

[80] *International Convention on the Elimination of All Forms of Racial Discrimination*, art. 5; *Convention on the Elimination of All Forms of Discrimination against Women*, arts. 7–14.

[81] See Freeman, Mark and Van Ert, *International Human Rights Law*, 31–32.

[82] Henry Shue, *Basic Rights: Subsistence, Affluence, and US Foreign Policy* (Princeton: Princeton University Press, 1980), 37–38; Stephen P. Marks, "Emerging Human Rights: A New Generation for the 1980s?" *Rutgers Law Review* 33, no. 2 (1980–1981): 438.

[83] *General Comment 3: Implementation at the National Level*, United Nations Human Rights Committee, UN Doc HRI/GEN/1/Rev.7 (1981).

[84] Shue, *Basic Rights*, 30.

[85] Ibid., 52.

duty of not depriving someone of their own security (avoidance), the duty to protect against harm or assault by third parties through proper social arrangements (protection) and the duty to aid the deprived (aid). In the same way, the right to subsistence entails the duty of not depriving people from their means of subsistence (avoidance), the duty to protect them from deprivation by others (protection) and the duty to supply necessities to those who are unable to provide for themselves (aid).[86] In this context, subsistence rights as economic rights do not automatically correlate with the duty of the state to deliver commodities, but with the availability of opportunities and appropriate social guarantees. This approach has practical implications because it brings both types of rights to the same level of priority and urgency. Although Shue's basic rights are restricted to entitlements to minimum social guarantees of physical security and subsistence, they are an attempt to reveal the fallacy of negative/positive rights and to highlight the urgency of subsistence rights that enable individuals to sustain their livelihoods without being jeopardized by the action or inaction of others. The notion of subsistence, as Shue defined it, includes "unpolluted air, unpolluted water, adequate food, adequate clothing, adequate shelter, and minimal preventive public health care."[87] From this perspective, environmental rights could be portrayed as subsistence rights that are necessary to the fulfilment of other rights. This view is compatible with the genesis theory discussed in Chapter 3.

In an attempt to transcend the dichotomy between political/civil rights and socio-economic rights, some writers have opted to categorise human rights on different grounds.[88] Of special importance is the taxonomy based on the concept of generations of human rights advanced by Vasak and outlined in the next section.[89]

2. *The Concept of Third-Generation Rights*

With the advent of new areas of interest into the family of human rights, a controversial taxonomy that divides human rights into three 'generations' has been proposed and subsequently widely debated. Vasak invoked the metaphor of 'generation' in his attempt to promote a new type of human rights and presented this new classification of human rights in the inaugural lecture at the Tenth Study Session of the International Institute of Human Rights in Strasbourg in July 1979.[90] According to Vasak, the first generation of rights

---

[86] Ibid., 52–53.
[87] Ibid., 23.
[88] For instance, Sieghart relied on the subject protected such as physical integrity, family, work, property, politics and democracy, and collective rights. See Eide, "Economic, Social and Cultural Rights," in Eide and Krause, 21–22.
[89] Vasak, "Troisième Génération."
[90] Ibid.

entails civil and political rights; the second generation of rights consists of social, economic and cultural rights; and the third generation of rights is a set of rights designed to protect human values that are likely to be severely violated as a result of rapidly evolving issues on the international stage (e.g., development, environmental pollution, nuclear proliferation and the North-South divide).[91] The list of new rights proposed by Vasak includes the right to development, the right to peace, the right to environment, the right to property over the common heritage of humankind, and the right to communicate.[92] Vasak's innovation stems from matching the three generations of rights with the famous three pillars of the French Revolution: *liberté, égalité* and *fraternité* (liberty, equality and brotherhood/sisterhood).[93] Accordingly, the first generation of rights represents freedoms or liberty, and the second generation of rights represents equality. Vasak drew upon the third pillar of brotherhood/sisterhood (*fraternité*) to label third-generation rights 'solidarity rights'.[94]

Many commentators have been critical of the use of the terms 'generation'[95] and 'solidarity'. For example, Wellman observed that the reference to 'generations' to describe different sets of rights can be 'misleading and potentially harmful' to understanding the reality of human rights or the intention of advocates of third-generation rights. In essence, the new wave of human rights is not intended to be a substitute of the earlier generations of human rights but to complement and promote them.[96] In addition to this linguistic objection, Alston listed reservations against the classification of rights into generations.[97]

---

[91] Ibid.

[92] Ibid. Third-generation rights are also called rights of developing countries. See V. T. Thamilmaran, *Human Rights in Third World Perspective* (New Delhi: Har-Anand Publications, 1992), 128.

[93] Vasak, "Troisième Génération," 839.

[94] Ibid.

[95] Instead of the generational approach, Sampford proposed a 'multi-dimensional' interpretation of the traditional conception of human rights that emphasises the non-interference of the state into the personal life of its citizens. Sampford broadened the scope of our understanding of human rights by exploring the possibility of viewing them through three or four dimensions. If negative rights, deeply rooted in our legal and social fabric, protect us from the state's infringement of our liberties, protective rights are those that prohibit other individuals from violating them, and therefore require more interference from the state to guarantee protection. Positive rights, a more complex and perplexing set of rights, are defined as 'the rights to resources necessary to act upon our choices.' He added a fourth dimension to his typology: the ability of right-holders to choose freely. This psychological dimension, as he called it, is a necessary step to the genuine realisation of all other rights. See Charles Sampford, "The Four Dimensions of Rights," in *Rethinking Human Rights*, ed. Brian Galligan and Charles Sampford (Sydney: The Federation Press, 1997), 52–56.

[96] Carl Wellman, "Solidarity, the Individual and Human Rights," *Human Rights Quarterly* 22, no. 3 (2000): 641.

[97] Philip Alston, "A Third Generation of Solidarity Rights: Progressive Development or Obfuscation of International Human Rights Law?" *Netherlands International Law Review* 29(1982): 316–17.

First, this 'generational terminology' leads to a conceptual misunderstanding that newer generations are more elaborate or better than the previous ones, which contradicts the international principle of indivisibility of human rights.[98] Second, there is a weak level of homogeneity among the putative new generation of human rights, so it is questionable whether they should be brought together under one umbrella.[99] Alston also questioned the need for a new generation of rights to meet current global challenges, rather than developing the content of existing and well-established human rights.[100] Alston added that the use of the word 'solidarity' to refer or 'launch' a new generation of rights is not appropriate because it implies that solidarity is restricted to third-generation rights. In Alston's words, "solidarity is an essential ingredient in the promotion and realisation of *all* human rights, and not just those of third generation."[101] However, the level and breadth of international cooperation needed to resolve complex issues such as peace and war, transnational pollution, climate change and development are greater than those required for the implementation of other kinds of rights.

Vasak justified the novelty of solidarity rights based on three factors.[102] First, they introduce the human rights dimension into areas traditionally confined to states, particularly development, peace, environment and common heritage of humankind. Second, these rights are negative and positive rights in the sense that they can be invoked by the state and against it at the same time. Finally, the implementation of such broad rights stretches beyond the responsibility of States to include individuals, non-state bodies and the international community.[103] The specific feature of joint responsibility of all relevant actors in global issues is what justifies the need for solidarity rights. In the case of humanitarian assistance, the international community as a whole is considered the right-bearer that is responsible for helping affected people.[104] Commenting on the notion of solidarity in Vasak's proposition of third-generation rights, Wellman noted that the new generation of rights, Vasak conceived it, is designed to fill a gap in the classical doctrine of human rights that is based on excessive individualism and egoism.[105] Filling this gap is achieved through *fraternité*, the solidarity component of human rights that creates a sense of social solidarity among citizens.

In summary, solidarity rights are inclined towards group or collective rights in that citizens, private groups, and the entire international community share

---

[98] Ibid.
[99] Ibid.
[100] Ibid.
[101] Ibid., 318.
[102] Vasak, "Troisième Génération," 839.
[103] Ibid.
[104] Marks, "Emerging Human Rights," 325.
[105] Wellman, "Solidarity," 642.

responsibility with the states in order to fulfil and guarantee these rights. Sen described the allocation of duties to such a wide range of duty-holders as the Kantien view of 'imperfect obligations', which contradicts the notion of 'perfect obligations' that links rights to 'agent-specific' duties.[106] According to Sen, the notion of 'imperfect obligations'—which implies that the fulfilment of rights can be the responsibility of a flexible range of duty-bearers such as the State or the international community—circumvents the traditional conception of states as the main duty-bearers in guaranteeing human rights.[107] In this respect, Vasak's theory of third-generation rights provides a useful contribution to the doctrine of human rights because it extends the scope of obligations to non-state actors. The main objection against socio-economic rights and solidarity rights lies in the ability of these rights to be judicially enforceable but the most common response to this objection is that a legal norm is not necessarily conditional on the means of its execution.[108] The implementation of second and third generations of rights necessitates more than a traditional bill of rights, judicial reviews and high courts. There is a pragmatic need for 'joint efforts' from other social and political institutions.[109] However, this sense of solidarity does not necessarily undermine the individualistic nature of universal human rights but complements it.

3. *Individualism versus Collectivism*

Third-generation rights and collective rights differ in several ways. Some human rights already recognised under the International Bill of Rights—including minority rights, the right to self-determination and cultural rights—have a collective element, while solidarity rights such as the right to development have an individual component.[110] Much suspicion surrounds the move towards the concept of collective human rights. Apart from Indigenous peoples, Donnelly asserted that groups such as women and minorities can have their rights protected through well-established international human rights, while some collective human rights, such as cultural rights, the right to self-determination and the right to cultural identity, lack viable bases.[111] The problem lies in the observance of individual human rights by states, rather than in the liberal individual rights approach.[112] In Donnelly's words, people's

---

[106] See Arjun Sengupta, "On the Theory and Practice of the Right to Development," in *Development as a Human Right: Legal, Political, and Economic Dimensions*, ed. Bård A. Andreassen and Stephen P. Marks (Boston: Harvard School of Public Health, 2006), 65.

[107] Ibid., 65.

[108] Vasak, "Troisième Génération," 843.

[109] Ibid.

[110] See Allan Rosas, "So-Called Rights of the Third Generation," in *Economic, Social, and Cultural Rights*, ed. Asbjørn Eide, Catarina Krause, and Allan Rosas (Dordrecht/Boston/London: Martinus Nijhoff Publishers, 1995), 244.

[111] Donnelly, *Universal Human Rights*, 211–14.

[112] Ibid., 221.

rights "are best seen as rights of individuals acting as members of social groups."[113]

Despite the growing enthusiasm for collective rights, individualism is—and always will be—at the core of human rights philosophy. Undermining individual rights for the sake of higher social interests strips the concept of human rights of its very foundation.[114] In some respects, classifying some rights into the category of group rights or collective rights does not affect the individualistic essence of human rights since it is a tactical approach related to the intrinsically complex nature of rights such as the right to environment and the right to development. According to Appiah, group rights should be perceived "as instruments in the service of enriching the lives and possibilities of individuals."[115] In the same vein, Ignatieff noted that "the ultimate purpose and justification of group rights is not the protection of the group as such but the protection of the individuals who compose it."[116] For instance, environmental disasters infringe on the rights of individuals as well as those of whole communities; it is impractical to address many human rights violations on an individual basis because thousands of people are affected. Thus, an innovative and suitable mechanism is necessary to remedy such situations.

E. *The Implementation of Human Rights*

1. *The Observance of International Human Rights*

As Thomas Hobbes once said, "[c]ovenants, without the sword, are but words!"[117] Most international human rights treaties are endowed with treaty-monitoring bodies the primary role of which is to monitor and promote States' compliance with treaties' provisions through reporting and complaints procedures. All States Parties to an international human rights treaty are required to submit to the relevant body periodic reports of the status of human rights within their territories. Apart from reporting and complaint procedures, some treaty bodies, such as the UNHRC and the Committee on the Elimination of Discrimination against Women, are also empowered to accept petitions from individuals.[118]

The implementation of international human rights is not confined to treaty-based procedures since some non-treaty based mechanisms derive from

[113] Ibid., 222.
[114] Fleiner, *What Are Human Rights?* 30.
[115] Appiah, "Grounding Human Rights," 115.
[116] Ignatieff, "Human Rights as Politics and Idolatry," 67.
[117] Thomas Hobbes, "Leviathan," in *Oxford World's Classics Series* (New York: Oxford University Press, 1998). Chapter XVII. Available at http://oregonstate.edu/instruct/phl302/texts/hobbes/leviathan-c.html#CHAPTERXVII.
[118] *First Optional Protocol to the International Covenant on Civil and Political Rights*; *Optional Protocol to the Convention on the Elimination of All Forms of Discrimination against Women*, Opened for signature 10 Dec. 1999, UN Doc A/54/L4 (Entered into force 22 Dec. 2000).

resolutions of the UN Human Rights Council or the General Assembly. These mechanisms are assigned to working groups of experts or individuals, such as Special Rapporteurs, Special Representatives or Independent Experts. All these appointed experts work independently from their governments to address serious human rights issues through either country-specific or thematic mandates. The Special Rapporteur on Afganistan and the Special Representative on Iran are examples of country-specific mandates, while thematic mandates include the Special Rapporteur on religious intolerance, the Special Rapporteur on the right to education, and the Independent Expert on the right to food, among others. The appointment of rapporteurs, representatives or working groups is of central importance to the development of international human rights.[119] In contrast to the international environmental law system, the international human rights system is endowed with the supervisory and judiciary mechanisms necessary for the protection and enforcement of human rights. A human rights approach to environmental issues relies on these mechanisms to defend both ecosystems and victims of environmental degradation.

2. *Role of Non-Governmental Organisations*

Apart from the judiciary's role, non-governmental organisations (NGOs) and public opinion have a constructive and complementary role to play in the observance of international human rights. NGOs, whether international, regional or local, carry out diverse functions. Through the submission of 'shadow reports', these NGOs keep track of the status of human rights violations and channel their information to specialised UN human rights bodies such as the CEDAW Committee.[120] Such records, whether or not facilitated by the official bodies, exert tremendous pressure on local authorities to act in conformity with international human rights norms. Of equal importance are the NGOs' efforts to lobby governmental bodies on behalf of human rights matters. It is a common practice for international human rights organisations, such as Amnesty International and Human Rights Watch, to reveal alarming governmental records to the media in order to mobilise public support for the environment. In reality, it is difficult to imagine a functioning and effective human rights law without the advocacy of NGOs.

---

[119] See Office of the High Commissioner for Human Rights, "Human Rights Bodies," http://www.ohchr.org/EN/HRBodies/Pages/HumanRightsBodies.aspx.

[120] WLP Women's Learning Partnership, "Shadow Reports: Holding Governments Accountable for Women's Human Rights," http://www.learningpartnership.org/news/enews/2003/iss4/shadow.

3. *The Justiciability of Socio-Economic and Cultural Human Rights*

One of the most debated issues in the implementation of human rights lies in the widespread belief that socio-economic rights are less justiciable or enforceable than civil and political rights. Since its inception, the ICCPR has been endowed with more explicit enforcement provisions than the ICESCR. In addition, the first *Optional Protocol* to ICCPR empowers individuals to lodge complaints with the UNHRC when all domestic legal avenues are exhausted. From a practical standpoint, such legal considerations lead to the supremacy of civil and political rights, perceived as 'real rights', over socio-economic rights.[121] If rights-holders can file suits against perpetrators only when the human right involved is a civil and political right, rather than a socio-economic right, then a certain degree of hierarchy exists amongst human rights. Accordingly, one might question the validity of the biased difference in the implementation between the two sets of rights. Many arguments have been unconvincingly advanced in an attempt to answer this legitimate question. Among them is the specious notion that political rights require a more acquiescent attitude from States and less governmental resources than do economic rights. Another argument reiterates the idea that the non-interference of states in the enjoyment of political and civil rights alone leads to their full and immediate implementation.[122] The first argument can be refuted on the grounds that expenditures are needed in support of both types of rights. For instance, the protection of the 'due process' rights of defendants does not occur without governmental expenditure on judicial institutions.[123] As for the second argument, a sovereign state should be held accountable not only for torturing its people but also for its inaction or involvement in or failure to prevent serious human rights abuses, such as when civilians are the victims of a genocide executed by unofficial armed groups acting within a state's boundaries.[124]

The reluctance to treat these rights as justiciable and the failure to apply the principle of *locus standi* under diverse national courts in related cases, used to be the main obstacles to their implementation.[125] However, this situation is changing in favour of more judicial recognition of ESCR, especially in national jurisdictions. The *Human Rights Development Report 2000* found that people are increasingly relying on the law—including international human rights

---

[121] Shelley Wright, *International Human Rights, Decolonization and Globalization* (London: Routledge, 2001), 187.

[122] Lauren, *Evolution of International Human Rights*, 711–12.

[123] Ibid., 711.

[124] Ibid., 713.

[125] Justice C. Nwobike, "The African Commission on Human and Peoples' Rights and the Demystification of Second and Third Generation Rights under the African Charter: *Social and Economic Rights Action Center (SERAC) and the Center for Economic and Social Rights (CESR) v. Nigeria*," *African Journal of Legal Studies* 1(2004–2005): 141.

law—to vindicate their social and economic rights such as housing rights.[126] Despite the complexity and difficulty of implementing the second generation of rights, the judiciary was, in many instances, able to achieve a breakthrough in the development of the jurisprudence of socio-economic rights. In the *Grootboom* case,[127] the South African Constitutional Court questioned the justiciability of socio-economic rights. Sachs, Justice of the Constitutional Court of South Africa, considered the case a major test of the enforceability of constitutional economic and social rights and of the influence that the judiciary can exert on the executive in order to guarantee such rights.[128]

This case law is indicative of the complexity of these rights and the judiciary's ability to adjudicate them. Mrs Grootboom was one of about a thousand squatters, half of them children, living in dreadful conditions in a Wallacedene sports field in South Africa.[129] After failing to get help from the municipality, Mrs Grootboom and members of her community launched an urgent application in the Cape High Court basing their claims on constitutional provisions related to the right to access to adequate housing and the right of children to shelter.[130] While the Cape High Court dismissed the right of the applicant to adequate housing, it held that the State is under the constitutional obligation to provide shelter and other basic services to homeless parents and children and issued a declaratory order that obligated public authorities to take the necessary measures to provide relief to the poverty-stricken community of Wallacedene.[131] The national government challenged the order in the Constitutional Court, which asserted the responsibility of the State to comply with its obligations regarding the constitutional right of access to adequate housing. Despite the State's poor compliance with the order, the *Grootboom* case, theoretically speaking, is an interesting example of how the judiciary can explicitly compel the executive to comply with the requirements of a socio-economic human right. State non-compliance with a judicial order is not the

[126] United Nations Development Programme (UNDP), "Human Development Report 2000: Human Rights and Human Development," http://hdr.undp.org/en/reports/global/hdr2006/. 76.

[127] *Government of Republic of South Africa and Others v. Grootboom*, 11 BCLR 1169 (2000).

[128] Hon. Mr. Justice Albie Sachs, "Enforcing Socio-Economic Rights," in *Sustainable Justice: Reconciling Economic, Social and Environmental Law*, ed. Marie-Claire Cordonier Segger and C.G. Weeramantry (Dordrecht/Boston/London: Martinus Nijhoff Publishers, 2005), 66.

[129] In fact, South Africa struggles with deep-rooted housing crises, a legacy of colonialism and apartheid. The advent of democracy and the Bill of Rights was supposed to rectify the inequity practiced for centuries against deprived and homeless people who lack basic rights like adequate housing and shelter for children.

[130] *Constitution of the Republic of South Africa* secs. 26(2) and 28 (1-c).

[131] *Grootboom v. Oostenberg Municipality and Others*, 3 BCLR 277(2000). Available at http://www.communitylawcentre.org.za/Childrens-Rights/05Legal-Resources/cases-judgements/high-courts/2_groot.pdf/.

responsibility of the courts but is primarily related to the peculiarities of the state's political system and does not necessarily affect the jurisprudential value of a judgment, although persistent non-compliance with judicial decisions may undermine the legitimacy of the judiciary.

On the regional level, the *SERAC* decision[132] of the African Commission on Human and Peoples' Rights (African Commission) is another groundbreaking case because of its role in the evolution of international jurisprudence on ESCR.[133] Two NGOs, the Social and Economic Rights Action Centre (SERAC) and the Centre for Economic and Social Rights, brought an action before the African Commission against the Nigerian government for violations related to two state-run oil companies operating in Ogoniland—National Nigerian Petroleum Company (NNPC) and Shell Petroleum Development Corporation—accusing them of gross human rights violations against the Indigenous Ogoni people. In this case, the African Commission refuted the common misunderstanding regarding the non-judicial enforcement of ESCR. Many human rights scholars and commentators have argued that individual petitions should not be confined exclusively to civil and political rights and have proposed that the right to individual petitions be advanced to socio-economic matters.[134] This approach would address the discrepancy in the protection of the human rights that belong to the so-called 'non-justiciable' category of rights. Scott argued that the concepts of 'interdependence' and 'permeability' justify expanding the expediency offered by individual petition procedures to some socio-economic rights that have the potential to 'permeate' the category of civil and political rights.[135] Scott defined permeability as "the openness of a treaty to the supervision of human rights norms from a different category of rights found in another treaty."[136] For instance, General Comment 6 of the UNHRC expanded the scope of the right to life enunciated in the ICCPR by interpreting the right to life in a wider context.[137] This right stretches beyond the physical integrity of a person to include socio-economic rights such as the rights to health, food and shelter. Therefore, if these socio-economic rights acquire the legal status of the right to life, they may become as justiciable as political and civil rights.

---

132 *The Social and Economic Rights Action Center and the Center for Economic and Social Rights v. Nigeria (SERAC Case)*, Communication 155/96, ACHPR/COMM/A044/1(2002).

133 See Nwobike, "Demystification of Second and Third Generation Rights."

134 Wright, *International Human Rights*, 187.

135 Craig Scott, "The Interdependence and Permeability of Human Rights Norms: Towards a Partial Fusion of the International Conventions on Human Rights," *Osgoode Hall Law Journal* 27(1989): 841.

136 Ibid.

137 *General Comment 6: The Right to Life*, United Nations Human Rights Committee, 16th sess, UN Doc HRI\GEN\1\Rev.7 (1982).

Moreover, General Comment 3 of the UN Committee on Economic, Social and Cultural Rights (CESCR) requires states to satisfy 'minimum core obligations' to fulfil socio-economic rights.[138] A state fails to comply with its core obligations under the ICESCR if "a significant number of individuals are deprived of essential foodstuffs, of essential primary health care, of basic shelter and housing, or the most basic forms of education."[139] Without such minimum requirements, the Committee argues, the Covenant loses its 'raison d'être'.[140] Therefore, lack of resources does not justify violations of ESCR.[141] The Limburg Principles on the Implementation of the ICESCR clarified that human rights listed in the ICESCR should be fulfilled gradually and that "some rights can be made justiciable immediately while other rights can be justiciable over time."[142] As a result of staunch advocacy for the promotion of ESCR as legal rights, the CESCR drafted an *Optional Protocol* to the *International Covenant on Economic Social and Cultural rights* (OP-ICESCR).[143] The aim of the Protocol is to establish an individual complaint mechanism in the UN that enables victims of alleged breaches of socio-economic and cultural rights to submit formal complaints to the CESCR in order to seek appropriate remedies where domestic avenues are lacking or insufficient.[144] The *Optional Protocol* to CEDAW also provides a communication procedure that enables both individuals and groups of individuals to submit complaints to the Committee on the Elimination of Discrimination against Women.[145]

4. *States' Obligations*

The tripartite obligations as elaborated by Eide, or quadruple obligations as expanded by Van Hoof, are presented as alternatives to the traditional notion of negative and positive duties. Eide, the UN's Special Rapporteur for Food in the early 1980s, identified three types of obligations regarding human rights: the obligations to *respect, to protect* and *to fulfil*.[146] The obligation to *respect* requires non-interference by the state in the enjoyment of human rights. The

---

[138] *General Comment 3: The Nature of States Parties Obligations*, Committee on Economic, Social and Cultural Rights, UN Doc E/1991/23 (1990), par. 10.

[139] Ibid.

[140] Ibid.

[141] Sachs, "Enforcing Socio-Economic Rights," 71.

[142] *The Limburg Principles on the Implementation of the International Covenant on Economic, Social and Cultural Rights*, UN ESCOR, 4th Comm, 43rd sess, Annex, UN Doc. E/CN.4/1987/17(1987), Principle 8.

[143] See *Draft Optional Protocol to the International Covenant on Economic, Social and Cultural Rights: Note by the Secretary-General*, UN CHR, 53rd sess, E/CN.4/1997/105(1996).

[144] See ESCR-Net, "Optional Protocol to the ICESCR Initiative," http://www.escr-net.org/actions_more/actions_more_show.htm?doc_id=433788.

[145] *Optional Protocol to the Convention on the Elimination of All Forms of Discrimination against Women*, art. 2.

[146] *General Comment 12: The Right to Self-Determination of Peoples (Art 1)*, United Nations Human Rights Committee, 21st sess, UN Doc HRI/GEN/Rev.1 (1984), par. 15.

obligation to *protect* requires states to protect its citizens' rights from being violated by a third party. The obligation to *fulfil* requires a more proactive role from states regarding the realisation of human rights and includes the duty of governments to *facilitate* and to *provide*.[147] Through the obligation to *facilitate*, the government guarantees the social and economic preconditions for its citizens to enjoy their socio-economic rights. A strong economy, for example, is a prerequisite for the fulfilment of the right to work and the right to an adequate standard of living. However, when, under exceptional circumstances, some people fail to provide for themselves through employment or personal resources, the government is under the obligation to *provide* the right to social security so the person involved is not subject to humiliation, hunger or disease.[148]

According to Eide, the obligations related to ESCR are not restricted to states; individuals are supposed to seek the fulfilment of their needs through their own resources, protected by the state.[149] Consequently, the responsibility of the state lies in its enabling and protective role and not necessarily in the provision of specific economic resources. The protective function of the state is often reflected in constitutional provisions and existing laws that can be administered by the judiciary, so the assumption that socio-economic and cultural rights are non-justiciable is not tenable.[150] The quadruple typology is similar to the tripartite one, with the exception that the obligation *to fulfil* is replaced by two more nuanced obligations: *to ensure and to promote*. These are called 'programmatic', meaning that they are positive actions taken by states with a progressive element.[151] The 'tripartite typology'[152] and the quadruple categorisation of obligations transcend the rigid dichotomy of negative and positive duties, taking it to a different level of understanding. The traditional argument raised against the legal status of social rights is diminishing gradually as a result of global awareness of the importance of these rights. These categorisations are more suited to the emerging environmental rights whose realisation requires a more sophisticated approach to obligations that goes beyond the traditional dichotomy of negative and positive duties.

5. *Limited Duty-Bearers*

Human rights are also criticised for having a limited number of duty-bearers. Most of the responsibility for guaranteeing human rights is placed upon the

---

[147] Kent, *Freedom from Want*, 106–7.
[148] Ibid.
[149] Eide, "Economic, Social and Cultural Rights," 37.
[150] Ibid.
[151] Scott, "Human Rights Norms," 835.
[152] See Ida Elisabeth Koch, "Dichotomies, Trichotomies or Waves of Duties?" *Human Rights Law Review* 5, no. 1 (2005): 82.

government, but many authors have argued that international law should not be static in a dynamic world and that it must move beyond the traditional conception of states as the primary abusers of human rights. In the sweeping era of globalisation, non-state entities are increasingly becoming a new threat to the status of human rights worldwide.[153] Terrorist and clandestine organisations, along with large corporations, are just some examples of the inability of governments to control new international actors. Practically and theoretically speaking, as long as human beings' rights are violated, the identity of the perpetrators makes little difference.[154] As Kennedy pointed out, "[h]uman rights implicitly legitimates ills and delegitimates remedies in the domain of private law and non-state action."[155] Typical of this view is the feminist criticism of a human rights system that is predominantly focused on states' violations while overlooking individual domestic violations that men inflict on women.[156]

The tripartite typology described above attempts to hold private entities accountable for human rights violations. It includes the obligation of the state to take measures to *protect* its citizens from private parties, not only from public authorities. To hold third parties accountable for their violations of human rights does not change the fact that the main obligation for fulfilling human rights remains in the hands of governmental bodies. On the international level, states are the main signatories of treaties, including human rights covenants. However, the power of multinational corporations (MNCs) and their influence on local economies reduce considerably the capacity of states to fulfil their obligations under the ICESCR.[157] As global businesses, many MNCs cross national boundaries in order to run their operations in host countries where social and environmental regulations are less stringent. Driven by profit maximisation and competitiveness, they are often insensitive to the sociocultural needs of local communities.[158] These MNCs are called upon to play a more positive role in host countries, particularly developing countries, by requiring an acceptable standard of human rights from local governments as a prerequisite to bringing in their investment operations.[159] When local governments are unable or unwilling to invest in the local communities where most of the impact from MNCs' operations occurs, MNCs are urged to step in and reinvest some of the profit generated from using local resources back into

---

[153] See Sampford, "Four Dimensions," 52.
[154] See Daniel Aguirre, "Multinational Corporations and the Realisation of Economic, Social and Cultural Rights," *California Western International Law Journal* 35(2004): 57.
[155] David Kennedy, *The International Human Rights Movement: Part of the Problem?* (Sydney: The Federation Press, 2001), 10.
[156] See Freeman, Michael, *Interdisciplinary Approach*, 128.
[157] Aguirre, "Multinational Corporations," 56.
[158] Ibid., 60–61.
[159] Ibid., 64.

those localities.[160] Accordingly, the responsibility for fulfilling human rights, especially the ESCR, can be transferred to the private sphere in cases where the state fails to comply with its international obligations. In this regard, MNCs should be held accountable for human rights' violations especially when those violations are endorsed by public authorities, such as the use of the military or security forces to suppress and torture local people who protest against harmful and inequitable development projects.[161] In such circumstances, the state cannot protect its own citizens from a third party when, by its own actions, it is condoning and facilitating the exploitative operations of MNCs.

The efforts of the international community have gradually moved towards breaking the complicity between MNCs and host countries by regulating the conduct of corporations at an international level. Large-scale industrial and nuclear environmental disasters, in particular, have raised the issue of corporate accountability worldwide. The Bhopal disaster of 1984, described as the world's worst industrial disaster, is a tragic illustration of the impact of the environmentally unsound management of dangerous industries on vulnerable communities and their environments. The Bhopal disaster caused by the release of 27 tons of toxic gases from a pesticide factory run by an Indian subsidiary of Union Carbide, a US-based company, killed an estimated 22,000 people as a result of the gas leak and left about 100,000 more with debilitating and chronic ailments.[162] The effects of the disaster still haunt the survivors of Bhopal and shockingly, neither Union Carbide nor Dow Chemical, who took over Union Carbide in 2001, were held accountable for their plight.[163] More recently, Shell agreed, after 14-year trial, to pay \$15.5 million to settle a legal suit in which the plaintiffs accused the oil giant of human rights violations in the Ogoni region of the Niger Delta, alleging that Shell was complicit in the 1995 executions of Ken Saro-Wiwa, leader of the Movement for the Survival of Ogoni People, and eight other leaders.[164] Although Shell never admitted its involvement in the death of the Ogoni Nine, this large settlement, portrayed by Shell as 'a humanitarian gesture', will undoubtedly have a significant impact on corporate responsibility in the future by encouraging MNCs to take their social and environmental responsibilities seriously when they operate in host countries.

In response to the increased pressure on multinational firms to comply with their social responsibilities, many corporations have adopted voluntary codes

---

[160] Ibid., 64–65.

[161] See Nwobike, "Demystification of Second and Third Generation Rights," 143.

[162] Amnesty International, *Clouds of Injustice: Bhopal Disaster 20 Years On* (London: Amnesty International Publications, 2004), 1.

[163] Ibid.

[164] The Case Against Shell, "Wiwa v. Shell: Victory Settlement!" http://wiwavshell.org/wiwa-v-shell-victory-settlement/.

of conduct. However, judging by the numerous cases of human rights violations by such corporations, these voluntary codes are often insufficient. In August 2003, the UN Sub-Commission on the Promotion and Protection of Human Rights approved the UN Human Rights Norms for Business (UNHRNB), which lists the human rights obligations of MNCs.[165] This international instrument refers to MNCs as 'transnational corporations' and to domestic companies as 'other business enterprises'. Although the UNHRNB reiterates that States are the primary duty-bearers of human rights on the international stage, it also mentions that "transnational corporations and other business enterprises have the obligation to promote ... and protect human rights recognised in international as well as national law, including the rights and interests of Indigenous peoples and other vulnerable groups."[166]

The duties of the states are also compromised by the work of welfare organisations, both national and international, that try to fill the gaps in basic services such as shelter, food and medical assistance. In this regard, Kent stressed the importance of differentiating between 'humanitarian assistance work and human rights work'.[167] While the excessive reliance on charitable work to meet people's needs strips the state of its own social responsibilities, human rights work targets the public sector in a bid to pressure the government to remedy the social and economic discrepancies in its own system.[168] Welfare assistance through either private or public entities is not desirable in the long-term because it leads to the disempowerment of communities, and the respect of human dignity is compromised when people of low socio-economic status have to rely on external financial assistance to survive. The state is obliged to secure appropriate employment strategies to empower the marginalised and to encourage them to participate in political and social systems. In this regard, democracy is often portrayed as an essential precondition for the implementation and enforcement of human rights.[169]

Conclusion

The culture of human rights is one of struggle and nobility. Despite the human aspect enshrined in its core concept, human rights cannot be fully associated with anthropocentrism since its scope goes beyond the mere immediate

---

[165] *Norms on the Responsibilities of Transnational Corporations and Other Business Enterprises with Regard to Human Rights*, UN Doc E/CN.4/Sub.2/2003/12/Rev.2 (2003).

[166] Ibid., sec. A.

[167] Kent, *Freedom from Want*, 124.

[168] Ibid., 121–23.

[169] It is worth noting that democracy has its own limitations and does not offer solutions to all social and political problems. Such critique is beyond the scope of this book. See generally Samuel Gregg, "The Tragedy of Democracy: 'Rights', Tolerance and Moral 'Neutrality'," *Comment* (Winter 2000). Available at http://www.cis.org.au/policy/winter00/win2k-8.pdf.

materialistic interests of human beings to the preservation of the integrity and dignity of humanity in its spiritual and ecological dimensions. There is great potential to defend the rights of nature through the human rights discourse because of the complementarities between humans and the environment. Moreover, the conceptualisation of human rights as solidarity rights and the elaboration of the tripartite obligations constitute significant legal bases for emerging environmental rights, as proposed in this book. Without necessarily adopting the generational classification of human rights advocated by Vasak, the current research views 'solidarity' as a concept that can address the complexities of environmental issues and the multiplicity of duty-bearers involved. Similarly, the tripartite typology of obligations, which is more detailed than the traditional dichotomy of negative and positive duties, is of central importance to the realisation of environmental rights.

The principle of sovereignty constitutes a constraint on the ability of the international community to hold states accountable for gross human rights violations. Despite this impediment, the strength of the human rights concept lies in its weaknesses. In essence, human rights advocates tend to target primarily powerful entities, such as governments and businesses, in order to protect the most vulnerable and, in doing so, position themselves as the voice of the voiceless. In the public conscience, human rights are endowed with a psychological puissance that can mobilise the masses around urgent global issues such as genocide, environmental degradation and poverty. Most important, human rights are endowed with a sense of urgency, a 'trumping' effect that counterbalances economic and financial interests. In the domestic realm, environmental rights, as defensive legal rights, have the potential to elevate environmental concerns above politics by providing an additional tool of checks and balances to offset the ever-increasing power of the legislative and executive branches of government in environmental matters.

PART TWO

THE CONCEPTUALISATION AND DEVELOPMENT OF ENVIRONMENTAL ISSUES AS HUMAN RIGHTS

CHAPTER THREE

THEORISATION OF THE VARIOUS HUMAN RIGHTS APPROACHES TO ENVIRONMENTAL ISSUES

Introduction

Previous chapters have explored the philosophical and theoretical bases underlying the evolution of the environment as a human right. Chapter 1 argued that one way of addressing ecological crises lies in mending the exploitative relationship between humankind and nature. To achieve this, the human rights concept, as explored in Chapter 2, can be expanded to include the environment and its components on the premise that the intrinsic value of non-human entities is part of human dignity. In other words, human beings can extend their human dignity beyond themselves, so there is no philosophical impediment to the inclusion of environmental interests in the human rights catalogue, from either an anthropocentric or an ecocentric perspective.

The interrelationship between human rights and the environment materialises in the various human rights approaches to environmental issues, which encompass the expansion or re-interpretation of existing human rights, the reliance on procedural rights, and the conceptualisation of a distinct human right to environment. The trend towards environmental protection constitutes an innovative and sophisticated legal tool of the 21st century. In order to critically examine these approaches, I devise three theories to explain and capture the various nuances, viewpoints and controversies surrounding the legal and philosophical conceptualisation of environmental issues as human rights: the expansion theory, the 'environmental democracy' theory and the genesis theory. The first two theories correspond to the greening of existing procedural and substantive human rights, while the genesis theory explains the development and emergence of a distinct right to environment in international law.

A. *The Expansion Theory*

The expansion theory bestows an environmental interpretation upon well-established human rights, like the right to life, the right to health and the right to privacy in what is known as the greening of existing human rights.[1] These

[1] See Patricia Birnie and Alan E. Boyle, *International Law and the Environment*, 2nd ed. (New York: Oxford University Press, 2002).

rights are often referred to as 'derivative rights',[2] which nomenclature implies that they have been or—could be—invoked in an environmental context. Although the expansion or reinterpretation of existing human rights is not sufficient to protect a wider environmental agenda, this approach is useful as a transitional stage that paves the way to the future recognition of a distinct right to environment.[3]

1. *The Right to Life*

The right to life is the essence of all other types of rights because it refers to the core existence of human beings.[4] A threatened or terminated human life cannot enjoy other rights. Vasak described the right to life as 'the first right of man.'[5] Because of its paramount importance, it is often recognised as a peremptory norm in international law that cannot be derogated under any circumstances. The right to life is a well-established international human right that is embodied in major international and regional instruments: Article 3 of the Universal Declaration of Human Rights (UDHR), Article 3 of the *International Covenant on Civil and Political Rights* (ICCPR), Article 4 of the *African Charter on Human and Peoples' Rights (Banjul Charter)*, Article 4 of the *American Convention on Human Rights* (ACHR) and Article 2 of the *European Convention on Human Rights (European Convention)*. The *jus cogens* nature of the right to life makes states, as traditional duty-bearers, accountable not only when it infringes on the right to life but also when it fails to take necessary measures to prevent its infringement. The idea of negative rights versus positive rights, which differentiates civil and political rights from socio-economic rights, is applicable only when states are viewed as the sole actors in the human rights arena. In a more complex setting, whether national or international, other powerful actors may violate a multitude of human rights, but a state cannot argue that its responsibility lies only in its non-involvement in the enjoyment of a specific human right. Instead, the state is required to take some positive measures to ensure that civil and political rights, traditionally considered negative rights, are sufficiently respected and guaranteed. The European Commission on Human Rights (ECHR) adopted this proactive approach by suggesting that the right to life, as embodied in Article 2 of the *European Convention*, requires states "not only to refrain from taking life intentionally but, further, to take appropriate steps to safeguard life."[6]

---

[2] Robin Churchill, "Environmental Rights in Existing Human Rights Treaties," in *Human Rights Approaches to Environmental Protection*, ed. Alan E. Boyle and Michael R. Anderson (Oxford: Clarendon Press, 1996), 90.

[3] See especially Patrick Ryan Hamilton, "Human Rights at the Doubling Point: Human Rights, the Environment and Climate Change in International Law" (LLM diss., University of Toronto, 2006), 15.

[4] See especially *General Comment 6: The Right to Life*.

[5] Frank C. Newman and Karel Vasak, "Civil and Political Rights," in *The International Dimensions of Human Rights*, ed. Karel Vasak (Paris: Greenwood Press, 1982), 144.

[6] Churchill, "Environmental Rights," 91.

General Comment 6 of the UNHRC describes the right to life as a 'supreme' and non-derogable human right that should not be interpreted in a narrow way.[7] In this regard, states are urged to take positive measures in order to protect human life, including the reduction of infant mortality, increase in life expectancy, and eradication of malnutrition and epidemics.[8] Through this Comment, the UNHRC opened the door for the right to life to stretch beyond the traditional threat coming from public authorities to include environmental threats affecting the welfare and livelihoods of millions of people around the world.

The 1989 Hague Declaration on the Environment is an important (non-binding) document because it linked the fundamental right to life to a healthy environment.[9] Several national and regional courts have drawn upon this link between environmental protection and the right to life. Of special importance is the Indian judiciary, which is known for its proactive role in defending the environment through the expansion of the right to life to include environmental interests and through its reliance on unenforceable directive principles to interpret and expand fundamental rights. The Indian Supreme Court interpreted the constitutional right to life in a broad way as to secure environmental protection in both its anthropocentric and ecocentric dimensions. This interpretation promoted the status of human rights and initiated a rich environmental jurisprudence in India. Decisions of an anthropocentric nature have linked environmental violation to human life, health and safety. For instance, in *Chinnappa and Godavarman*,[10] the Indian Supreme Court found that a "hygienic environment is an integral facet of the right to a healthy life and it would be impossible to live with human dignity without a humane and healthy environment."[11] Some environmental decisions went further in the protection of the environment by requiring pollution-free air and water or even the more ecocentric goal of 'ecological balance'.[12] In the *Subhash Kumar* case, the Supreme Court stated that the right to life "includes the right to enjoyment of pollution-free water and air for full enjoyment of life."[13] In another case, it reiterated "that every citizen has a right to fresh air and to live in a pollution-free environment."[14] In the *Kendra* case,[15] the Supreme Court

[7] *General Comment 6: The Right to Life*, par. 1.

[8] Ibid., par. 5.

[9] *Hague Declaration on the Environment*, 28 ILM 1308 (1989).

[10] *K.M. Chinnappa and T.N. Godavarman Thirumalpad v. Union of India and Others*, 10 SCC 606(2002).

[11] Ibid., par. 18.

[12] Michael R. Anderson, "Individual Rights to Environmental Protection in India," in *Human Rights Approaches to Environmental Protection*, ed. Alan E. Boyle and Michael R. Anderson (Oxford: Clarendon Press, 1996), 217.

[13] *Subhash Kumar v. State of Bihar*, AIR 1991 SC 420(1991).

[14] *M.C. Mehta v. Union of India and Others*, 1991 SCC (2) 353, 360 (1992).

[15] *Rural Litigation and Entitlement Kendra v. Uttar Pradesh* (1985) AIR SC 652.

ruled that the limestone quarries in the Dehra Dun area should be closed and the cost borne by the lessees for the sake of "protecting and safe-guarding the right of the people to live in a healthy environment with minimal disturbance of ecological balance."[16] In this case, the Supreme Court stood by peoples' right to ecological balance without direct reliance on fundamental rights such as life or health. In addition to its weak anthropocentric orientation, this case reflects the collective nature of the right to environment. The right to environment in all its forms (free from pollution, the right to livelihood, the right to ecological balance and so on) is derived from a fundamental right to life, which is traditionally considered a negative right. However, by combining Directives 48A and 51A on affirmative environmental obligations to the expansive interpretation of the right to life, the Indian jurisprudence allowed the new right to environment to acquire the characteristics of both negative and positive rights.[17]

Environmental provisions in the Indian Constitution are in the form of environmental duties. From a legal standpoint, these provisions are not by themselves enforceable because they fall under the Directive Principles of State Policy (DPSP). According to Article 37 of the Indian Constitution, these Principles "shall not be enforceable by any court, but are nevertheless fundamental in the governance of the country and it shall be the duty of the State to apply these principles in making laws."[18] Most provisions in the DPSP (Articles 36–50) can be associated with social, economic and cultural rights of the ICESCR.[19] The reason for including these rights under the title of DPSP is to distinguish them from enforceable fundamental rights, a distinction which coincides with the traditional division between civil and political rights enshrined in the ICCPR, and the socio-economic rights of the ICESCR. Despite the constitutional impediment to the justiciability of DPSP, the Indian judiciary was able to narrow the gap between fundamental rights and Directive Principles on Environmental Protection through an ingenious interpretation of constitutional provisions.[20]

It is argued that the DPSP are introduced in the constitution to encourage future environmental legislation, rather than to create new fundamental rights.[21] Among its provisions are Articles 48A and 51A, which place 'fundamental duties' regarding environmental protection on the Indian State and its citizens, respectively. Article 48A provides that the "state shall endeavour to protect and improve the environment and to safeguard the forests and

---

[16] J. Mijin Cha, "A Critical Examination of the Environmental Jurisprudence of the Courts of India," *Albany Law Environmental Outlook Journal* 10, no. 2 (2005): 219.

[17] *Constitution of India* arts. 48A and 51A.

[18] Ibid., art. 17.

[19] University of Minnesota: Human Rights Resource Center, "Justiciability of ESC Rights-the Indian Experience," http://www1.umn.edu/humanrts/edumat/IHRIP/circle/justiciability.htm.

[20] Ibid.

[21] Anderson, "Environmental Protection in India," 213.

wildlife of the country", while 51A posits that it "shall be the duty of every citizen of India ... to protect and improve the natural environment including forests, lakes, rivers and wildlife, and to have compassion for living creatures."[22] These constitutional provisions, which obligate respectively the state and the citizen to protect the environment, were referred to in many judicial decisions, and therefore led to the creation of a new right to a clean environment.[23] In *L.K.Koolwal v. State of Rajasthan and Others,* the High Court concluded that, while every citizen has a constitutional duty under Article 51A to protect and preserve the environment, the citizen also has the right "to move the Court for the enforcement of the duty cast on the State instrumentalities [and] agencies."[24]

As in the Indian cases, the Inter-American Commission on Human Rights (IACHR) did not limit its interpretation of the right to life as recognised in Article 4 of the ACHR to the 'protection against arbitrary killing'. The IACHR affirmed that the "realisation of the right to life, and to physical security and integrity is necessarily related to and in some ways dependent upon one's physical environment."[25] In *Sawhoyamaxa Indigenous Community v. Paraguay,* the IACHR held that Paraguay failed to respect the right to life of the members of the Sawhoyamaxa Community "since the lack of recognition and protection of their lands forced them to live on a roadside and deprived them from access to their traditional means of subsistence."[26] Due to precarious living conditions, such as lack of appropriate nutrition and medical care, many members of the community, including children, died. Based on the inalienability of the right to life, the Court ruled that "States have the duty to guarantee the creation of the conditions that may be necessary in order to prevent violations of such an inalienable right."[27] Thus, respect of the right to life is warranted through positive obligations. According to the Court, "States must adopt any measures that may be necessary to create an adequate statutory framework to discourage any threat to the right to life."[28] Despite its recognition in the *San Salvador Protocol,* the right to a healthy environment has not been invoked in neither this case nor other cases, instead, most cases revolved around the respect of Indigenous rights to communal property and resources

---

[22] *Constitution of India* art. 48A.

[23] Shubhankar Dam and Vivek Tewary, "Polluting Environment, Polluting Constitution: Is a 'Polluted' Constitution Worse Than a Polluted Environment?" *Journal of Environmental Law* 17(2005): 386.

[24] *L.K.Koolwal v. State of Rajasthan and Others,* AIR 1988 Raj.2(1998).

[25] *The Report on Human Rights Situation in Ecuador,* Inter-American Commission on Human Rights, OEA/Ser.L/V/II.96, Doc.10 rev.1(1997), chap. VIII.

[26] *Sawhoyamaxa Indigenous Community v. Paraguay,* 146 Inter-Am Ct HR (ser c), par. 145(a) (2006).

[27] Ibid., par. 151.

[28] Ibid., par. 153.

as a prerequisite for the enjoyment of their basic right to life.[29] However, by defending the rights of Indigenous communities to their ancestral lands, the Inter-American System has indirectly advanced the protection of nature for present and future generations, in addition to the conservation and preservation of natural ecosystems. I argue in Chapter 4 that the right to communal or Indigenous ownership of land is an integral part of substantive environmental rights. In essence, the loss of Indigenous peoples' connection with nature is equal to the loss of economic entitlements to natural resources like shelter, food, water and medicinal plants and to the loss of spiritual and cultural rights necessary for their social fabric.

There are, however, limitations to the extent to which the right to life can be relied upon to protect the environment.[30] The invocation of the right to environment based on the link to life-threatening conditions is a very narrow approach because environmental danger must be severe to imperil human life directly. As Ramcharan pointed out, although the right to life has the potential to include protection against serious environmental risks to life, the reliance on such an expansive formulation is limited to incidents of direct threats to life.[31] It is preferable to take preventive measures well before environmental degradation occurs. In some cases, such as the Bhopal crisis, it might be too late or too costly to reverse the environmental damage by the time a case gets to court.

2. *The Right to Privacy*

The right to privacy belongs to civil and political rights. The ICCPR provides that "[n]o one shall be subjected to arbitrary or unlawful interference with his privacy, family, home or correspondence ... Everyone has the right to the protection of the law against such interference or attacks."[32] Similar provisions are embodied in Articles 11(2) and 21 of the ACHR, and in Article 8(1) of the *European Convention*.[33] Many cases have been brought to the attention of the European Court of Human Rights (ECtHR) based on the allegation that environmental hazards affect the claimants' right to privacy under Article 8 of the *European Convention*.[34] The absence of explicit environmental provisions in

[29] Before November 1999, the right could not be invoked because the Protocol was not yet in force.

[30] See especially Sumudu Atapattu, "The Right to a Healthy Life or the Right to Die Polluted?: The Emergence of a Human Right to a Healthy Environment under International Law," *Tulane Environmental Law Journal* 16(2002–2003): 100–1.

[31] Luis E. Rodriguez-Rivera, "Is the Human Right to Environment Recognized under International Law? It Depends on the Source," *Colorado Journal of International Environmental Law and Policy* 12(2001): 20.

[32] *International Covenant on Economic, Social and Cultural Rights*, art. 17.

[33] *American Convention on Human Rights*, arts. 11(2) and 21; *European Convention on Human Rights*, art. 8(1).

[34] See Malgosia Fitzmaurice and Jill Marshall, "The Human Right to a Clean Environment-Phantom or Reality? The European Court of Human Rights and English Courts Perspective

the *European Convention* did not prohibit the ECtHR from successfully addressing the negative implications of environmental pollution on the enjoyment of the individual right to privacy (Article 8). In *Lopez Ostra*, the ECtHR pointed out the impact of an environmental harm on individuals' well-being, their private and family life and the enjoyment of their homes, even when their health was not seriously endangered.[35] In *Guerra and Others v. Italy*,[36] the ECtHR reiterated its view regarding the impact of environmental pollution on the enjoyment of a person's home and family life.[37] Although, in recent cases, the ECtHR maintained the trend towards the protection of individual environmental interests through the invocation of the right to privacy, it stressed that applicants should invoke this right only when the polluting source affects them in a direct and severe manner. In contrast to *Lopez Ostra*, where the link to health was not required to establish a violation of Article 8, the ECtHR emphasised the need for a strong causal connection between environmental harm and the polluting factory.[38]

The Court's interpretation of the right to privacy is very narrow and anthropocentric and does not allow the emergence of a distinct environmental human right. In *Fadeyeva v. Russia*, the ECtHR reiterated that "no right to nature preservation is as such included among the rights and freedoms guaranteed by the Convention … Thus, in order to raise an issue under Article 8 the interference must directly affect the applicant's home, family or private life."[39] In fact, the right to privacy and other rights that are enshrined in the Convention have their limitations in the defence of individual environmental rights. As the ECtHR clarified in *Kyrtatos*, "[n]either Article 8 nor any of the other Articles of the *European Convention* are specifically designed to provide general protection of the environment as such; to that effect, other international instruments and domestic legislation are more pertinent in dealing with this particular aspect."[40] In the absence of substantive environmental rights, the interpretation of existing human rights will be subject to whether the judiciary adopts a proactive or a traditional approach.[41]

Moreover, the use of the 'margin of appreciation' as a way to interpret the *European Convention* and as a test of the balance between individual rights

---

on Balancing Rights in Environmental Cases," *Nordic Journal of International Law* 76(2007). See also Alan E. Boyle, "Human Rights or Environmental Rights? A Reassessment," *Fordham Environmental Law Review* 18(2006–2007).

35 *Lopez Ostra v. Spain*, App. No. 16798/90, 20 Eur. H. R. Rep. 277, par. 51 (1994).

36 *Guerra and Others v. Italy*, App. No. 14967/89, 26 Eur. H.R. Rep. 357(1998).

37 Mariana T. Acevedo, "The Intersection of Human Rights and Environmental Protection in the European Court of Human Rights," *New York University Environmental Law Journal* 8(2000): 489.

38 Ibid.

39 *Fadeyeva v. Russia*, App. No. 55723/00, 45 Eur. H. R. Rep. 10, par. 68 (2005).

40 *Kyrtatos v. Greece*, App. No. 41666/98, 40 Eur. H. R. Rep. 16(2003).

41 Hamilton, "Human Rights at the Doubling Point," 39–40.

and governmental interests, is double-edged.[42] While the ECtHR has applied the margin of appreciation in many cases to protect the environment, it is not guaranteed that it won't use the same legal approach in future cases that it used in the *Second Hatton* case, which allowed wider economic concerns to take precedence over the environmental interests of individuals. In *Fadeyeva*, the ECtHR found that the applicant's health had deteriorated as a result of prolonged exposure to toxic emissions from a nearby steel manufacturing plant and that her right to private life and home had been violated.[43] Therefore, the ECtHR held the Russian Federation accountable for failing to take positive measures to regulate the level of emissions near the steel plant.[44] It also stated that "despite the wide margin of appreciation left to the respondent state, it has failed to strike a fair balance between the interests of the community and the applicant's effective enjoyment of her right to respect for her home and her private life. There has accordingly been a violation of Article 8."[45] However, in the *Second Hatton* case, the Court granted national authorities a wide margin of appreciation when complainants failed to prove a severe violation of their right to privacy.[46] It confirmed that sovereign states are better suited to weigh competing interests in conflicts involving Article 8.

3. *The Right to an Adequate Standard of Living and the Right to Health*

A strong connection can be established between the right to an adequate standard of living and the state of the natural environment since a healthful environment is a prerequisite for human health and well-being. According to Article 11 of the ICESCR, States Parties recognise "the right of everyone to an adequate standard of living for himself and his family, including adequate food, clothing and housing and to the continuous improvement of living conditions."[47] This Article also includes 'the right of everyone to be free from hunger.'[48] Similarly, the realisation of the right to health cannot be limited to medical care and assistance but includes protection from environmental hazards such as, radioactive contamination, water pollution and food

[42] The margin of appreciation is defined as the "breadth of deference the Strasbourg Organs will allow to national legislative, executive, administrative and judicial bodies before they will allow or disallow a national derogation from the Convention." Howard Charles Yourow, "The Margin of Appreciation Doctrine in the Dynamics of European Human Rights Jurisprudence," *Connecticut Journal of International Law* 3(1987–1988): 118.

[43] *Fadeyeva v. Russia*, par. 88.

[44] Ibid., par. 133.

[45] Ibid., par. 134. In this regard, the Russian government was obligated to pay the applicant €6,000 in respect of non-pecuniary damages in addition to other costs and expenses related to the litigation. Ibid., par. 152(2).

[46] See especially Fitzmaurice and Marshall, "The Human Right to a Clean Environment-Phantom or Reality? The European Court of Human Rights and English Courts Perspective on Balancing Rights in Environmental Cases," 124–27.

[47] *International Covenant on Economic, Social and Cultural Rights.*

[48] Ibid.

pollution.[49] The right to health is embodied in many human rights conventions, including Article 12 of the ICESCR, Article 24 of the *UN Convention on the Rights of the Child*, Article 10 of the *Protocol of San Salvador*, and Article 16 of the *Banjul Charter*. Article 12 of the ICESCR provides that States Parties "recognise the right of everyone to the enjoyment of the highest attainable standard of physical and mental health."[50] One of the preconditions advanced for the realisation of this standard is 'the improvement of all aspects of environmental and industrial hygiene.'[51] In its General Comment 14 on the right to the highest attainable standard of health, the CESCR provides a broader interpretation of the right to health by stating that it is "an inclusive right extending … to the underlying determinants of health, such as access to safe and potable water and adequate sanitation, an adequate supply of safe food, nutrition and housing, healthy occupational and environmental conditions."[52] This Comment clearly indicates that the enjoyment of the right to health is inextricably dependent on environmental conditions.

Paul Hunt, the Special Rapporteur on the Right to Food, reiterated the view of the Committee's 2003 Report that environmental conditions are one of the 'underlying determinants of health' in pointing out that the right to health is a broader concept requiring more specific entitlements like the right to healthy workplace and natural environments.[53] For instance, in his visit to various polluted areas in Peru, Hunt identified many of the environmental causes that affect the health of local communities. Lack of clean drinking water, poor sanitation and pollution are the main causes of the environmental health problems that strike the weakest and most vulnerable groups, especially children, Indigenous peoples and the poor.[54] Hunt found serious violations of the right to health in polluted areas like Belen, Callao and San Mateo de Huanchor.[55]

The right to health is often invoked in regional and national tribunals in relation to environmental protection, pollution problems, the scarcity of

---

[49] See Thorme, "Establishing Environment as a Human Right," 322.

[50] *International Covenant on Economic, Social and Cultural Rights*, art. 12(1).

[51] Ibid., art. 12(2) (b).

[52] *General Comment 14: The Right to the Highest Attainable Standard of Health*, Committee on Economic, Social and Cultural Rights, UN Doc E/C.12/2000/4 (2000), par. 11.

[53] *Report of the Special Rapporteur: The Right of Everyone to the Enjoyment of the Highest Attainable Standard of Physical and Mental Health*, Paul Hunt, UN Doc E/CN.4/2003/58 (2003), pars. 23, 25.

[54] *Report of the Special Rapporteur: Mission to Peru*, Paul Hunt, E/CN.4/2005/51/Add.3 (2005), par. 52.

[55] Due to the scarcity of safe water and the contamination of the River Nanay with mercury caused by mining companies, acute diarrhoea, water-related illnesses and infant mortality are common among poor people living in Belen. In Callao, a city known for its export and storage of minerals including lead ore, 50% of local children have high levels of lead in their blood. In San Mateo de Huanchor, the Rapporteur was informed about the high level of toxic mine tailings in the area and its negative impact on local residents' health especially Indigenous peoples and children. Ibid., par. 52.

potable water and the lack of sufficient food. For instance, the Yanomami Indians filed a suit with the IACHR against Brazil regarding the construction of the trans-Amazonian highway that crosses their homelands and forced them to resettle without any compensation.[56] Moreover, the discovery of mineral deposits drew mining companies to their areas, leading to further displacement and the spread of epidemics, including influenza and tuberculosis.[57] The petitioners claimed that these developments and commercial projects infringed on their basic human rights as embedded in the American Declaration of the Rights and Duties of Man,[58] including the right to life, to liberty and personal security; the right to residence and movement; and the right to the preservation of health and well-being.[59] The Commission ruled in favour of the Yanomami Indians in their struggle with the Brazilian authorities and recommended the Brazilian government take appropriate measures to protect Indigenous peoples' health and life and that it set and demarcate the boundaries of the Yanomami Park.[60] Unfortunately, the outcome of the lawsuit did not compel the government to halt or reverse the environmental degradation that occurred on the Yanomami lands.

Similarly, many claims presented to the African Human Rights System have invoked the violation of the right to health as a result of environmental disruption, rather than the right to environment explicitly embodied in Article 24 of the *Banjul Charter*.[61] This trend has left the impression that the right to environment may not be effectively invoked on its own.[62] As Van der Linde and Louw noted, it is not clear whether a claim to environmental protection based on Article 24 can be successfully invoked without linking it to the right to health or other human rights in the *Banjul Charter*.[63] This argument is part of the constant debate about the anthropocentric nature of environmental rights and the efficacy of invoking them regardless of their concrete and direct relationship to the physical and spiritual integrity of humankind.

---

[56] *Yanomami Community v. Brazil*, Inter-Am Comm HR, Brazil, Resolution No. 12/85, Case No. 7615(1985).

[57] Ibid., par. 3(a).

[58] *American Declaration of the Rights and Duties of Man*, OAS Res XXX, Opened for signature in Apr. 1948, OEA/Ser.L.V/II.82 doc.6 rev.1 (1992) (Entered into force in Apr. 1948).

[59] *Yanomami v. Brazil*, par. 1.

[60] Ibid., par. 3 (under sub-heading 'The Inter-American Commission on Human Rights, resolves).

[61] See Dinah Shelton, "The Environmental Jurisprudence of International Human Rights Tribunals," in *Linking Human Rights and the Environment*, ed. Romina Picolotti and Jorge Daniel Taillant (Tucson, Arizona: The University of Arizona Press, 2003).

[62] Morné Van der Linde and Lirette Louw, "Considering the Interpretation and Implementation of Article 24 of the African Charter on Human and Peoples' Rights in Light of the SERAC Communication," *African Human Rights Law Journal* 3, no. 1 (2003): 178.

[63] See Ibid., 176.

B. *The 'Environmental Democracy' Theory*

The environmental democracy theory brings democratic governance into the realm of ecological sustainability.[64] According to this theory, environmental procedural rights such as the rights to participation, remedies and access to justice are necessary to empower citizens, communities and civil society groups to challenge industrial projects and influence public environmental decisions and policies. Procedural rights, an essential part of international human rights law are already embedded in the UDHR.[65] Similarly, the ICCPR recognises general procedural rights such as the right to a fair and public hearing, the right to freedom of expression, the right to seek information and the right to participate in public affairs.[66] Principle 10 of the Rio Declaration articulates the link between procedural rights and environmental issues. Of special importance is the 1998 *Aarhus Convention*, which explicitly recognizes environmental procedural rights.[67] Many international organisations and UN agencies have adopted policies that encourage access to environmental information and public participation in decisions that affect the environment. To some extent, the wide recognition of the interdependence between human rights and environment since the 1992 United Nations Conference on Environment and Development (UNCED) is the result of the development and acceptance of environmental procedural rights.[68]

1. *International Provisions of Environmental Procedural Rights*

Many international environmental instruments include provisions on procedural rights in relation to the environment. The 1982 *World Charter for Nature* provides that "[a]ll persons, in accordance with their national legislation, shall have the opportunity to participate, individually or with others, in the formulation of decisions of direct concern to their environment, and shall have access to means of redress when their environment has suffered damage or degradation."[69] Similarly, Principle 6 of the Proposed Legal Principles for Environmental Protection and Sustainable Development of the Brundtland Report urges states to "inform in a timely manner all persons likely to be

---

[64] See generally Michael Mason, *Environmental Democracy: A Contextual Approach* (London: Earthscan, 1999).

[65] *Universal Declaration of Human Rights*, arts. 8, 19, 21, and 26.

[66] See *International Covenant on Civil and Political Rights*, arts. 14, 19 and 25.

[67] However, the Rio Declaration did not couch these well-established rights in terms of human rights. See Dinah Shelton, "What Happened in Rio to Human Rights?" *Yearbook of International Environmental Law* 3(1992): 83–84.

[68] *Report of the Joint OHCHR-UNEP Seminar on Human Rights and the Environment 16 Jan. 2002*, UN Doc E/CN.4/2002/WP.7 (2002), AnnexII(15).

[69] *UN World Charter for Nature*, GA Res 37, UN GAOR, 48th plen mtg, III(23), UN Doc A/Res/37/7 (1982).

significantly affected by a planned activity and to grant them equal access and due process in administrative and judicial proceedings."[70] Chapter 23 of Agenda 21 on strengthening the role of major groups stresses the rights of individuals, groups and organisations to request information from public authorities regarding projects or products that may negatively impact the environment and to participate in environmental impact assessment processes.[71] Principle 10 of the Rio Declaration provides that:

> Environmental issues are best handled with the participation of all concerned citizens, at the relevant level. At the national level, each individual shall have appropriate access to information concerning the environment that is held by public authorities, including information on hazardous materials and activities in their communities, and the opportunity to participate in decision-making processes. States shall facilitate and encourage public awareness and participation by making information widely available. Effective access to judicial and administrative proceedings, including redress and remedy, shall be provided.[72]

The procedural rights described in Principle 10 received only qualified support at the World Summit on Sustainable Development (WSSD) in 2002, which proposed no specific timing in which to achieve them. However, the Partnership for Principle 10 (PP10), an outcome of the 2002 WSSD, is considered a step forward in the promotion of procedural rights on the national level because it allows governments, international organisations and non-governmental organisations to work together towards the implementation of Principle 10.[73] Moreover, some environmental treaties contain provisions in relation to informational, participatory and remedial rights. For instance, the *UN Framework Convention on Climate Change* (UNFCCC) stipulates that Parties "shall promote and facilitate at the national ... sub-regional and regional levels, and in accordance with national laws and regulations, and within their respective capacities, public access to information and public participation."[74] On the institutional level, the United Nations Environment Programme (UNEP) plays a significant role in the collection and dissemination of environmental information through its Global Environmental Monitoring Service. Because of the specificity of environmental problems, it is more effective to adopt the approach of the *Convention on Access to Information, Public Participation in Decision-Making and Access to Justice in Environmental Matters (Aarhus Convention)*, which establishes a detailed and specific link between procedural rights and environmental issues.

---

[70] The World Commission on Environment and Development, *Our Common Future*, 349.

[71] Agenda 21, chap. 23(2). Available at http://www.un.org/esa/dsd/agenda21/res_agenda21_23.shtml.

[72] *Rio Declaration on Environment and Development*, Principle 10.

[73] World Resources Institute, "Partnership for Principle 10," http://www.wri.org/governance/project_description2.cfm?pid=133.

[74] *The UN Framework Convention on Climate Change*, art. 6.

In a paper presented to the joint UNEP-OHCHR seminar, Fabra showed that none of the UN agencies and international organisations whose main competence is unrelated to human rights "recognises or expressly addresses the right to a healthy environment."[75] However, many of the organisations and agencies Fabra examined do acknowledge the close interdependence between human rights and environmental protection from an instrumental perspective. There is a tendency among these international bodies to recognise environmental procedural rights such as access to information and participation in decision-making. Other international organisations refer explicitly to environmental protection as they relate to human rights in their field of competence. For instance, the World Health Organisation (WHO) addresses the right to health, and the Food and Agriculture Organisation (FAO) addresses the right to food.[76]

2. Aarhus Convention

Former UN Secretary-General, Kofi Annan described the *Aarhus Convention*, adopted on 25th June 1998, as "the most impressive elaboration of Principle 10 of the Rio Declaration and ... the most ambitious venture in the area of environmental democracy so far undertaken under the auspices of the United Nations."[77] The unique nature of the *Aarhus Convention*, which extends procedural rights to environmental issues stems from its adoption of existing participatory rights anchored in the ICCPR and other regional human treaties to the field of environmental law. It is the first international environmental agreement whose main objective is to determine states' obligations towards their citizens and NGOs.[78] By establishing these obligations, the Convention demonstrates a 'close affinity' with the international human rights system.[79]

The environmental procedural rights embedded in the *Aarhus Convention*, often referred to as the 'three pillars', are the right to access to environmental information, the right to participate in environmental decision-making procedures and the right to access to justice. Most important, the Convention broadened the right to access to environmental information beyond what is

---

[75] Fabra, "Intersection of Human Rights and Environmental Issues," 5.

[76] Ibid., 33.

[77] UNECE, "Aarhus Convention: Convention on Access to Information, Public Participation in Decision-Making and Access to Justice in Environmental Matters," http://www.unece.org/env/pp/. Despite its European coverage, the Convention is open to members and consultative members of the UN Economic Commission for Europe which includes North America, Israel and the Central Asian Republics.

[78] Marc Pallemaerts, "Introduction: Human Rights and Environmental Protection," in *Human Rights and the Environment*, ed. Dejeant-Pons Maguelonne and Marc Pallemaerts (Strasbourg: Council of Europe Publishing, 2002), 18.

[79] Ibid.

practiced in European national jurisdictions. It also widened the definition of 'public authorities' to include regional bodies, along with national and local authorities.[80] According to Article 2 of the *Aarhus Convention*, environmental information encompasses all forms of information on the state of all components of the environment including air, water, soil and biological diversity. The Convention also includes factors that affect the state of the environment and human health such as substances, activities, administrative measures, and cost-benefit and other economic analyses and assumptions used in environmental decision-making.[81] As a result, individuals request environmental information without having to prove their specific interest in the disclosure of such information. In addition, public authorities are required to periodically collect, disseminate and release information on the state of the environment.[82] Each Signatory Party is also urged to "take steps to establish progressively ... a coherent, nationwide system of pollution inventories or registers."[83] The Convention lists many restrictions on the obligation to disclose environmental information to the public: If the information requested is unavailable, 'unreasonable', 'formulated in too general a manner' or in the process of completion, the State may refuse to answer such requests.[84] The information requested may also be withheld if the disclosure would negatively affect issues such as the confidentiality of the public proceedings, international relations, public security, the course of justice and intellectual property rights.[85]

Access to environmental information is a prerequisite for public participation in environmental decision-making. According to the *Aarhus Convention*, States Parties are required to assign fixed periods, to publish draft rules and to allow the public to express its opinion through representative consultative bodies.[86] The Convention facilitates the involvement of the public in the preparation of executive rules and regulations but does not extend that involvement to legislation.[87] States Parties are obligated to facilitate the participation of their citizens in decisions involving the granting of permits or licenses in vital activities such as energy production, metal production and processing, mineral and chemical production and installation, waste management and other activities with potential effect on the environment.[88]

As for access to justice, Article 9 of the Convention obligates each Signatory Party to ensure that its citizens have access to judicial review procedures before courts and administrative authorities if requested information is denied.

---

[80] *Aarhus Convention*, art. 2(2).
[81] Ibid.
[82] Ibid., art. 5.
[83] Ibid., art. 5(9).
[84] Ibid., art. 4(3).
[85] Ibid., art. 4 (4).
[86] Ibid., art. 8.
[87] Ibid.
[88] Ibid., Annex I.

Judicial review is defined as the "scrutiny by the courts of the acts of other government organs to ensure that they act within the limits of the constitution."[89] States Parties are also required to ensure that members of the public have access to review procedures and remedies, including injunctive relief, in relation to the substantive and procedural legality of decisions, acts and omissions by private persons and public authorities.[90] The *Aarhus Convention* is unique among multilateral environmental agreements (MEAs) in its openness to the involvement of civil society in public interest actions. It introduces innovative compliance mechanisms at both the structural and the procedural levels. On the structural level, it allows NGOs to appoint members of the independent body while on the procedural level, individual members of the public and NGOs are allowed to contribute in the preparation of national reports and to lodge complaints regarding a party's compliance with the Convention's provisions.[91] The empowerment of civil society groups through broad public participation and the relaxation of standing rules are effective and innovative tools in the protection of the environment and the pursuit of sustainable development.

The *Aarhus Convention* establishes a strong link between environmental procedural rights and a substantive right to environment, described as "the right of every person of present and future generations to live in an environment adequate to his or her health and well-being."[92] The Convention requires States Parties to guarantee procedural rights in environmental matters in order to contribute to the protection of the right to environment.[93] This guarantee highlights the instrumental nature of procedural rights that have the purpose of protecting the right to environment as an 'objective' and not as an obligation on States Parties.[94] The Convention's focus on the procedural aspect of environmental rights reflects the resistance of the Organisation for Economic Cooperation and Development (OECD) countries to the idea of a substantive right to environment.[95]

3. *Benefits of Environmental Procedural Rights*

The idea behind the mobilisation of procedural rights—the right to information, the right to public participation, and the right to seek redress in relation to the environment—rests upon the argument that because of their paramount

---

[89] S. P. Sathe, "Judicial Activism: The Indian Experience," *Washington University Journal of Law and Policy* 6(2001): 33.
[90] *Aarhus Convention*, art. 9.
[91] Svitlana Kravchenko, "The Aarhus Convention and Innovations in Compliance with Multilateral Environmental Agreements," *Colorado Journal of International Environmental Law and Policy* 18, no. 1 (2007): 10.
[92] *Aarhus Convention*, art. 1.
[93] Ibid.
[94] Pallemearts, "Human Rights and Environmental Protection," 18.
[95] See Birnie and Boyle, *International Law and the Environment*, 263.

importance, environmental issues should not be left to the discretion of governments. Accordingly, the public should be empowered to seek information and participate in decision-making processes related to environmental policies, regulations and legislation. Participatory rights have a preventive and proactive role in managing and protecting the environment. By participating in environmental policy-making, citizens can influence decisions that have potential implications for the environment and propose effective ways of dealing with polluting activities.[96] In other words, environmental protection is attained through the democratic principles embodied in procedural rights.[97] By inducing gradual changes in the attitudes and practices inherited from the Soviet culture of governance, the *Aarhus Convention* plays a crucial role in strengthening and promoting the ongoing democratization in Eastern European countries, Caucasus and Central Asia (EECCA).[98] The implementation of the Aarhus provisions in post-socialist countries entails the harmonization of national laws and practices with the requirements of the European Union.[99] This type of participatory democracy constitutes a more suitable avenue to deal with complex environmental issues than does the representative version of democracy.[100]

Douglas-Scott noted that procedural rights may lead to the "liberalisation of the standing rules or a shifting of the burden of proof onto those whose action may damage the environment."[101] Procedural rights have been used successfully on behalf of future generations in cases such as *Minors Oposa*.[102] The broad legal standing adopted in *Minors Oposa* enables citizens and public interest environmental groups to represent present and future generations and to bring proceedings before the court against environmental offenders without necessarily proving that they themselves have been the victims of direct environmental harm.[103] As early as 1972, US Supreme Court Justice Douglas

---

[96] See especially Janusz Symonides, "The Human Right to a Clean, Balanced and Protected Environment," *International Journal of Legal Information* 20(1992): 33–34.

[97] S. Douglas-Scott, "Environmental Rights in the European Union-Participatory Democracy or Democratic Deficit," in *Human Rights Approaches to Environmental Protection*, ed. Alan E. Boyle and Michael R. Anderson (Oxford: Clarendon Press, 1996), 113.

[98] See generally Tatiana R. Zaharchenko and Gretta Goldenman, "Accountability in Governance: The Challenge of Implementing the Aarhus Convention in Eastern Europe and Central Asia," *International Environmental Agreements: Politics, Law and Economics* 4, no. 3 (2004). The 12 EECCA countries are: Armenia, Azerbaijan, Belarus, Georgia, Kazakhstan, Kyrgyzstan, Moldova, Russian Federation, Tajikistan, Turkmenistan, Ukraine and Uzbekistan.

[99] Ibid., 232.

[100] See John E. Bonine, "The Construction of Participatory Democracy in Central and Eastern Europe," in *Human Rights in Natural Resource Development*, ed. Donald N. Zillman, Alistair Lucas, and George Pring (New York: Oxford University Press, 2002).

[101] Douglas-Scott, "Environmental Rights in the European Union," 112.

[102] *Minors Oposa et al. v. Secretary of the Environment and Natural Resources Fulgencio Factoran*, 33 ILM 173(1994).

[103] Rodolfo Ferdinand N. Quicho, *Watching the Trees Grow: New Perspectives on the Standing to Sue* (Manila: IUCN-CEL Philippine Group, 1995), 37.

suggested in a remarkable dissenting opinion in the *Sierra Club* case that inanimate objects of the ecological community should be granted legal standing.[104] Drawing upon Leopold's land ethic, he argued that "before these priceless bits of Americana (such as a valley, an alpine meadow, a river, or a lake) are forever lost ... the voice of the existing beneficiaries of these environmental wonders should be heard ... Perhaps they will not win. That is not the present question. The sole question is who has standing to be heard?"[105] This point of view is in keeping with Stone's 1971 article "Should Trees Have Standing?" through which Stone sought to influence the outcome of the *Sierra Club* case. In the absence of a direct injury to the plaintiff (the Sierra Club), Stone suggested that the natural site itself (the Mineral King Valley in the Sierra Nevada Mountains in California) ought to have legal standing.[106] This ecocentric approach made its way to the *US Endangered Species Act* of 1973, whose citizen-suit provision allows any person to sue on behalf of a listed threatened or endangered species.[107]

On the international level, participatory rights allow the non-state actors to be involved in international policy-making and dispute settlement processes.[108] Through their participation in global forums, NGOs represent global public interests, which role is complementary to the role of government representatives. For instance, Indigenous NGOs played a central role in bringing Indigenous' interests to international forums and in furthering the recognition of Indigenous rights.[109] It is common for states in which Indigenous peoples reside to neglect or violate Indigenous rights.

In summary, environmental procedural rights encourage citizens to claim their rights to environmental information and to have their say in decision-making related to the environment in which they live. Of central importance is that environmental litigation has the potential to introduce democratic practices in developing countries. However, procedural rights should not be perceived as a substitute for substantive environmental rights. Many legal scholars are in favour of adopting procedural rights in assertions of environmental matters, rather than a substantive right to environment. For instance, Douglas-Scott contended that, as a result of the ambiguous definition of a substantive right to environment, it is preferable to dispense with the notion

---

104 *Sierra Club v. Morton*, 405 U.S. 727, 742 (1972).

105 Ibid., 751.

106 J. Baird Callicott and William Grove-Fanning, "Should Endangered Species Have Standing? Toward Legal Rights for Listed Species," *Social Philosophy and Policy* 26, no. 2 (2009): 321.

107 Ibid., 325.

108 See generally, James Cameron and Ruth Mackenzie, "Access to Environmental Justice and Procedural Rights in International Institutions," in *Human Rights Approaches to Environmental Protection*, ed. Alan E. Boyle and Michael R. Anderson (Oxford: Clarendon Press, 1996).

109 Ibid., 150.

entirely and to replace it with procedural or participatory rights.[110] Similarly, Macrory argued that environmental procedural rights, unlike the conceptual difficulties that accompany the express right to a 'healthy' environment, are more likely to be accepted and to be legally enforceable before the courts.[111] In the same vein, Handl, a staunch opponent of a 'generic environmental human right', questioned the usefulness of such a right in international law and contended that only environmental procedural rights should be considered in the human rights-based approach to environmental protection.[112] Nevertheless, because of the ethical, conceptual and legal association between the intrinsic worth of nature and the notion of human dignity, the case for substantive environmental rights should not be dismissed.

C. *The Genesis Theory*

The genesis theory dovetails with the 'indispensability theory' that Rich identified in his analysis of the genesis of the right to development.[113] According to this theory, the right to development is necessary for the enjoyment of basic human rights although in some cases this approach may lead to the sacrifice of basic human rights for the sake of development goals or environmental protection.[114] As Rich warned, the 'indispensability theory' may open the door for the "deprivation of many civil and political rights until development is achieved."[115] By applying Rich's rationale to environmental protection, it can be argued that, as with the right to development, a human right to environment is indispensable to the fulfilment of basic human rights.

In contrast to the expansion theory, exponents of a new human right to environment maintain that the reliance on already existing human rights, including procedural rights—while useful in combating environmental damage—is limited in scope and restricted in its effect.[116] Therefore, the recognition of substantive environmental rights allows environmentalists to tackle the human rights implications of environmental degradation without having to invoke extant human rights, which would require "fitting the potentially round peg of environmental concerns into the square hole of staunchly

---

[110] Douglas-Scott, "Environmental Rights in the European Union," 112.

[111] Richard Macrory, "Environmental Citizenship and the Law: Repairing the European Road," *Journal of Environmental Law* 8, no. 2 (1996): 232–33.

[112] Günther Handl, "Human Rights and Protection of the Environment," in *Economic, Social, and Cultural Rights*, ed. Asbjørn Eide, Catarina Krause, and Allan Rosas (Dordrecht/Boston/London: Martinus Nijhoff Publishers, 2001), 327.

[113] Ronald Rich, "The Right to Development as an Emerging Human Right," *Virginia Journal of International Law* 23(1982–1983): 320.

[114] Ibid.

[115] Ibid., 321.

[116] See Joshua P. Eaton, "The Nigerian Tragedy: Environmental Regulation of Transnational Corporations and the Human Right to a Healthy Environment," *Boston University International Law Journal* 15(1997): 297.

anthropocentric human rights."[117] Plaintiffs are often required to show a causal connection between the undesirable environmental factor and the violation of an extant human right.[118] For instance, if because of scientific uncertainty the petitioners cannot prove that a certain environmental pollutant is affecting their health, the case might risk dismissal.

In *X and Y v. Federal Republic of Germany*, the ECHR rejected the application filed by an environmental organisation complaining about the use of adjacent marshlands for military purposes on the grounds of incompatibility with the *European Convention*. The ECHR stated that "no right to nature preservation is as such included among the rights and freedoms guaranteed by the Convention."[119] Similarly, in *Tauira and 18 Others v. France*, the ECHR declared inadmissible the application submitted by residents in Tahiti, French Polynesia, regarding potential human rights violations associated with French nuclear testing in Mururoa Atoll.[120] Because of the divergence of scientific reports presented by the contending parties to the ECHR and the lack of scientific consensus among experts in relation to nuclear contamination, the ECHR found itself unable to base its decision on hypothetical and supposed risks. It stated that the risks often alleged to be associated with the use of nuclear power, whether for civil or military purposes; do not constitute a sufficient reason for litigation because many human activities involve risks.[121] In this case, the recognition of environmental rights was deemed necessary in order to overcome the requirement of establishing a direct causation between the environmental incident and a personal harm. Instead, the plaintiffs had to prove that a certain acceptable environmental standard, such as the permissible level of a pollutant in the air, was breached, rendering the environment unfit or unhealthful to live in.[122]

Because of the irreversibility and long-term effects of many ecological problems, the precautionary principle is of central importance to substantive environmental rights. The precautionary principle is designed to 'prevent serious irreversible harm' and "urges the authorities to act, or to abstain from action, in cases of uncertainty."[123] Scientists and environmental experts must often undertake extensive and lengthy scientific research in order to prove that certain environmental hazards, such as exposure to nuclear radiation or chemical pollutants, are harmful to human beings and their natural environment. The precautionary principle suggests that the lack of solid scientific data in

---

117 Hamilton, "Human Rights at the Doubling Point," 82.
118 Atapattu, "Emergence of a Human Right," 98.
119 *X and Y v. Federal Republic of Germany*, 15 Eur Comm HR 161, 161 (1976).
120 *Tauira and 18 Others v. France*, App. No. 28204/95, 83-B Eur Comm HR 112(1995).
121 Ibid.
122 Atapattu, "Emergence of a Human Right," 99.
123 Sadeleer, *Environmental Principles*, 221.

environmental issues is not sufficient reason to dismiss a case but that factors should be taken into consideration. Environmental protection and conservation requires the judiciary to rely more on precautionary measures such as injunctive relief than on mere penalties and compensations in their decisions. Practically speaking, the aim of filing a suit against a company whose developmental project is polluting or risks polluting a nearby river and disturbing the ecological balance of a whole area is to halt the damage to the environment by imposing strict environmental requirements, such as restoring damaged ecosystems, granting compensation to the plaintiffs and imposing penalties on the defendants. The imposition of heavy penalties on a polluting factory may have a deterrent effect on other enterprises since the high costs involved in compensating the victims and restoring the ecological damage may compel these enterprises to weigh carefully the environmental implications of their activities.

In order to make the case for a 'right to an adequate environment' to be conceived as a universal human right, Hayward applied Cranston's tests[124] for a genuine right: universality, practicability and paramount importance.[125] The universality criterion implies that a right that does not apply to all people is not a universal right. The practicability test follows the narrow and traditional line of argument that civil and political rights are more realisable than socio-economic rights because they involve the non-interference of states into the enjoyment of those rights.[126] Therefore, socio-economic rights, such as the right to work or the right to social security, are perceived to be less achievable on the global scale because most developing countries will not have the necessary resources to provide their citizens with such entitlements.[127] As for the nuance of 'paramount importance', it allows the distinction between the duty to give relief to a vital problem, which justifies the adoption of a new right, and the less important duty of granting pleasure.[128]

In Hayward's view, the putative right to environment can pass all three tests.[129] First, environmental protection touches upon the lives of all people, which guarantees its universality.[130] Second, regarding the criterion of universal practicability, Hayward refuted Cranston's presumption that a universal right leads to specific universal correlative duties, since these have a dynamic nature and can be held by some parties and not necessarily by all.[131] Hayward

---

[124] Cranston, *What Are Human Rights?* 66–67.
[125] Tim Hayward, *Constitutional Environmental Rights* (New York: Oxford University Press, 2005), 47.
[126] Cranston, *What Are Human Rights?* 66.
[127] Ibid.
[128] Ibid., 67.
[129] Hayward, *Constitutional Environmental Rights*, 48–52.
[130] Ibid., 48.
[131] Ibid.

concluded that "one can claim that there is a right to an adequate environment without necessarily being able to pinpoint (in advance) which duties it entails."[132] Finally, environmental problems are of 'paramount moral importance' because they threaten human life and well-being.[133]

Some exponents of the right to environment support the adoption of the right to environment but in an anthropocentric context. Nickel argued that the use of the rights discourse should not be extended beyond human beings; otherwise, rights will be assigned to non-human entities such as species, animals or other components of nature. In his opinion, these entities should be approached through non-rights notions, such as "*environmental goods*, *respect* for, and *responsibilities* towards nature, and *obligations* to future generations".[134] However based on people's perception of nature's worth and role in their life, environmental rights can be conceived as both anthropocentric and ecocentric, a concept which will be elaborated upon in Chapter 4.

1. *Definitional Issues*

Definitional ambiguity and vagueness are the first objections raised against the adoption of the right to environment. 'Healthy', 'decent', 'clean', 'ecologically balanced', 'safe' and 'sound' are examples of the multitude of adjectives commonly used to describe the desired quality of the environment. Terms like 'clean' or 'safe' are deemed 'too nebulous to be justiciable'.[135] The most commonly used formulation is the 'right to a healthy environment' and those who use it believe that the term 'healthy' is sufficiently versatile to be used to describe all environmental ills. This adjective is also viewed as 'broad enough' to include all other adjectives used in connection with the environment and 'specific enough' to describe expressly the quality of a right to environment.[136] According to Ledewitz, "the right to a healthy environment is more than a functioning biosphere not degraded in its systems by people. The right that we have is to a planet that has not been unalterably changed by man, and that right is grossly threatened today."[137]

Some commentators have distinguished between the right to environment and environmental rights. The latter are seen as the application of procedural rights to environmental issues, so they are not considered the manifestation of

[132] Ibid.
[133] Ibid., 52.
[134] Nickel, "Human Right to a Safe Environment," 282.
[135] Karrie A. Wolfe, "Greening the International Human Rights Sphere? An Examination of Environmental Rights and the Draft Declaration of Principles on Human Rights and the Environment," *Journal of Environmental Law and Practice* 13(2003): 123.
[136] Eaton, "Nigerian Tragedy," 299.
[137] Bruce Ledewitz, "Establishing a Federal Constitutional Right to a Healthy Environment in US and in Our Posterity," *Mississippi Law Journal* 68, no. 2 (1998–1999): 583.

a new human right.[138] However in many cases, environmental rights are placed in a broader context in which they are used interchangeably with the emerging right to environment. For instance, Atik differentiated between three formulations of environmental claims: environmental justice, environmental human rights and 'strong environmental rights', the last of which is equated with the ecocentric right to nature where non-human beings are protected for their inherent worth. Both environmental justice and environmental human rights aim to protect human beings from environmental degradation.[139] The main objective of environmental justice is to rectify inequalities in the distribution of the environmental burden among citizens. Environmental human rights have a more expansive agenda that encompasses the assessment of the environmental harm's impact on people's basic rights. According to Atik, environmental rights entail "the right to clean air and water, or more generally the right to a safe environment."[140]

One way of defining a complex term is by negation. The right to environment is not a right to an ideal environment with zero pollution or a right to a pristine nature, but a right to an appropriate degree of environmental protection and conservation necessary for the enjoyment of basic human rights. According to Thorme, one of the earliest to write on the subject, the right to environment may include "the right not to be exposed to man-made environmental contaminants injurious to health, the right not to be subjected to life-shortening influences, the right not to be subjected to extraordinary noise, and the right to know that natural ecosystems containing wild flora and fauna still exist in the world."[141] Some have proposed a much narrower formulation of the right to environment that revolves around the protection of human health and well-being from environmental hazards and argued that such a formulation has more potential to be accepted as a valid human right.[142] This anthropocentric formulation has its limitations because it does not cover broader issues such as resource management or species extinction.[143] For instance, in *Kyrtatos*, the ECtHR found no violation of the right to private life as a result of urban development because the applicants were unable to prove "that the alleged damage to the birds and other protected species living in the

---

[138] Atapattu, "Emergence of a Human Right," 72.

[139] Jeffery Atik, "Commentary," *Human Rights Dialogue* 2, no. 11 (Spring 2004): 26.

[140] Ibid., 72.

[141] Melissa Thorme, "Establishing Environment as a Human Right," *Denver Journal of International Law & Policy* 19(1990–1991): 309.

[142] See especially James W. Nickel, "The Human Right to a Safe Environment: Philosophical Perspectives on Its Scope and Justification," *Yale Journal of International Law* 18(1993): 284. See also John Lee, "The Underlying Legal Theory to Support a Well-Defined Human Right to a Healthy Environment as a Principle of Customary International Law," *Columbia Journal of Environmental Law* 25(2000): 287.

[143] Atapattu, "Emergence of a Human Right," 112.

swamp was of such a nature as to directly affect their own rights under Article 8.1 of the Convention."[144]

On the other hand, some authors have preferred a more expansive and detailed definition of the right to a healthy environment, arguing that such a broad approach is more effective than narrow formulations. For instance, Eacott suggested a 'possible broad and effective' definition for the violation of a right to healthy environment:

> A right to a healthy environment is violated when land, water, and/or air is polluted to the extent that present and future individuals suffer or likely suffer disruption of their quality or way of life, or significant health problems, including death. Injury or destruction of the plants, animals or ecological balance upon which humans depend also violates the right to a healthy environment. Such a strong right is necessary for sustainable development where a healthy environment must be balanced against the equally strong pressure to development.[145]

This definition indicates that the protection of biotic and non-biotic components of nature and sustainable development are necessary for human and ecological health. It also reflects the recent trend in international law towards a more extensive formulation of the right to environment (environmental rights). The Ksentini Report used the terms 'satisfactory environment' and 'healthy and flourishing environment' in referring to the right to environment. The 1994 Draft Declaration of Principles on Human Rights and the Environment (1994 Draft Declaration) annexed to Ksentini's Final Report conceives of environmental rights in the form of 'the right to a secure, healthy and ecologically sound environment.'[146] In a commentary on the 1994 Draft Declaration, Popovic defined the Declaration's formulation as the right to an environment 'sufficiently free of human intervention to maintain its essential natural processes' and the right to an environment 'that can sustain its own biodiversity' as well as 'human life'.[147] This definition contains a clear ecocentric component of the right to environment, in addition to the anthropocentric one.

The ambiguity and indeterminacy inherent in trying to define a controversial concept reflects two opposing realities. On one hand, an uncertain definition could constitute an impediment to the adoption or recognition of the alleged right. On the other hand, such uncertainty is a sign of the richness and flexibility of the concept and its ability to cover a wide range of complex issues.

---

[144] *Kyrtatos v. Greece*, par. 53.

[145] Erin Eacott, "A Clean and Healthy Environment: The Barriers & Limitations of This Emerging Human Right," *Dalhousie Journal of Legal Studies* 10, no. 1 (2001): 92.

[146] See *The 1994 Draft Declaration of Principles on Human Rights and the Environment*, UN Doc E/CN.4/Sub.2/1994/9, Annex I (1994).

[147] Neil A.F. Popovic, "In Pursuit of Environmental Human Rights: Commentary on the Draft Declaration of Principles of Human Rights and the Environment," *Columbia Human Rights Law Review* 27(1996): 504.

Many sceptics who doubt that a new human right to environment can add up to the existing international and national environmental law and policy base their arguments on the ambiguous definition of the emerging right. Others with a more optimistic perspective emphasise the role of the judiciary in developing the content of environmental rights. As Eaton put it, "[a]s with all human rights, nuances and interpretive extensions of the right to a healthy environment will develop through adjudication on a case-by-case basis."[148] It has been often agreed that this defect of ambiguous definition is not exclusive to the right to environment; most human rights lack a specific and clear definition, which did not constitute an impediment to their implementation and enforcement.[149] Boyle pointed out that this problem is not 'necessarily an insurmountable one', arguing that the same problem encountered by the concept of sustainable development did not refrain the UN from promoting sustainability.[150] In summary, a broader formulation of the right to environment is best suited to addressing the complexities and diversities of environmental issues. A broad right to environment will concentrate not only on the limited scope of guaranteeing legal redress for victims of environmental harm, but on the more ambitious scope of protecting and preserving natural processes and ecosystems for present and future generations.

2. *Other Objections to a Substantive Right to Environment*

In addition to the issue of definition and the anthropocentric critique discussed in Chapter 1, four critiques are often raised against the adoption of a substantive right to environment. The first critique is raised against the usefulness of the rights-based approach to adjudication altogether; the second highlights the overlapping of international environmental rights with international environmental law and its consequential redundant nature; the third emphasises the practical impediments to the implementation of the new right in an international context; and the fourth warns of the inflation of the human rights system by unnecessarily transforming claims into rights.

As to the first critique, many authors do not believe in the supremacy and absoluteness of rights over other social values. As Debeljak put it, "[i]t is a myth that rights are absolute 'trumps' over majority desires or whims ... Rights are balanced against and limited by many other values and communal needs."[151]

---

[148] Eaton, "Nigerian Tragedy," 300.

[149] See Rodriguez-Rivera, "Is the Human Right to Environment Recognized under International Law?" 11.

[150] Alan E. Boyle, "The Role of International Human Rights Law in the Protection of the Environment," in *Human Rights Approaches to Environmental Protection*, ed. Alan E. Boyle and Michael R. Anderson (Oxford: Clarendon Press, 1996), 51.

[151] Julie Debeljak, "Rights Protection without Judicial Supremacy: A Review of the Canadian and British Models of Bills of Rights," *Melbourne University Law Review* 26(2002): 305.

Similarly, Ignatieff dismissed the idea of rights as trump cards able to resolve a conflict in an ongoing political debate because, when rights conflict, there is no 'unarguable moral priority in rights claims'. In other words, when a political or social claim is transformed into a legal right, it suppresses any possible compromise in a political context. Accordingly, Ignatieff questioned the usefulness of rights that function as trump cards because they are conducive of a 'spirit of non-negotiable confrontation'.[152] On the Other hand, although the rights-based approach has its limitations, couching environmental claims in human rights terms places environmental issues on an equal footing with other well-established rights, especially property rights.

Second, the recognition of an international right to environment is also criticised for being unnecessary in the presence of international human rights law and international environmental law.[153] For instance, Boyle questioned the necessity for a substantive human right to environmental quality in the presence of an extensive body of international environmental rules and principles. In his opinion, "[i]t is far from certain whether much would be added by reformulating these rules in explicit human rights terms."[154] He concluded that, unlike national legal systems, international law does not need a human right to the environment.[155] In the same vein, Shelton argued that all global and regional human rights bodies have considered the link between environmental degradation and human rights and questioned whether "a recognised and explicit right to a safe and environmentally-sound environment would add to the existing protections and further the international values represented by environmental law and human rights."[156]

A corollary to the second critique is the idea that environmental rights might weaken the role of sustainable development in the reconciliation between developmental and environmental objectives.[157] Developing countries often resist the recognition of an international right to environment because it contradicts the principle of sovereignty over natural resources and the right to economic development exercised by developed countries.

---

[152] Ignatieff, "Human Rights as Politics and Idolatry," 20.

[153] See Boyle, "Protection of the Environment," See especially Paula M. Pevato, "International Law and the Right to Environment: Encouraging Environmental Cooperation Via the International Protection of Human Rights" (PhD diss., London School Economics and Political Science, 1998).

[154] Boyle, "Protection of the Environment," 51.

[155] Birnie and Boyle, *International Law and the Environment*, 64.

[156] Dinah Shelton, "Human Rights and the Environment: Jurisprudence of Human Rights Bodies" (paper presented at the Joint UNEP-OHCHR Expert Seminar on Human Rights and the Environment, Geneva, 14–16 Jan. 2002).

[157] Ximena Fuentes, "International Law-Making in the Field of Sustainable Development: The Unequal Competition between Development and the Environment," *International Environmental Agreements: Politics, Law and Economics* 2(2002): 126–27.

They fear that environmental accountability, backed by the industrialised world, will restrict their development options and increase their economic dependency. However, this critique fails to acknowledge that the overlap between emerging environmental rights and international environmental law does not preclude the need for such rights. While the implementation of international environmental law is the responsibility of States Parties, the function of international human rights is to empower vulnerable and poor communities living within the confines of sovereign states to voice their concerns regarding human rights violations. Dommen pointed out that, while "international environmental law offers little possibility of recourse for individual victims of domestic environmental problems, the usefulness of human rights mechanisms and institutions is easily apparent."[158] In this sense, the recognition of an international right to environment may be necessary. In addition, most environmental problems, such as climate change, are trans-boundary in nature, so the international recognition of the right to environment will provide a new focus on the human rights implications of environmental degradation and open the door for judicial and non-judicial avenues to defend environmental human rights, whether individual or collective. In the same vein, Popovic doubted the usefulness of state-centred international environmental law in protecting environmental rights, arguing that the "international community has already spilled much ink and consumed forests of paper developing international environmental instruments ... But the fact remains, those instruments have not done enough."[159] Accordingly, Popovic proposed the establishment of international environmental rights as 'a complementary alternative to traditional international environmental law.'[160] In this case, one can argue that the incompatibility between the principle of state sovereignty and compliance with international norms will apply to international environmental rights as well. Even the presence of an international treaty on environmental rights is not considered adequate because such a treaty requires ratification by legislatures in order to be implemented in national jurisdictions. However, international human rights can be differentiated from all other international norms because they were conceived to protect individuals from state abuse by challenging the principle of sovereignty.

A related objection contends that environmental rights may be necessary in the national legal system but not in the international system. However, this argument is ill-founded because both systems are intimately interwoven.

---

[158] Caroline Dommen, "Claiming Environmental Rights: Some Possibilities Offered by the United Nations Human Rights Mechanisms," *Georgetown International Environmental Law Review* 11(1998): 3.

[159] Popovic, "In Pursuit of Environmental Human Rights," 494.

[160] Ibid.

For instance, the enforcement of broad constitutional environmental provisions in Eastern European countries that depends, for the most part, on judicial interpretation, is not sufficient to address the urgency of environmental problems in these countries.[161] Therefore, Gravelle suggested that "East Europeans may have to look to international legal structures to help enforce their right to the environment while national or constitutional courts are in their infancy."[162] A well-developed set of environmental rights along with appropriate environmental adjudicatory and supervisory bodies will facilitate the task of implementing constitutionally entrenched environmental rights in these emerging democracies.

The third criticism is that the lack of appropriate compliance mechanisms in the international human rights system makes environmental rights an empty rhetoric.[163] For instance, the international trade law system is endowed with sophisticated enforcement mechanisms, while international environmental and human rights regimes lack appropriate systems of sanctions.[164] The lack of compliance mechanisms, Hancock argued, illustrates a blatant bias towards economic interests over all other social interests. He suggested 'ecological rationality' as an alternative to counterbalance the effects of rampant 'economic rationality' in order to change the political mood towards a more environmentally friendly attitude. In this regard, he advocated the adoption of "environmental human rights as an anti-systemic instrument to prioritise social and environmental concerns over economic ones."[165]

Despite the clear prevalence of economically oriented values over all non-capitalist values, including ecological ones, Hancock's emphasis on 'economic rationality' seems lopsided because it overlooks the growing impact of international environmental principles and the concept of sustainable development on international and domestic law and policy. Although the law is not sufficient by itself to induce changes in what society values, legal mechanisms and other means interact in a complex and dynamic way to achieve desired behavioural changes in social and political arenas. Moreover, while the issue of enforceability may constitute a serious impediment to the advancement and recognition of environmental rights on the international level, the genesis of new rights follows a separate process from the means of their implementation. In some instances, setting the legal and philosophical foundations of an emerging right could precede its recognition and realisation by relevant stakeholders.

---

161 Ryan K. Gravelle, "Enforcing the Elusive: Environmental Rights in East European Constitutions," *Virginia Environmental Law Journal* 16, no. 4 (1997): 660.

162 Ibid.

163 Wolfe, "Examination of Environmental Rights," 126.

164 Hancock, *Environmental Human Rights,* 161.

165 Ibid., 73.

The fourth criticism of the adoption of a substantive right to environment is that the proliferation of new rights undermines the credibility of traditional rights. In other words, the haphazard couching of new issues, goals or values in human rights language will lead to the debasement of the human rights currency.[166] In fact, "[m]any political movements would like to see their main concerns categorised as matters of human rights, since this would publicise, promote, and legitimate their concerns at the international level."[167] As Nickel contended, "[i]f the language of rights is used loosely in environmental discourse, people may begin to claim rights that are excessively metaphorical and rhetorical."[168] For instance, the World Tourism Organisation stated that "tourism has become increasingly a basic need, a social necessity, a human right."[169] Several authors have come up with a list of unusual claims to human rights that includes the right to sleep, the right to social transparency, the right to co-existence with nature and the right to be free to experiment with alternative ways of life.[170] However, it is necessary, as Alston suggested, to strike a balance between the need to safeguard the integrity and credibility of the human rights tradition and the need to maintain the flexibility of the human rights concept when new threats jeopardise human dignity and well-being.[171] Because of the complexity of environmental matters, and in order to prevent the mushrooming of environmental human rights, I propose the adoption of the international 'Right to Environment' as a general right and consider all other corollary rights, such as the right to water and the right to a healthy or clean environment, as part of the general right. This viewpoint is developed in Chapter 4.

3. *From Procedural and Derivative Rights to Substantive Environmental Rights*

The development in the human rights approaches to environmental issues is not limited to environmental procedural rights and derivative rights. In addition to national constitutions and regional treaties, a distinct right to environment can be inferred from many international instruments. An increasing number of states have inserted some form of environmental provisions into their constitutions that often equip their citizens with environmental rights and/or place duties on their governments to protect the environment. While 56 of these constitutions explicitly recognise the right to a 'healthy' environment, 97 constitutions impose a duty on the government to prevent harm to

---

[166] See Philip Alston, "Conjuring up New Human Rights: A Proposal for Quality Control," *American Journal of International Law* 78(1984): 614.

[167] Stanford Encyclopaedia of Philosophy, "Human Rights," http://plato.stanford.edu/entries/rights-human/.

[168] Nickel, "Human Right to a Safe Environment," 283.

[169] Alston, "Conjuring Up," 611.

[170] Ibid., 610.

[171] Ibid., 609.

the environment.[172] The constitutitionalisation of environmental concerns is noticeable in many countries of the developing world[173] and the new democracies in Eastern Europe because most of these constitutions are relatively new and because of the severity of environmental problems in those countries. Some newly created constitutions adopted in the 1970s and the 1980s, such as those of Portugal, Spain and Brazil, incorporated environmental provisions to offset the extensive inclusion of economic interests. In contrast, older constitutions reflect less concern for counterbalancing economic and environmental interests because it was less compelling at the time of their writing to introduce such environmental provisions.[174] Older constitutions can adopt amendments that address environmental provisions.

Unlike the European human rights system, both the Inter-American and the African human rights systems explicitly recognise a separate right to environment, albeit under various formulations. However, the *Additional Protocol to the American Convention on Human Rights in the Area of Economic, Social, and Cultural Rights (Protocol of San Salvador)* is the first and only binding international agreement to recognise an individual right to environment; unlike the *Banjul Charter*, it recognises an explicit individual right to a 'healthy environment'.[175] Article 11(1) of the Protocol specifies that "[e]veryone shall have the right to live in a healthy environment and to have access to basic public services."[176] The same Article requires States Parties to "promote the protection, preservation and improvement of the environment."[177] The Protocol requires that states take appropriate legislative and other measures to make these rights a reality in the absence of legislative or other provisions necessary for the exercise of the conferred rights.[178] It can be inferred from the title of the

---

[172] Earthjustice, "Environmental Rights Report 2005: Human Rights and the Environment," http://www.earthjustice.org/library/references/2005_ENVIRONMENTAL_RIGHTS_REPORTrev.pdf.

[173] In fact, the incorporation of charters of rights in the constitutions of newly decolonised countries in the 1950s and 1960s was not necessarily the outcome of a sudden acknowledgement of the sacredness of individual rights. Instead, it emanated from the will of colonising powers to guarantee the rights of their settlers. See Gearty, 78. Tracking the evolution of constitutional rights in African British colonies, Vivien Hart emphasised the role that Britain played in diffusing human rights in Africa. The drafting of independence constitutions in former British colonies was accompanied by the entrenchment of rights clauses. However, this role was a matter of pragmatism rather than principle. It was instigated by wealthy British settlers who sought protection from possible human rights violations. Drafters were mostly concerned about fundamental rights, especially property rights, of European minorities and other foreign investors. Vivien Hart, "The Contagion of Rights: Constitutions as Carriers," in *Identity, Rights and Constitutional Transformation*, ed. Patrick J. Hanafin and Melissa S. Williams (Aldershot: Ashgate, 1999), 54.

[174] Brandl and Bungert, "Constitutional Entrenchment," 85.

[175] Marie Soveroski, "Environment Rights versus Environmental Wrongs: Forum over Substance?" *RECIEL* 16, no. 3 (2007): 264.

[176] *Protocol of San Salvador*, art. 11.

[177] Ibid.

[178] Ibid., art. 2.

Protocol that the right to a 'healthy' environment is classified among social, economic and cultural rights. It follows that the duties placed on states are similar to those provided in the ICESCR regarding the progressive implementation of the specified rights. Article 1 stipulates that states are obligated to take necessary measures "to the extent allowed by their available resources ... for the purpose of achieving progressively and pursuant to their internal legislations, the full observance of the rights recognised in this Protocol."[179] In addition, States Parties are required to "establish restrictions and limitations on the enjoyment and exercise of the rights ... for the purpose of preserving the general welfare in a democratic society."[180]

Some commentators have argued that the provisions of the *Protocol of San Salvador* weaken the realisation of the right to a 'healthy' environment.[181] Most Latin American governments use their lack of resources as an excuse for inaction in response to environmental problems.[182] Eventually, the implementation of Article 11 will be subject to the proactive role of the IACHR and the Inter-American Court of Human Rights (Inter-American Court). Although the IACHR plays a vital role in adjudicating environmental disputes and human rights violations and can make recommendations to governments of Member States, only the Inter-American Court can render binding judgments.[183] Practically speaking, victims seeking legal redress will benefit only from the Court's decision, although the IACHR's findings and recommendations are beneficial to the development of human rights jurisprudence.

The Organisation of African Unity (OAU) adopted *the Banjul Charter* in 1981 following mounting pressures on African countries to adopt a specific regional human rights regime, particularly in reaction to enormous human rights violations by African leaders such as Idi Amin of Uganda, Banda of Malawi, Emperor Bokassa of Central African Republic, and Mengistu of Ethiopia.[184] Unlike other regional human rights treaties, the *Banjul Charter* was hailed for including both categories of rights—civil and political rights as well as socio-economic and cultural rights—in one binding treaty. Provisions related to socio-economic and cultural rights were conceived as direct entitlements to individuals and groups, in contrast with the progressive nature of the rights enshrined in the ICESCR.[185] The *Banjul Charter* was the first binding instrument to recognise explicitly the fundamental right to environment. Article 24 of the Charter provides that "[a]ll peoples shall have the right to a

[179] Ibid., art. 1.
[180] Ibid., art. 5.
[181] Churchill, "Environmental Rights," 100.
[182] Ibid.
[183] *American Convention on Human Rights*, art. 41(b).
[184] Danwood Mzikenge Chirwa, "Toward Revitalizing Economic, Social, and Cultural Rights in Africa: Social and Economic Rights Action Centre and the Center for Economic and Social Rights v. Nigeria," *Human Rights Brief* 10, no. 1 (2002): 14.
[185] Churchill, "Environmental Rights," 104–5.

general satisfactory environment favourable to their development."[186] This provision indicates that African people are entitled to a collective right to environment, rather than an individual one and that achieving development is the main objective of recognising such a right. This objective can also be understood through Article 21, which provides that "peoples shall freely dispose of their wealth and natural resources. This right shall be exercised in the exclusive interest of the people. In no case shall a people be deprived of it."[187] The Charter widens the scope of the right to environment by including the right to natural resources necessary to people's well-being and development. The realisation of these rights in the African continent is guaranteed through provisions that establish a general institutional framework for the implementation of human rights enshrined in the *Banjul Charter*.

To determine whether the right to environment exists on the international level, it is necessary to differentiate between two forms of international norms, traditionally known as hard law and soft law.[188] To a certain extent, this distinction coincides with the one corresponding to legally binding instruments and non-legally binding instruments. Hard law represents traditional sources of international law as enumerated in the Statute of the International Court of Justice (ICJ): international conventions, international custom, general principles of law, judicial decisions and the teachings of the most highly qualified publicists.[189] In contrast to hard law, soft law often "refers to any international instrument other than a treaty that contains principles, norms, standards, or other statements of expected behaviour."[190] There is no consensus among international legal scholars on the nature and legal significance of soft law. From a traditionalist approach, soft law norms are less persuasive than hard law norms, so they do not create rights and obligations.[191] As Klabbers contended, the soft law thesis is based on 'shaky presumptions' and lacks the support of state practice and judicial practice.[192] Others have suggested that the norms emanating from soft law instruments, although not legally binding, reflect the changing nature of modern international law into 'a more political and diplomatic order, and less of a legal order.'[193] In this context, soft law norms are

---

[186] *Banjul Charter*, art. 24.

[187] Ibid., art. 21(1).

[188] See generally Rodriguez-Rivera, "Is the Human Right to Environment Recognized under International Law?"

[189] *Statute of the International Court of Justice*, 3 Bevans 1179; 59 Stat. 1031; T.S. 993; 39 AJIL Supp. 215 (1945), art. 38(1).

[190] Dinah Shelton, "Normative Hierarchy in International Law," *American Journal of International Law* 100(2006).

[191] See Rodriguez-Rivera, "Is the Human Right to Environment Recognized under International Law?" 40–41.

[192] Jan Klabbers, "The Redundancy of Soft Law," *Nordic Journal of International Law* 65(1996): 182.

[193] See Rodriguez-Rivera, "Is the Human Right to Environment Recognized under International Law?" 41.

perceived as moral and political commitments necessary to circumventing the impediment of the sovereignty doctrine.[194] Soft law provides sovereign states with a flexible tool that attracts more compliance from states.[195] Therefore, states' willingness to abide by their international commitments, rather than the legal nature of the norms concerned, is what determines compliance with international norms.

Unlike many regional treaties and national constitutions, there is no legally binding right to environment in international law. On the other hand, several soft law instruments contain provisions on emerging environmental rights. The Stockholm Declaration is often cited as the first international instrument to establish strong links between basic rights and environmental protection. Principle 1 of the Declaration provides that a person "has the fundamental right to freedom, equality and adequate conditions of life, in an environment of a quality that permits a life of dignity and well-being, and he bears a solemn responsibility to protect and improve the environment for present and future generations."[196] According to this formulation, the quality of the environment constitutes a *sine qua non* for 'a life of dignity and well-being.' This Principle did not expressly recognise a distinct international right to environment, despite its role in motivating the inclusion of constitutional environmental law in national jurisdictions after 1970.[197]

The Brundtland Report includes a list of proposed legal principles for environmental protection and sustainable development from which the right to environment can be inferred.[198] The first principle proclaims that all human beings have the fundamental right to an environment adequate for their health and well-being, while Principle 6 advocates environmental procedural rights such as the right to information, equal access and due process in administrative and judicial proceedings.[199] The 1989 Hague Declaration on the Environment clearly recognises the right to a viable environment in the context of atmospheric pollution, stating that remedies should go beyond the fundamental duty to preserve the environment to "the right to live in dignity in a

---

[194] Ibid.

[195] See generally Hartmut Hillgenberg, "A Fresh Look at Soft Law," *EJIL* 10, no. 3 (1999).

[196] *Stockholm Declaration*, UN Doc A/CONF.48/14/Rev.1 (1972). The formulation proposed by the USA at the Stockholm Conference was so advanced, detailed and straightforward regarding the human implications of environmental degradation. It states that "[e]very human being has a right to a healthful and safe environment, including air, water and earth, and to food and other material necessities, all of which should be sufficiently free of contamination and other elements which detract from the health or well-being of man." This formulation reflected the American mood or mindset towards environmental issues where environmentalism was at its highest peak in the seventies.

[197] See Pallemaerts, "Human Rights and Environmental Protection," 11.

[198] The World Commission on Environment and Development, *Our Common Future*, Annexe 1.

[199] Ibid.

viable global environment, and the consequent duty of the community of nations vis-à-vis present and future generations."[200] This provision emphasises the need for a human rights-based approach to address the severity of ecological problems and considers the 'community of nations' as the duty-bearers of the 'right to live in dignity in a viable global environment.' This notion of collective responsibility places the Hague Declaration in the context of third-generation rights.

Two decades after the Stockholm summit, the UNCED placed the rights-based approach to environmental issues into the sweeping concept of sustainable development. Principle 1 of the Rio Declaration, issued at the UNCED, declared that "[h]uman beings are at the centre of concerns for sustainable development. They are entitled to a healthy and productive life in harmony with nature."[201] The drafters avoided the term 'rights' altogether indicating uneasiness in bringing the environment into the sphere of human rights.[202] This omission, as Shelton argued, is a regressive step compared to what had been proclaimed in Principle 1 of the Stockholm Declaration.[203] Although the Rio Declaration and Agenda 21 examined issues closely related to the basic rights of groups like youth, children, and Indigenous peoples, they avoided adequate references to human rights.[204] Shelton listed many reasons for such an omission, but the main reason was the lack of consensus among states regarding the usefulness and validity of adopting or committing to a right to environment.[205] The theme of the Rio Conference revolved around striking a balance between economic development and environmental protection in a North-South context. Thus, states were reluctant to frame their responsibilities, especially nations of the developing world that were not ready to commit to both environmental protection and human rights agendas, in terms of the human rights discourse. The low level of NGO representation, with the exception of some Indigenous organisations and women's groups, at the UNCED preparatory meetings and at the Conference of State Representatives is thought to be another reason behind the final texts' omission of references to human rights.[206] Moreover, many states, especially Latin American states, did not welcome the focus on Indigenous human rights, which are integrally linked to environmental protection.[207] Finally, developing countries pushed for the

---

[200] *Hague Declaration on the Environment.* Available at http://www.nls.ac.in/CEERA/ceerafeb04/html/documents/lib_int_c1s2_hag_230300.htm.

[201] *Rio Declaration on Environment and Development,* Principle 1.

[202] See especially Boyle, "Protection of the Environment," 43.

[203] Shelton, "What Happened in Rio to Human Rights?" 83.

[204] Ibid., 85.

[205] Ibid., 89.

[206] Ibid., 89–99.

[207] Ibid., 90.

inclusion of developmental provisions in the Rio Declaration in order to attenuate its emphasis on environmental issues.[208] This retreat from the human rights agenda was compensated for by the inclusion of Principle 10 in the Rio Declaration, which provides for environmental procedural rights.[209]

At the initiative of the Executive of the Provincial Council of Bizkaia, the International Seminar of Experts on the Right to the Environment was held in Bilbao, Spain, in February 1999 under the auspices of the United Nations Educational, Scientific and Cultural Organisation (UNESCO) and the Office of the High Commissioner for Human Rights (OHCHR). The Declaration of Bizkaia, adopted at the seminar, recognised that "[e]veryone has the right, individually or in association with others, to enjoy a healthy and ecologically balanced environment."[210] The Plan of Implementation adopted at the 2002 World Summit on Sustainable Development in Johannesburg urges states to "[a]cknowledge the consideration being given to the possible relationship between environment and human rights, including the right to development."[211] The Plan suggests that the right to an adequate standard of living is a prerequisite to the implementation of food security and poverty eradication.[212] In order to lessen environmental health threats, the Plan recommends that states comply with human rights and fundamental freedoms.[213]

Among human rights bodies, the UN Sub-Commission on Prevention of Discrimination and Protection of Minorities has been the most active in exploring the interaction between the environment and human rights. In 1990, the Sub-Commission appointed Fatma Zohra Ksentini as the Special Rapporteur on Human Rights and the Environment primarily to investigate and examine the potential relationship between the state of the environment and that of human rights worldwide. Ksentini submitted four successive reports to the Sub-Commission and put forward in her 1994 final report the view that the legal foundations of the right to environment stem from the existence of a rich environmental law system replete with environmental regulations. Ksentini viewed the links established by the Stockholm Declaration among the environment, development and basic individual rights as a legal foundation for the recognition of the 'right to a healthy and decent environment'.[214] Accordingly, her report concluded that there is a "shift from

---

208 Ibid.

209 Boyle, "Protection of the Environment," 60.

210 *Declaration of Bizkaia on the Right to the Environment*, UNESCO, 30th sess, UN Doc C/INF.11 (1999), art. 1(1).

211 *Plan of Implementation of the World Summit on Sustainable Development*, par. 138.

212 Ibid., par. 40.

213 Ibid., par. 54.

214 *Final Report Prepared by the Special Rapporteur on Human Rights and the Environment*, par. 22.

environmental law to the right to a healthy and decent environment."[215] Critics of the conclusions advanced by the Ksentini reports, have argued that Ksentini's argument is ill-founded because the alleged right to environment is not yet recognised at an international level, and that she had gone too far in concluding that international law recognises the emerging right to environment.[216]

In addition, the 1994 Draft Declaration annexed to the Ksentini Report establishes a cause-effect relationship between human rights violations and environmental degradation. Popovic described the Draft as a "cohesive and comprehensive package of the essential components of environmental human rights."[217] The 1994 Draft Declaration, consisting of a preamble and five untitled parts, reiterates the principle of interdependence and indivisibility of all human rights.[218] The preamble fleshes out the legal foundation of the principles of the 1994 Draft Declaration by grounding these principles in international human rights and environmental principles, and concludes that human rights violations lead to environmental degradation and vice versa. Principle 5 of the 1994 Draft Declaration defines the 'right to a secure, healthy, and ecologically sound environment' as the right of all peoples to be free "from pollution, environmental degradation and activities that adversely affect the environment, threaten life, health, livelihoods … across or outside national boundaries."[219] Principle 6 specifies the parts of the environment that need to be protected and preserved as "air, soil, water, flora and fauna, and the essential processes and areas necessary to maintain biological diversity and ecosystems."[220]

The 1994 Draft Declaration considers the "right to benefit equitably from natural resources and sites of cultural and religious significance" as an integral part of the right to a healthy environment, especially in the context of Indigenous peoples.[221] It also includes many internationally recognised human rights—such as the rights to health, to food and water, to a safe and healthy working environment, and to adequate housing—as part of the principles that govern the relationship between human rights and environment. In addition to the substantive rights listed as part of the right to environment, the 1994 Draft Declaration contains procedural rights necessary for the implementation of environmental rights.[222] Despite the many advantages that the 1994 Draft

---

[215] Ibid.
[216] See especially Atapattu, "Emergence of a Human Right," 108–9.
[217] Popovic, "In Pursuit of Environmental Human Rights," 493.
[218] *The 1994 Draft Declaration of Principles on Human Rights and the Environment* Principle 2.
[219] Ibid., Principle 5.
[220] Ibid., Principle 6.
[221] Ibid., Principles 13–14.
[222] Ibid., Principle 11.

Declaration offers to the field of environmental human rights, the international community has not yet recognised it. As one critic put it, "[b]y framing environmental concerns as simply component parts of existing human rights, actual protection of the environment receives little energy."[223]

On 26 March 2008, the UN Human Rights Council passed a breakthrough resolution on human rights and climate change that constitutes a leap towards the recognition of environmental human rights. The resolution was triggered by the 2007 Fourth Assessment Report of the Intergovernmental Panel on Climate Change (IPCC), which illustrates the drastic environmental consequences of global warming.[224] The Council, in cooperation and consultation with other state and non-state stakeholders, asked the OHCHR to undertake "a detailed analytical study of the relationship between climate change and human rights."[225] The Council was particularly aware of the negative repercussions of climate change on the world's poor, especially those living in low-lying and small island countries.

After this exploration of the many non-binding rules and principles relating to the human rights-based approach to environmental protection, one might wonder whether it is even possible to talk about an emerging right to environment in international law. In fact, soft law instruments are a central part of the international law-making process and, in many instances, they constitute transitional and practical steps towards legally binding norms.[226] As Rodriguez-Rivera put it, "[t]o expect new international norms to derive exclusively from binding or hard law instruments is, in effect, to oversimplify the dynamics of modern international law."[227] The adoption of many declarations on human rights paved the way to the establishment of most recent human rights treaties.[228] Similarly, non-binding norms and agreements may play the same role in advancing environmental protection and preservation.[229] Soft law is a non-traditional alternative to multilateral environmental agreements in dealing with environmental problems and has the potential to harden into legally binding instruments. For instance, the 1989 *Basel Convention of the Control of Trans-boundary Movement of Hazardous Waste* adopted the UNEP's Cairo Guidelines and the Principles for the Environmentally Sound

---

223 Wolfe, "Examination of Environmental Rights," 121.

224 IPCC Intergovernmental Panel on Climate Change, "IPCC Fourth Assessment Report: Climate Change 2007," http://www.ipcc.ch/ipccreports/assessments-reports.htm.

225 *Draft Resolution on Human Rights and Climate Change*, par. 1.

226 See especially Shelton, "Normative Hierarchy," 320–21.

227 See Rodriguez-Rivera, "Is the Human Right to Environment Recognized under International Law?" 44.

228 Shelton, "Normative Hierarchy," 321.

229 See especially Pierre-Marie Dupuy, "Soft Law and the International Law of the Environment," *Michigan Journal of International Law* 12(1991–1992).

Management of Hazardous Waste.[230] It is certainly possible for non-binding rules and principles relating to the right to environment to 'harden' in a similar way through a treaty, if the necessary political will exists, or through state practice and the judicial activism of international judges and arbiters.[231]

Conclusion

The human rights approaches to environmental issues, often depicted as mutually exclusive, are, in reality, complementary since each approach has its own uses and limitations. The expansion theory is instrumentally valuable because it allows a certain degree of ecological protection in the absence of distinct environmental rights or provisions. The environmental democracy theory is conducive to democratization through higher accountability and transparency in matters of environmental protection and resource management. This approach is compatible with the precautionary principle. By requesting the disclosure of vital environmental information and by participating in environmental decision-making, individuals and NGOS are empowered to lobby against what they perceive as ecologically harmful policies or regulations. The genesis theory favours the conceptualisation and recognition of a distinct right to environment. In contrast to the expansion theory, which relies essentially on well-established human rights, substantive environmental rights can be invoked on both anthropocentric and ecocentric bases.

As utopian as they may appear at this stage of their development, environmental rights may facilitate the protection of natural ecosystems and Indigenous collective rights without the legal hurdles of standing and burden of proof. Moreover, granting attributes of human rights to complex concepts such as ecosystems, water resources, and indigenous communal ownership of land may contribute to a less utilitarian approach to nature and provide future generations with an alternative understanding of the relationship between humans and nature. This extra-judicial role of environmental rights is what makes them ethically and practically valuable: they can lead to a paradigm shift in our societal value system.

To go beyond the theorisation presented in this chapter, I lay out in Chapter 4 a two-level conceptualisation of environmental rights. The first level of conceptualisation emphasises the mutually reinforcing correlations between

---

230 See Ayesha Dias, "Human Rights, Environment and Development: With Special Emphasis on Corporate Accountability," UNDP, http://hdr.undp.org/en/media/hdr_2000_ch0.pdf.

231 See especially Shelton, "Normative Hierarchy." In Shelton's opinion, "soft law is not law or a formal source of norms. Such [soft law] instruments may express trends or a stage in the formulation of treaty or custom, but law does not come with a sliding scale of bindingness, nor does desired law become law by stating its desirability, even repeatedly."

the environment, development and democracy. Since development and environment are inappropriately pitted against each other, they can be brought together under the wings of human rights. Based on the recent developments in the concept of environmental rights, I advocate the adoption of a distinct 'Right to Environment' in international law whose role is to provide a broad legal and policy framework for international cooperation in matters involving the human rights implications of ecological degradation. Next, I offer a set of specific environmental rights that are justiciable in international and domestic courts and that can be invoked by both individuals and groups. This approach leads to the re-conceptualisation or reconfiguration of the human rights discourse in light of sustainable development, the notion of solidarity, the principle of indivisibility of human rights, and democratic entitlements.

CHAPTER FOUR

RECONFIGURATION OF THE HUMAN RIGHTS SYSTEM IN LIGHT OF SUSTAINABLE DEVELOPMENT AND THE TWO-LEVEL CONCEPTUALISATION OF ENVIRONMENTAL RIGHTS

Introduction

This chapter locates the evolving 'Right to Environment' in the broader framework of sustainable development and a new categorisation of human rights. The chapter explores whether the emergence of sustainable development has played a role in furthering or hindering the development of the international 'Right to Environment' and its sub-rights, as proposed in this book. It also builds a theoretical connection among the concepts of environment, development, democracy and human rights. In fact, the right to development has been greatly influenced by the concept of sustainable development. As for the right to democracy, it is not yet recognised as a human right, although the *Aarhus Convention* on environmental procedural rights is illustrative of the intimate connection between environmental issues and democratic accountability, especially in Eastern Europe.[1]

Labelling broad concepts like those of development and environment as 'human rights' does not easily fit within the traditional framework of human rights. Therefore, a more evolutionary and proactive approach is needed in order to overcome the theoretical stalemate between these new rights and the requisites of individualism and judicial enforceability. The conceptualisation of a distinct 'Right to Environment' in international law and the reconfiguration of the human rights system into generalist and specialist rights fit squarely within this context. This conceptualisation conforms to the principle of interdependence and indivisibility of human rights. By emulating the more advanced right to development and the less developed right to democracy, it is possible to conceive a 'Right to Environment' as a generalist or umbrella right. This approach will provide a broad legal and policy framework necessary to take on the complexities of environmental issues and the multiplicity of duty-bearers involved.

The first section of this chapter explains the meaning of sustainable development, its three pillars and its role as an umbrella concept for the right to development, the right to democracy and the 'Right to Environment'. The second section examines the rationale behind the proposed reconfiguration

---

[1] See generally Zaharchenko and Goldenman, "Accountability in Governance."

of human rights and establishes the connection between each generalist right and its corresponding covenant, including a detailed description of a draft covenant on environmental rights.

A. *Sustainable Development: A Marriage of Convenience between Environment and Development*

The concept of sustainable development can mean different things to different people. For instance, in the *Hungary v. Slovakia* case, both contending parties used the concept of sustainable development to defend their differing interests: Slovakia stressed the economic aspect of sustainable development, Hungary focused on the environmental impact of the Gabčíkovo-Nagymaros project.[2] Extensively defined, the concept of sustainable development is one of the most hotly debated topics of international concern. Its opponents question whether sustainable development aims to sustain nature or to sustain 'economic' development, while its advocates believe in the concept's ability to restructure and 'green' existing development paradigms. The concept of sustainable development is often marketed as the magic wand that can sustain, on one hand, economic development and the lifestyle of modern societies and, on the other, the environment and the livelihoods of local and traditional communities—at least, this is the common rationale behind most definitions of sustainable development. The Brundtland Report states that "ecology and economy are becoming ever more interwoven—locally, regionally, nationally, and globally—into a seamless net of causes and effects."[3] Instilling ecological concerns into the dominant economic paradigm will eventually change our perception of economic growth, so it is important to clarify the place of environmental human rights and the proposed 'Right to Environment' in the sustainable development discourse, which has become the dominant discourse in relation to the global environmental movement.

1. *What is Sustainable Development?*

The ambiguity and versatility of the term 'sustainable development' stem from the difficulty of defining development itself. If development is simply equated with economic growth, sustainable development may appear to be an oxymoronic concept par excellence.[4] For its critics, sustainable development seems unattainable because it entails the reconciliation between two traditionally opposing notions—economic development and environmental protection. They often differentiate between sustainability and sustainable

---

[2] *Gabčikovo-Nagymaros Project (Hungary v. Slovakia)*, ICJ Rep 7(1997). See below Section B.2.

[3] The World Commission on Environment and Development, *Our Common Future,* 5.

[4] See especially Wolfgang Sachs, *Planet Dialectics* (London: Zed Books, 1999), 17.

development. Sachs maintained that sustainable development shifts the focus from sustainability of nature to sustainable growth.[5] Bosselmann contended that, without the principle of ecological sustainability, there is no sustainable development; he distinguished between strong sustainability, which is highly critical of growth and economic development and focuses on ecological sustainability, and weak sustainability, which puts economic growth on equal footing with environmental sustainability and social justice.[6] To a certain extent, the concept of sustainable development, as promoted by the Brundtland report and subsequent instruments, oscillates between these two definitions. It is a dynamic concept, not frozen in time or definition. Sustainable development will finally ripen when it conveys the message that ecological and social values should not be sacrificed at the altar of economic development. Doing so will not be easy since modern societies have to move gradually from unsustainable ways of production and consumption to a wiser and more ecologically friendly lifestyles. Despite its recent appearance on the international stage, the concept of sustainability is rooted in the practices of ancient communities that successfully applied the precepts of sustainable development.[7] The modern approach to the concept lies primarily in placing these old ideas and practices into contemporary legal and policy frameworks.

The Brundtland definition of sustainable development, the most commonly quoted definition, describes sustainable development as "development that meets the needs of the present without compromising the ability of future generations to meet their own needs."[8] Some commentators have contended that the focus on development in the Brundtland definition is misleading because it gives the impression that environmental considerations are secondary to developmental goals and that the term 'needs' is difficult to define because individuals' needs are subject to social and cultural variations. To overcome such confusion, some opt for the term 'Ecologically Sustainable Development' (ESD), which emphasises the ecological aspect of sustainability. For instance, the Australian Government defines ESD as "using, conserving and enhancing the community's resources so that ecological processes, on which life depends, are maintained, and the total quality of life, now and in the future, can be increased."[9] However, the Australian definition is not immune from criticism: Beder noted that the phrase 'total quality of life', like the term

---

[5] Ibid., 81.

[6] Klaus Bosselmann, *The Principle of Sustainability: Transforming Law and Governance* (Aldershot: Ashgate, 2008), 53, 27.

[7] *Gabčikovo-Nagymaros Project (Hungary v. Slovakia)(Separate Opinion of Judge Weeramantry)*, ICJ Rep 7, 98–107 (1997).

[8] The World Commission on Environment and Development, *Our Common Future*, 43.

[9] The Ecologically Sustainable Development Steering Committee, "National Strategy for Ecologically Sustainable Development," Australian Government, Department of the Environment and Heritage, http://www.deh.gov.au/esd/national/nsesd/strategy/intro.html#WIESD.

'needs', varies with the cultural specificities and value systems of individuals and communities.[10]

The Brundtand definition also implies that a 'development' that is concerned about the fate of nature and future generations is incompatible with the classical notion of economic growth, which will open the door to broader and alternative conceptions of development that regard the process of development as involving material and non-material needs. A broader conception of development, as advocated by Sen, views the creation of norms and social ethics as part of the process of development, along with markets and other institutions.[11] An alternative view of development that is more critical of the market economy advocates a bottom-up approach to development and favours small-scale projects over large capital investments, and sufficiency and self-reliance over profit maximization and the free market system.[12] These conceptions of development tend to be more socially and ecologically friendly and are better suited to describing the essence of sustainable development as conveyed by the Brundtland report and other instruments.

Since the Brundtland Report, sustainable development has been the core concept in subsequent global conferences and corollary instruments. Of specific importance is the Rio Declaration, which played a seminal role in launching and activating the principle of sustainable development. Principle 4 of the Rio Declaration highlights the inextricable link between environmental protection and development, stating that "[i]n order to achieve sustainable development, environmental protection shall constitute an integral part of the development process and cannot be considered in isolation from it."[13] Similarly, the Millennium Declaration affirms the necessity of managing environmental resources according to the principles of sustainable development and states that "[p]rudence must be shown in the management of all living species and natural resources, in accordance with the precepts of sustainable development."[14] In addition, the concept of sustainable development was the cornerstone of major international environmental agreements adopted at the Rio Conference: the 1992 *UN Framework Convention on Climate Change* (UNFCCC), the 1992 *UN Convention on Biological Diversity*, and the 1994 *UN Convention to Combat Desertification*. The UNFCCC mentions the right to

---

[10] Sharon Beder, *The Nature of Sustainable Development* (Newham, Australia: Scribe Publications, 1993), 3.

[11] Amartya Sen, *Development as Freedom* (New York: Oxford University Press, 2001), 297.

[12] Caroline Thomas, "Poverty, Development, and Hunger," in *The Globalization of World Politics*, ed. John Baylis, Steve Smith, and Patricia Owens (New York: Oxford University Press, 2008), 473.

[13] *Rio Declaration on Environment and Development*, Principle 4.

[14] *United Nations Millennium Declaration*, GA Res 55/2, UN GAOR, 55th sess, 8th plen mtg, UN Doc A/55/L.2 (2000), I(6).

sustainable development as a right of States Parties and proclaims that states "have a right to, and should, promote sustainable development."[15]

2. *The Three Pillars of Sustainable Development*

The Brundtland Report emphasises the transformative and dynamic nature of sustainable development. It describes sustainable development as "a process of change in which the exploitation of resources, the direction of investments, the orientation of technological development, and institutional change are all in harmony and enhance both current and future potential to meet human needs and aspirations."[16] Therefore, it identifies three pillars of sustainable development: economic development, social equity and environmental protection.[17] The ILA New Delhi Declaration of Principles of International Law Relating to Sustainable Development (ILA Declaration) reaffirms in its preamble the interconnectedness of the three pillars of sustainable development identified by the Brundtland Report:

> The objective of sustainable development involves a comprehensive and integrated approach to economic, social and political processes, which aims at the sustainable use of natural resources of the Earth and the protection of the environment on which nature and human life as well as social and economic development depend and which seeks to realise the right of all human beings to an adequate living standard.[18]

Sands provided a definition of sustainable development that highlights the dynamic, formless, inconsistent and ambiguous nature of sustainable development. In his words, sustainable development "is not independent and free-standing of principles and rules, and it is still emerging. As such, it is not coherent or comprehensive, nor is it free from ambiguity or inconsistency."[19] He perceived sustainable development as "a broad umbrella accommodating the specialised fields of international law which aim to promote economic development, environmental protection and respect for civil and political rights."[20] The IUCN Draft International Covenant on Environment and Development (IUCN Draft Covenant) is a perfect illustration of this integrative

---

[15] *The UN Framework Convention on Climate Change*, art. 3(4).

[16] The World Commission on Environment and Development, *Our Common Future*, 46.

[17] Ibid.

[18] *New Delhi Declaration of Principles of International Law Relating to Sustainable Development*, Res 3/2002, 70th Conference of the International Law Association, New Delhi, 2–6 Apr. 2002.

[19] Philippe Sands, "International Courts and the Application of the Concept of "Sustainable Development"," in *Law and Development: Facing Complexity in the 21st Century: Essays in Honour of Peter Slinn*, ed. John Hatchard and Amanda Perry-Kessaris (Newport, Australia: Cavendish Publishing, 2003), 147.

[20] Ibid.

approach towards varying fields of international law. Its drafters described it as "a blueprint for an international framework (or umbrella) agreement consolidating and developing existing legal principles related to environment and development."[21]

In contrast to the common integrative approach mentioned above, Mary Robinson, the UN High Commissioner for Human Rights, perceived the interconnectedness among the environment, human rights and sustainable development through the metaphor of a triangle, where the achievement of every concept is conditioned on the support of the other two.[22] In Robinson's opinion, the image of the triangle reflects 'the intersection not the integration of these three goals.'[23] It follows that all three discourses are to be viewed as goals in themselves and not as mere instruments, each for the implementation of the other. Sustainable development, then, is not portrayed as a concept of integration between human rights and environment, but as a distinct entity that needs to be implemented as a separate goal of international law. Robinson's view reflects a certain level of confusion regarding the meaning and place of sustainable development in international law.

In fact, Principle 7 of the ILA Declaration affirms the integrative nature of sustainable development by stating that the "principle of integration reflects the interdependence of social, economic, financial, environmental and human rights aspects of principles and rules of international law relating to sustainable development."[24] This statement demonstrates that the goals of sustainable development are inferred from the goals of other international rules and principles and should not be perceived as separate goals. The usefulness of sustainable development lies in its practical approach to complex global issues, which often involve more than one field of international law and policy. In this regard, one can argue that the originality of sustainable development stems from its role as an 'umbrella' or framework concept for crossover principles of international law, such as the principles of sustainable development identified by the ILA Declaration. For instance, the principle of equity and eradication of poverty that encompasses the realisation of both inter-generational equity and intra-generational equity requires the integration of a complex web of environmental and socio-economic goals.[25] Drawing upon the Brundtland

---

[21] IUCN Commission on Human Rights, *Draft International Covenant on Environment and Development*, 3rd ed. (Gland and Cambridge: IUCN, 2004), xi.

[22] Mary Robinson, "Civil Society Workshop on Human Rights, Sustainable Development and Environmental Protection (Speech Delivered at the World Summit on Sustainable Development, Johannesburg, South Africa, 1 Sept. 2002)," http://www.unhchr.ch/huricane/huricane.nsf/0/A551686D4B5905D0C1256C28002BF3D6?opendocument.

[23] Ibid.

[24] *New Delhi Declaration of Principles of International Law Relating to Sustainable Development*, Principle 7.

[25] Ibid., Principle 2.

Report, Sands' definition and the work of leading scholars on sustainable development,[26] I constructed the diagram shown in Figure 2, which represents the three pillars of sustainable development and the main corollary fields of international law.

As Figure 2 shows, sustainable development brings together scattered international laws and principles in areas that are best addressed in a holistic way. The figure also places both the 'Right to Environment' and the right to development in the sustainable development context. This choice is best illustrated in the background paper prepared by the UN Commission on Sustainable Development (CSD), which considers the right to development and the right to a 'healthy' environment as principles and concepts of international law for sustainable development.[27] The purpose of this diagram is to show that sustainable development as a theoretical and normative framework provides a valid justification for a human rights approach to the concepts of democracy, development and environment.

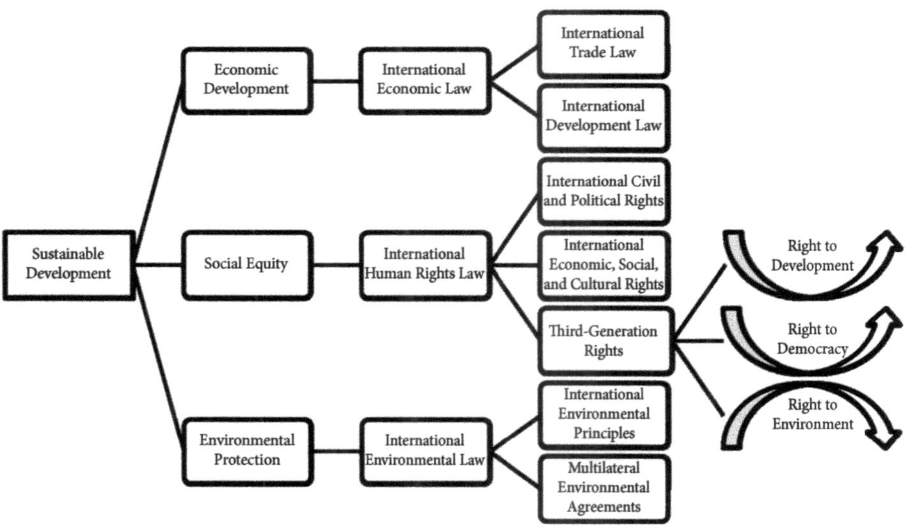

Fig. 2. Sustainable Development as a Conceptual and Legal Framework for the Right to Environment.

---

[26] See Peter P. Rogers, Kazi F. Jalal, and John A. Boyd, *An Introduction to Sustainable Development* (London: Earthscan, 2008); Segger and Khalfan, *Sustainable Development Law*; Beder, *Nature of Sustainable Development*.

[27] *Report of the Expert Group Meeting on Identification of Principles of International Law for Sustainable Development*, United Nations Commission on Sustainable Development, UN CSD 4th Session (1996).

B. *Sustainable Development as a Theoretical and Normative Framework for the Right to Development and the Right to Environment*

1. *Sustainable Development as a Link between Trade and Environment*

International law presents the sustainable development concept as an innovative approach to the way modern economies should be performing in the 21st century. Some commentators have wondered whether sustainable development can be an alternative to conventional economic thought.[28] That the application of the concept of sustainable development is important in the context of international trade has been made clear in the many international trade disputes involving environmental components.

Broadly speaking, there is no integration of environmental principles and trade under the current trade regime. However, the *WTO Case on Sea Turtle Conservation* provides an example of the judicial use of sustainable development as a reconciliatory concept between environmental considerations and trade.[29] Under the *US Endangered Species Act* of 1973, the USA adopted strict conservation legislation regarding the protection of endangered species such as the sea turtles. The Act also allows the USA to provide free technical support to countries willing to use safe fishing methods in order to avoid the accidental ensnaring of sea turtles in their nets. Moreover, *Section 609 of the 1989 US Public Law 101–162* prohibits the import of certain shrimp and shrimp products from countries whose fishing methods may threaten the life of certain types of sea turtles and requires the use of 'turtle-excluder devices' (TEDs) by US shrimp trawlers to protect sea turtles from being accidentally caught in fishing nets.[30] Four Asian shrimp exporters directly affected by the ban–India, Malaysia, Pakistan and Thailand–brought a joint complaint against the USA.

Pursuant to an appeal lodged by the USA regarding the decision reached by a panel set up by the Dispute Settlement Body, the Appellate Body found that the panel erred in its interpretation of Article XX(g) of GATT 1994. This Article, which is an exception to the rules of GATT, allows WTO members to put restrictions on trade practices if they do not comply with some environmental and conservation requirements. It stipulates that, unless the measures adopted by states do not constitute "means of arbitrary or unjustifiable discrimination between countries where the same conditions prevail, or a disguised restriction on international trade, nothing in this Agreement shall be

---

[28] W.M. Adams, *Green Development: Environment and Sustainability in the Third World*, 2nd ed. (London/New york: Routledge, 1990), 11.

[29] *United States-Import Prohibition of Certain Shrimp and Shrimp Products*, WTO Doc WT/DS58/AB/R, AB-1998-4 (1998) (Report of the Appellate Body).

[30] World Trade Organization, "India etc versus US: 'Shrimp-Turtle'," http://www.wto.org/english/tratop_e/envir_e/edis08_e.htm.

construed to prevent the adoption or enforcement by any Member of measures ... relating to the conservation of exhaustible natural resources if such measures are made effective in conjunction with restrictions on domestic production or consumption."[31]

The WTO Appellate Body reversed the conclusions reached by the panel on the grounds of an 'error in legal interpretation' because the Appellate Body relied on the concept of sustainable development in its interpretation of Article XX(g).[32] In contrast with the panel's decisions, it considered sea turtles part of the 'exhaustible natural resources' that need to be protected and conserved. It concluded that the measures taken by the USA to protect the endangered turtles do not violate the provisions of Article XX(g). It ruled that, while the USA's conservation measures are 'provisionally justified', fault lies in that they were applied in an unjustifiable and discriminatory manner among WTO members.[33]

According to the Appellate Body, the essence of Article XX(g) falls within the wider scope of sustainable development, an internationally recognised concept that mirrors the trend towards the acknowledgement of environmental concerns in all economic activities that rely heavily on natural resources. The Preamble of the 1994 WTO Agreement states that the rules of trade should be 'in accordance with the objective of sustainable development' and should seek to 'protect and preserve the environment'.[34] This statement conforms with Principle 2 of the Rio Declaration, which acknowledges the sovereign right of states "to exploit their own resources pursuant to their own environmental and developmental policies, and the responsibility to ensure that activities within their jurisdiction or control do not cause damage to the environment of other States or of areas beyond the limits of national jurisdiction."[35] Despite the fact that international law is predicated on the principle of state sovereignty, this principle is often portrayed as a hindrance to the implementation of environmental policies. According to Weeramantry, each state has the duty to surrender some of its absolute sovereignty to the well-being of the global environment and future generations.[36]

---

[31] *General Agreement on Tariffs and Trade (GATT)*, 1867 UNTS 187, 33 ILM 1153 (1994), art. XX(g).

[32] *United States-Import Prohibition of Certain Shrimp and Shrimp Products*, par. 122; Sands, "International Courts and the Application of the Concept of "Sustainable Development"," 152–56.

[33] *United States-Import Prohibitions of Certain Shrimp and Shrimp Products*, par. 186.

[34] Ibid., par. 17.

[35] *Rio Declaration on Environment and Development*, Principle 2.

[36] H.E. Judge Christopher G. Weeramantry, "Sustainable Development: An Ancient Concept Recently Revived (Speech Delivered at the Global Judges Symposium on Sustainable Development and the Role of Law, Colombo, 4–5 July 1997)," United Nations Environment Programme (UNEP), http://www.unep.org/law/symposium/Speeches.htm.

2. *Sustainable Development as a Reconciliatory Concept between Development and Environment*

Sustainable development as a concept forged its way for the first time into the International Court of Justice (ICJ) in the *Hungary v. Slovakia* case.[37] In 1977, Hungary and Czechoslovakia signed a treaty 'concerning the construction and operation of the Gabčíkovo-Nagymaros System of Locks.'[38] The Treaty established a joint investment project to construct two water barrages, one at Gabčíkovo, in Czechoslovak territory, and the other at Nagymaros, in Hungarian territory. The main objectives of the project were to generate hydroelectric power, to facilitate navigation and to prevent flooding along the Danube riverbanks.[39] The treaty proscribed the contracting parties from impairing the quality of the Danube. Twelve years later, the Hungarian government unilaterally suspended work on the project, claiming serious ecological hazards to the region of Szigetköz.[40] In an attempt to mitigate the economic harm caused by Hungary's unilateral suspension of the joint investment, Czechoslovakia reverted to an alternative project named 'Variant C', which consisted of a diversion of the Danube in Czechoslovakian territory and the construction at Cunovo of an overflow dam and a levee linking that dam to the south bank of the bypass.[41] The Hungarian government complained that the unilateral diversion of the Danube River affected its access to water and decided to terminate the 1977 treaty in May 1992. Negotiations between the contracting parties failed to settle the dispute, so they agreed to submit the dispute to the ICJ.[42]

The ICJ found Hungary's concerns about the environmental implications of the project were legitimate and related to an 'essential interest' of that State but that its unilateral suspension could not be justified under the law of treaties, nor could its abandonment of the treaty altogether.[43] Similarly, the ICJ found the unilateral diversion of water by Czechoslovakia incompatible with the Treaty.[44] In the end, the ICJ left the two contending states dissatisfied with its decision because it advised them to pursue further negotiations in order to reach a workable solution for the thorny issue. To an extent, the ICJ's decision was a plea for the litigants to rectify their implementation of the Treaty by adopting the concept of sustainable development as a reconciliatory tool

[37] See Bukhosi Fuyane and Ferenc Madai, "The Hungary-Slovakia Danube River Dispute: Implications for Sustainable Development and Equitable Utilization of Natural Resources in International Law," *International Journal of Global Environmental Issues* 1, no. 3 (2001): 330.
[38] *Hungary v. Slovakia*, 16.
[39] Ibid.
[40] Ibid., 35.
[41] Ibid., 25.
[42] Ibid., 11.
[43] Ibid., 39, 45.
[44] Ibid., 65.

between their divergent interests. The ICJ emphasised the historical roots of the practice of sustainable development and its validity for modern economic practices in stating that:

> Throughout the ages, mankind has, for economic and other reasons, constantly interfered with nature. In the past, this was often done without consideration of the effects upon the environment. Owing to new scientific insights and to a growing awareness of the risks for mankind–for present and future generations–of pursuit of such interventions at an unconsidered and unabated pace, new norms and standards have been developed, set forth in a great number of instruments during the last two decades. Such new norms have to be taken into consideration, and such new standards given proper weight, not only when States contemplate new activities but also when continuing with activities begun in the past. This need to reconcile economic development with protection of the environment is aptly expressed in the concept of sustainable development.[45]

In a separate opinion, Judge Weeramantry described in detail the historical underpinnings of the sustainable development concept demonstrating that sustainable development, widely recognised by the international community, is rooted in traditional cultures, which accord more respect for and awe of the natural environment than do modern societies. Drawing upon these cultures, Weeramantry suggested the integration of these ancient environmental principles into our modern international legal systems.[46] The tension between environmental and developmental prerogatives in this case is actually simply a clash of interests between two sovereign states. The root cause of the problem lies in the interpretation and application of the right to development as the right of states to pollute and damage the environment for the sake of economic necessities. This point of view contradicts the spirit of the UN Declaration on the Right to Development (DRTD), which proclaims that "the human person is the central subject of the development process."[47]

The *Gabčíkovo-Nagymaros* case is illustrative of the growing impact of the sustainable development concept on the fields of international law. As Weeramantry put it, "the principle of sustainable development is thus a part of modern international law by reason not only of its inescapable logical necessity, but also by reason of its wide and general acceptance by the global community."[48] To some extent, the solution to the above conflict lies in the harmonization and balance of two competing rights: the right to development and the right to environmental protection.[49] In the *Pulp Mills* case, the ICJ interpreted the concept of sustainable development as the need to safeguard

---

[45] *Hungary v. Slovakia*, 78.
[46] See *Hungary v. Slovakia (Separate Opinion of Judge Weeramantry)*, 88–119.
[47] *Declaration on the Right to Development*, GA Res 41/128, UN GAOR, 41st, 97th plen mtg, UN Doc A/Res/41/128 (1986).
[48] *Hungary v. Slovakia (Separate Opinion of Judge Weeramantry)*, 95.
[49] Ibid., 89.

shared natural resources while pursuing lucrative economic projects by emphasizing the "need to safeguard the continued conservation of the river environment and the rights of economic development of the riparian States."[50]

In this dispute, Argentina brought proceedings before the ICJ against Uruguay alleging that Uruguay violated its international obligations under the 1975 River Uruguay Statute by failing to notify and negotiate with the Argentine government regarding the polluting effect of the paper mills on the banks of the Uruguay River. In its decision of 13/06/2006, the Court refused Argentina's request for an injunction to halt construction of the mills and suggested that both riparian states should proceed with negotiations in good faith according to the terms of the 1975 Statute. The Court concurred with Uruguay that "the provisional measures sought by Argentina would therefore irreparably prejudice Uruguay's sovereign right to implement sustainable economic development projects in its own territory ... and that, once in service, the mills would have an economic impact of more than $350 million per year."[51] In the presence of two independent studies from the World Bank Group's International Finance Corporation (IFC) and Multilateral Investment Guarantee Agency (MIGA) asserting that the mills will be safe environmentally, the Court could only err on the side of Uruguay regarding the economic benefits generated by the projects. Moreover, the Uruguayan authorities claimed that the mills would be using the 'best available technology' in their wood pulp processing, known as Elemental Chlorine-Free (or ECF) bleaching, adopted by both the United States and the European Union. In order to dissipate Argentina's concerns about the credibility of the environmental impact studies, Uruguay reiterated its willingness to comply in full with the 1975 Statute and offered to conduct continuous joint monitoring with Argentina regarding the environmental consequences of the mills' future operations.[52] Although the Court vindicated Uruguay's right to pursue its economic development in the absence of any evidence of imminent or irreparable harm to the river environment, it acknowledged "the right of Argentina to submit in the future a fresh request for the indication of provisional measures ... based on new facts."[53]

These two cases—the *Gabčíkovo-Nagymaros* case and the *Pulp Mills* case—suggest that the ICJ's interpretation of sustainable development encompasses both economic and ecological interests. To the dismay of deep ecologists, the concept of sustainable development does not guarantee a pristine environment but offers a platform from which judges and politicians can weigh, based

---

[50] *Pulp Mills on the River Uruguay (Argentine v. Uruguay)*, ICJ Rep 135(2006).
[51] Ibid., 48.
[52] Ibid., 56.
[53] Ibid., 86.

on factual evidence, the various interests at stake. As Birnie et al. pointed out, sustainable development is not yet a legal obligation but a policy that affects judicial decisions, state practices, international organisations and the development of international environmental law.[54] In my opinion, sustainable development is a move away from the strong anthropocentrism of last centuries to the weak anthropocentrism promoted by sustainable development and environmental human rights discussed in this book.

3. *The Human Rights Discourse as a Common Denominator for Environment and Development*

Human rights law is an important part of the social dimension of sustainable development. In this regard, the eradication of poverty is necessary for the achievement of social equity, one of the main pillars of sustainable development. The 2005 Human Development Report highlights the severity of poverty in the world by revealing alarming figures about the status of human development. It estimates that "10.7 million children every year do not live to see their fifth birthday, and more than 1 billion people survive in abject poverty on less than $1 a day."[55] Moser and Norton found a legitimate benefit in using the human rights concept in the context of poverty alleviation and designed a conceptual framework based on the links among sustainable development, human rights and 'sustainable livelihoods' of the poor.[56] The study emphasises the role of human rights in empowering the poor in pursuit of poverty reduction and more equitable and sustainable livelihoods.[57] Fabra observed that many international institutions, such as the International Monetary Fund and the World Health Organisation, refer to the concept of

[54] Patricia Birnie, Alan E. Boyle, and Catherine Redgwell, *International Law and the Environment*, 3nd ed. (New York: Oxford University Press, 2009), 127.

[55] United Nations Development Programme (UNDP), "Human Development Report 2005: International Cooperation at a Crossroads: Aid, Trade and Security in an Unequal World," http://hdr.undp.org/en/reports/global/hdr2005/. The MDGs have not been attained and the plight of the poor has worsened since then instead of improving. The 2007 Update on Africa and the Millennium Development Goals (MDGs) shows that only a slight improvement has been achieved in the social and economic situation of the sub-Saharan African people since the adoption of the MDGs in 2000. Unlike the ambitious goals set by the MDGs to halve extreme poverty and hunger by 2015, the report found that the proportion of people living on one dollar a day has declined 4.8 percent and that the proportion of children under five who suffer from hunger declined only by four percent. It is estimated that one African woman in every sixteen is at risk of dying from complications in pregnancy and childbirth and that the number of HIV/AIDS cases has increased dramatically. On the other hand, the report shows some progress in other areas. The number of poor people has levelled off and the percentage of children enrolled in primary school has increased from 57 percent in 1999 to 70 percent in 2005. United Nations, "Africa and the Millennium Development Goals: 2007 Update" http://www.un.org/millenniumgoals/docs/MDGafrica07.pdf.

[56] Caroline Moser and Andy Norton, *To Claim Our Rights: Livelihood Security, Human Rights and Sustainable Development* (London: Overseas Development Institute, 2001), 40–41.

[57] Ibid.

sustainable development when formulating links between human rights and environment.[58] Similarly, Pathak observed that "that the framework of human rights, with its emphasis on the social dimension and participation, was more appropriate than the framework of international ecological security."[59]

Figure 2 shows that the human rights approach to environment and development, materialised in the 'Right to Environment' and the right to development, respectively, serves as a common denominator between the development discourse and the environment discourse. Both the right to development and the 'Right to Environment', which belong to third-generation rights, attempt to achieve social goals such as poverty eradication and the respect for human dignity and nature. Moreover, based on the indivisibility of human rights, human rights law as a common denominator between environmental concerns and developmental prerogatives may constitute a legal basis for the adoption of a third covenant on environmental rights to complement the 1966 Covenants. The connection between the 'Right to Environment' and the proposed covenant on environmental rights is fully explored below.

Based on these discussions of sustainable development, two contrasting observations emerge. On one hand, the concept of sustainable development hovers over the international environmental agenda and may impede the development of a distinct 'Right to Environment' and environmental human rights in general. This observation is made clearest in the formulation of Principle 1 of the Rio Declaration, which moved away from the emerging idea of the right to environment, as fleshed out in Principle 1 of the Stockholm Declaration, towards the emerging concept of sustainable development. On the other hand, the concept of sustainable development, as the dominant global discourse relating to environment and development, has the potential to provide an appropriate conceptual and normative framework for the proposed 'Right to Environment' through the integration of the three pillars of sustainable development and the principles provided in the ILA Declaration. As an umbrella concept, sustainable development offers an integrative approach to the scattered fields of international law, facilitating the adoption of a human rights-based approach to environmental issues.

C. *Reconfiguration of the Human Rights System*

Figure 3 illustrates the interconnectedness of all human rights by classifying rights into two categories: umbrella rights and sub-rights (or generalist and specialist rights).

---

[58] Fabra, "Intersection of Human Rights and Environmental Issues," 33–34.

[59] See R.S. Pathak, "The Human Rights System as a Conceptual Framework for Environmental Law," in *Environmental Change and International Law: New Challenges and Dimensions*, ed. Edith Brown Weiss (Tokyo, Japan: United Nations University Press, 1992), 221.

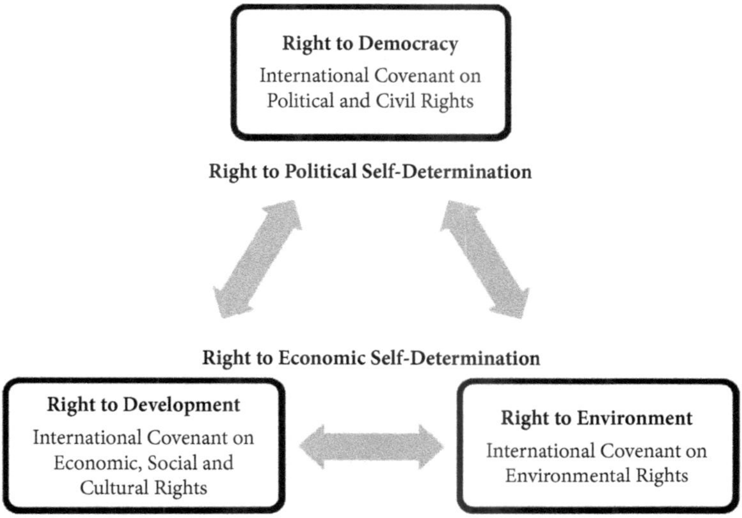

Fig. 3. Reconfiguration of the Human Rights System.

The rationale behind this re-conceptualisation of rights is grounded in the 'synthetic'[60] or 'integrated'[61] nature of the umbrella or generalist rights: the right to democracy, the right to development and the 'Right to Environment'. The idea of synthetic rights is invoked in the context of the right to development since it has been argued that the right to development cannot be considered a new right because it is extracted from rights already enshrined in the 1966 Covenants. Therefore, it is better to adhere to the traditional framework of human rights by incorporating new concepts and emerging claims into additional protocols, rather than jumping the hurdles of justifying and recognising new rights.[62]

However, one can also argue that synthetic rights transcend their synthetic nature. As Alston observed, the "vital characteristic of syntheses is indicated by the maxim which states that the whole is greater than the sum of parts."[63] In other words, despite their synthetic nature, umbrella or generalist rights are new rights because of the solidarity component that injects the notion of international cooperation into the well-established set of human rights. This perspective reflects the severity and importance of challenges that humanity is

[60] See Philip Alston, "Peace as a Human Right," *Security Dialogue* 11(1980): 321.

[61] See Siddiqur Rahman Osmani, "An Essay on the Human Rights Approach to Development," in *Reflections on the Right to Development*, ed. Arjun Sengupta, Archna Negi, and Moushumi Basu (New Delhi: Sage Publications 2005), 124.

[62] Ibid., 322.

[63] Ibid.

facing in the 21st century, all of which require more attention and more joint effort in order to reach valid solutions. The complexities of these generalist rights require a different classification, which makes the concept of third-generation rights useful. Without necessarily adopting the generational classification of rights advanced by Vasak, I regard the notion of joint responsibility as a sound theoretical basis for the proposed differentiation between 'generalist' rights and 'specialist' rights. Accordingly, the nature of generalist rights such as the right to development and the proposed 'Right to Environment' is different from other international individual rights. Rights assigned to broad and complex concepts such as development, environment and democracy are not easily recognised as individual and justiciable rights and can be difficult to enforce in courts and tribunals. Much of their usefulness comes from their extra-judicial meaning, and their legal worth stems from associating them with well-established individual human rights.

Based on the proposed reconfiguration of rights, the political and civil rights that first appeared on the international stage can be associated with the right to democracy. It is theoretically and empirically obvious that human rights cannot flourish without democracy. Even when a government pledges its commitment to economic and social welfare, human dignity is unlikely to be preserved if individual freedoms and liberties are squashed by an authoritarian regime, and it is unlikely that unelected or falsely elected governments that tend to systematically violate civil and political rights will guarantee their citizens' basic needs for food, work or shelter. Sen fervently refuted the argument that people should forgo their political freedoms and democratic rights in order to fulfil their economic needs, arguing that democracy, because of its instrumental and constructive aspects, is essential to furthering the process of development. Democratic institutions, rules and procedures constitute a buffer zone against economic disasters and deprivations. In Sen's words, "no substantial famine has ever occurred in any independent country with a democratic form of government and a relatively free press."[64] In addition to this instrumental element, democracy plays a constructive role by creating values, norms and priorities. Through public discussions and debates, people become more enlightened about their economic needs and tend to make more informed and rational decisions.[65]

Sen's conceptualization of development as freedom, rather than pure economic growth, highlighted the mutual dependency and strong theoretical and empirical connection between the concepts of democracy and development.

---

[64] Sen, *Development as Freedom*, 152.
[65] Ibid., 153.

The two sets of rights embedded in both 1966 Covenants can be associated with the right to democracy and the right to development. Regarding the right to development, Osmani argued that the "integrated nature of the right to development brings into sharp focus the dimension of international obligation in a way that pre-occupation with separate rights cannot."[66] The same rationale could apply to both the 'Right to Environment' and the right to democracy.

Drawing upon the nature of the right to development in international law, I propose the conceptualisation of an international 'Right to Environment' as a generalist right. The main purpose of this proposal is to enhance cooperation among states in addressing the human rights implications of ecological problems and the development of distinct environmental human rights in both the international and the domestic spheres. The essence of generalist rights is to bring the human person to the centre of state and non-state activities that were previously viewed as separate from the concept of human rights. As a new conceptualisation of rights, generalist rights integrate complex concepts such as development, environment and democracy in order to provide a more holistic approach to international laws and policies. In this case, states are perceived as both the rights-holders and the duty-bearers of generalist rights. As a rights-holder, the state represents its citizens on the international stage and acts on their behalf. As a rights-bearer, the state is compelled to cooperate with other states in order to achieve the goals and objectives of these new rights within the context of sustainable development as a legal and policy framework. Moreover, the fact that the right to self-determination is recognised as a legally binding collective right in international law constitutes a suitable conceptual and legal basis for the recognition of generalist rights as collective rights. As Figure 3 suggests, generalist rights can be intimately connected and associated with the right to self-determination in both its political and economic dimensions.

In summary, generalist rights are not individual rights per se, but are contingent on a set of fundamental and basic rights. While generalist rights are primarily of a collective nature, their corresponding sub-rights or specialist rights could be assigned to individuals or groups of individuals. Accordingly, the right to democracy, the right to development and the 'Right to Environment' are of a synthetic nature and can be associated with the corollary rights embedded in the *International Covenant on Civil and Political Rights* (ICCPR), the *International Covenant on Economic, Social and Cultural Rights* (ICESCR), and the proposed covenant on environmental rights, respectively.

---

[66] Osmani, "Human Rights Approach to Development," 125.

1. *The Right to Democracy and the ICCPR*

The 1993 Vienna Declaration and Programme of Action reiterated the core concept of democracy by stating that "democracy is based on the freely expressed will of the people to determine their own political, economic, social and cultural systems and their full participation in all aspects of their lives."[67] By its nature, democracy provides political and legal channels to hold rulers accountable for their misdeeds; as Dershowitz asserted, "rights serve as a check on democracy, and democracy serves as a check on rights."[68] Accordingly, a democratic regime is built on solid institutional arrangements that are able to fulfil and monitor democratic processes such as transparent and periodic elections. In addition, the respect of citizens' civil and political rights is a fundamental sign of a democratic society. Since democratic principles are undermined in a society whose people lack socio-economic and cultural rights, democracy is a *sine qua non* for the respect of human rights, and vice versa. The 1993 Vienna Declaration highlighted this intimate link by stating that "[d]emocracy, development and respect for human rights and fundamental freedoms are interdependent and mutually reinforcing."[69]

Human rights are more likely to thrive in democracies predicated on the rule of law[70] and government accountability than in non-democratic political systems. In fact, where corruption reigns, injustice and inequity flourish. The international community is becoming increasingly aware of the detrimental impact of corrupt practices on good governance, democracy and human rights. The 1993 Final Declaration on Defeating Corruption described corruption as "a virus capable of crippling governments, discrediting public institutions and private corporations, and having devastating impact on the human rights of populations."[71] The 2007 Corruption Perceptions Index shows that corruption is a dominant feature of the world's poorest countries.[72] The index uses a scale of zero to ten, with zero indicating the highest level of corruption in running public affairs; while most developed countries score above five, the majority of developing nations fall below five.[73]

---

[67] *Vienna Declaration and Programme of Action*, par. 8.

[68] Alan Dershowitz, *Rights from Wrongs: A Secular Theory of the Origins of Rights* (New York: Basic Books, 2004), 109.

[69] *Vienna Declaration and Programme of Action*, par. 8.

[70] The rule of law often implies limitations over arbitrary executive actions. See generally Jeffrey A. Brauch, "The Margin of Appreciation and the Jurisprudence of the European Court of Human Rights: Threat to the Rule of Law," *Columbia Journal of European Law* 11(2004–2005): 121–25.

[71] Revista Inter-Forum, "*Final Declaration on Defeating Corruption through Integrity, Transparency and Accountability* (the Second Global Forum on Fighting Corruption, Hosted by the Dutch Government and Co-Sponsored by the United States, Held in May 2001 at the Hague, Netherlands)," http://www.revistainterforum.com/english/articles/121701artprin_en.html.

[72] See Transparency International, "2007 Transparency International Corruption Perceptions Index," http://www.transparency.org/policy_research/surveys_indices/cpi/2007.

[73] Ibid.

This global awareness culminated with the 2003 adoption of the *UN Convention against Corruption,* whose preamble states that corruption undermines 'the institutions and values of democracy.'[74] During a mission to Mozambique, the Special Rapporteur on the Right to Health stated that corruption constitutes a serious impediment to the enjoyment of the right to health because health funds and resources are directed into 'private pockets' instead of alleviating the pain of the poor. The Rapporteur identified 'participation, access to information, transparency, monitoring and accountability' as necessary features to fighting corruption, but these features identified by the Rapporteur cannot flourish in an undemocratic environment.[75]

Respect for individual human rights is one of the main features of democratic governments. The resistance of non-democratic governments to human rights, especially their civil and political aspects, is understandable because the genuine implementation of such rights poses a drastic threat to dictatorial or unrepresentative regimes. Many Third World countries have been uncomfortable with the sweeping idea of international human rights in large part because the human rights concept puts some serious constraints on states' sovereignty. As Donnelly put it, "sovereignty is typically the mantle behind which rights-abusive regimes hide when faced with international human rights criticism."[76] Thus, one should be sceptical of claims based on sovereignty or cultural peculiarities when it is actually factors such as regime survival, national security or economic interests that lie behind these claims. China is a perfect illustration of a political regime that tolerates human rights violations on the grounds of cultural relativity and economic development. Among developing countries, China is the staunchest advocate of cultural relativism, arguing that the protection of human rights should be subject to cultural standards and values.[77] Chinese officials often defend China's prioritisation of the right to subsistence and development over other human rights on the grounds that it improves the socio-economic conditions of the Chinese people.[78]

Even when appropriate human rights mechanisms are in place, the realisation and efficacy of these rights are intimately related to the political and legal system in which they operate. For instance, the enforcement and compliance machinery related to the *European Convention* is far more efficient and practical than that of the African Commission on Human and Peoples'

---

[74] *United Nations Convention against Corruption*, GA Res 58/4, UN GAOR, 58th sess, UN Doc A/RES/58/4 (2003) (Entered into force 14 Dec. 2005).

[75] *Report of the Special Rapporteur: Mission to Mozambique*, Paul Hunt, UN Doc E/CN.4/2005/51/Add.2 (2005), par. 69.

[76] Donnelly, *Universal Human Rights*, 108.

[77] Jiangyu Wang, "China and the Universal Human Rights Standards," *Syracuse Journal of International Law and Commerce* 29(2001–2002): 148.

[78] Ibid., 145.

Rights.[79] While the acceptance and adherence to a regional human rights treaty does not guarantee the respect of citizens' rights in the presence of dictatorships and military regimes, the absence of such a treaty or commission on human rights, as is the case in Asia and the Pacific, is not a positive sign.[80] Still, even democracies are not immune from violating human rights. For instance, despite a deep-rooted tradition of democracy, the United States Congress has historically encountered problems with the norms of international human rights because the US adheres only to the primacy of the rights in its Constitution. For example, despite the fact that the death penalty defies the human right to life, as enshrined in Article 3 of the Universal Declaration, the American people see it as an incarnation of the will of the people given to them by the Constitution.[81]

In his 1992 article 'The Emerging Right to Democratic Governance', Franck argued that 'democratic entitlement' is emerging as a legal right in international law.[82] Democratic entitlement consists of three subsets of democratic norms: self-determination, freedom of expression, and the right to free and open elections.[83] Self-determination played a seminal role as a political principle and legal right in the creation of new states in the 20th century. Apart from its secessionist aspect, the right to self-determination evolved towards a more inclusive norm, interpreted as the right of people to participate in the democratic process of governance.[84] Franck emphasised this aspect of self-determination to establish the link between democracy and governance. The second and third norms of democratic entitlement, the right of free political expression and the right to free and open elections, are legally binding rules embedded in the Universal Declaration, the ICCPR and regional human rights treaties.[85] By establishing the connection between basic civil and political rights and democracy, Franck constructed a strong conceptual basis for democratic governance as a global legal entitlement.

In fact, the legal basis of the right to democracy can be drawn from several non-binding international instruments. The 1993 Vienna Declaration and Programme of Action acknowledges the interdependence among democracy, development and human rights.[86] The UN Commission on Human Rights and the General Assembly have issued many resolutions aimed at linking

---

[79] Kirby, 18.
[80] Ibid., 19.
[81] Ignatieff, "Human Rights as Politics and Idolatry," 13.
[82] Thomas M. Franck, "The Emerging Right to Democratic Governance," *American Journal of International Law* 86, no. 1 (1992).
[83] Ibid., 52.
[84] Ibid., 59.
[85] Ibid., 61–65.
[86] *Vienna Declaration and Programme of Action*, par. 8.

democracy and human rights,[87] particularly resolution 1999/57: 'Promotion of the right to democracy', which lists many well-established international political and civil rights as rights of democratic governance:

> a) The rights to freedom of opinion and expression, of thought, conscience and religion, and of peaceful association and assembly; (b) The right to freedom to seek, receive and impart information and ideas through any media; (c) The rule of law, including legal protection of citizens' rights, interests and personal security, and fairness in the administration of justice and independence of the judiciary; (d) The right of universal and equal suffrage, as well as free voting procedures and periodic and free elections; (e) The right of political participation, including equal opportunity for all citizens to become candidates; (f) Transparent and accountable government institutions; (g) The right of citizens to choose their governmental system through constitutional or other democratic means; (h) The right to equal access to public service in one's own country.[88]

This passage shows that the right to democracy is inherently related to the rights embedded in the ICCPR. As a result of this interrelatedness, democratic rights become prerequisites for the implementation of socio-economic rights and emerging environmental rights. The right to democracy, if recognised, allows the courts to determine the level of corruption in the government involved (which is more relevant in transnational disputes) and the responsibilities of the state regarding the procedural rights necessary for a viable and functional democracy. If citizens are unable to participate through a transparent voting system and other corollary mechanisms in the political life of their country, it is unlikely they will have a say in the enactment and implementation of environmental laws and policies. Moreover, the ecocentric-anthropocentric debate associated with the concept of environmental rights opens the door to a more holistic and equitable approach to environmental issues. In this respect, the judiciary may be compelled to examine the validity of non-anthropocentric environmental claims like conservation issues and to examine whether sacrificing some economic interests would be useful for the preservation of nature for present and future generations. The rights of present and future generations to a healthy environment and natural resources constitute an integral part of sustainable development, a necessary conceptual tool in determining which rights should prevail in the extreme situations where developmental and environmental issues collide.

---

[87] See Office of the United Nations High Commissioner for Human Rights, "Commission on Human Rights and General Assembly Resolutions Relating to Democracy and Governance 1998–2003," http://www.unhchr.ch/democracy/resolutions.htm.

[88] *Resolution on the Promotion of the Right to Democracy*, HRC Res 1999/57, UN HRC, 55th sess, 57th mtg, 2, UN Doc A/HRC/1999/57 (1999).

2. *The Right to Development and the ICESCR*

a. *The Right to Development: Convergence between Development and Human Rights*

Conceived after World War II at the height of decolonisation, the notion of development was initially coined as the demands of newly decolonised countries that the industrialised world rectify the dire consequences of Western colonial exploitation.[89] According to Kennedy, the right to development emerged out of a political tension among members of the international community, rather than as a response to global poverty.[90] Left with enormous economic and social challenges, newly independent developing countries aspired to a more equitable economic order that took into consideration people's socio-economic needs. This aspiration, reflected in the Declaration on the Establishment of a New International Economic Order (NIEO), emphasised the need for greater international cooperation in the achievement of global developmental goals.[91] It asserted that the "political, economic and social well-being of present and future generations depends more than ever on cooperation between all the members of the international community on the basis of sovereign equality and the removal of the disequilibrium that exists between them."[92]

Despite its inception as a reaction to the vestiges of colonialism, the notion of development transcended this legacy to become a full-fledged human right.[93] Some writers have expressed scepticism about the human rights approach to development. For instance, Rosas et al. perceived the right to development as an 'umbrella concept and programme rather than a specific human right'. In their opinion, this right could "play a role in planning and implementing *policies and programmes*, rather than function[ing] as a legal mechanism per se."[94] As the quest for an equitable international economic order proved to be too hard to achieve, developing countries turned to the human rights discourse to promote rapid economic development.[95] In 1986,

---

[89] For a brief overview of the historical evolution of the right to development see Rajeev Malhotra, "Right to Development: Where Are We Today?" in *Reflections on the Right to Development*, ed. Arjun Sengupta, Archna Negi, and Moushumi Basu (New Delhi: Sage Publications, 2005).

[90] Kennedy, *The International Human Rights Movement: Part of the Problem?* 21.

[91] *Declaration on the Establishment of a New International Economic Order*, GA Res 3201, UN GAOR, 6th special sess, 2229th plen mtg, Agenda item 7, A/RES/S-6/3201(1974).

[92] Ibid., art. 3.

[93] Malhorta, "Right to Development," 132.

[94] Allan Rosas and Martin Scheinin, "Implementation Mechanisms and Remedies," in *Economic, Social and Cultural Rights*, ed. Allan Rosas, Eide Asbjørn, and Catarina Krause (Dordrecht/Boston/London: Martinus Nijhoff Publishers, 1995), 255.

[95] See Balakrishnan Rajagopal, "Counter-Hegemonic International Law : Rethinking Human Rights and Development as a Third World Strategy," in *International Law and the Third World : Reshaping Justice* ed. Richard Falk, Balakrishnan Rajagopal, and Jacqueline Stevens (London/ New York: Routledge-Cavendish, 2008).

the UN General Assembly adopted the DRTD, which describes the right to development as 'an inalienable human right'.[96] The 1993 Vienna Declaration and Programme of Action reaffirmed the inalienability and universality of the right to development and considered it an integral part of fundamental human rights.[97] On 22 April 1998, the UN Commission on Human Rights adopted a resolution on the right to development that led to the establishment of the Open-Ended Working Group (OEWG) and the Independent Expert.[98] While the former's mandate involves the monitoring and fulfilment of the right to development, the latter is entitled to present focused studies on the state of the right to development to the Working Group at each of its sessions.[99]

The DRTD defines development as "a comprehensive economic, social, cultural and political process, which aims at the constant improvement of the well-being of the entire population and of all individuals."[100] Accordingly, the right to development is considered both an individual and a collective right. As with all human rights, states are the primary duty-bearers of the right to development. Their obligations consist of designing appropriate 'national development policies' necessary for the 'constant improvement of the well-being of the entire population and of all individuals.'[101] At the same time, states are urged to cooperate on the international level to create appropriate conditions for the fulfilment of the right to development.[102] The DRTD points out that failure in the observance of human rights, whether of civil, political, socio-economic or cultural rights constitutes an impediment to the implementation of the right to development.[103]

b. *Nature of the Right to Development*

In his analysis of the human rights approach to development, Rich identified three theories: The indispensability theory, the generational theory and the synthesis theory.[104] The indispensability theory perceives development as a prerequisite to the enjoyment of other human rights and is predicated on the belief that a state that fails to achieve its developmental goals is unable to guarantee its citizens' socio-economic rights.[105] This theory, Rich argued, allows the state to justify the violation of political and civil rights on the grounds that

---

96 *Declaration on the Right to Development*, art. 1.
97 *Vienna Declaration and Programme of Action*, par. 10.
98 *Resolution on the Right to Development*, CHR Res 1998/24, UN ESCOR Supp No. 3, 58th mtg, UN Doc E/CN.4/1998/24 (1998).
99 Ibid.
100 *Declaration on the Right to Development*, Preamble.
101 Ibid., art. 2(3).
102 Ibid., arts. 3 and 4.
103 Ibid., art. 6(3).
104 Rich, "Right to Development," 320.
105 Ibid., 320–21.

it is pursuing its economic development.[106] The generational theory considers the right to development a new right that belongs to third-generation rights or solidarity rights, a highly controversial issue at the international level.[107] The synthesis theory views the right to development as a synthesis of existing human rights and is more in line with the traditional conception of human rights than the other two theories. It implies that the right to development allows both an expansive re-interpretation of existing human rights and the inclusion of new principles such as those enshrined in the NIEO.[108] The synthesis theory has the potential to bridge the gap between the traditional rights as enshrined in the International Covenants and the newly emerging rights, especially the right to development, the 'Right to Environment' and the right to democracy. The synthesis theory facilitates the re-configuration of the field of international human rights.

The right to development can be associated with the ICESCR. Although the DRTD does not provide a clear definition of the right to development, it does offer some useful clues as to its content. Article 1 states that the right to development "is an inalienable human right by virtue of which every human person and all peoples are entitled to participate in, contribute to, and enjoy economic, social, cultural and political development, in which all human rights and fundamental freedoms can be fully realised."[109] In other words, the right to development as an inalienable right is intrinsically tied to economic, social and cultural rights along with political rights, an idea that conforms with the principle of indivisibility of human rights.[110] Article 1 portrays the right to development as a broad framework where all other human rights are fulfilled. As Rich notes, "the right to development will reinforce existing human rights, enhance their effectiveness, and make them more relevant to governments and individuals."[111] In addition, Article 1 considers the right to development both an individual and a collective right and portrays the participation of duty-holders in decision-making processes as a necessary step for the enjoyment and implementation of the right to development.

The DRTD conceives the right to development in the context of the right to self-determination and sovereignty over natural resources.[112] It also pledges to "promote more rapid development of developing countries", a statement that makes the international community accountable for ensuring this right.[113] The developing world has embraced the right to development as the right of states

---

[106] Ibid.
[107] Ibid., 322–23.
[108] Ibid., 323–24.
[109] *Declaration on the Right to Development*, art. 1.
[110] See Osmani, "Human Rights Approach to Development," 112.
[111] Rich, "Right to development," 325.
[112] *Declaration on the Right to Development*, art. 1(2).
[113] Ibid., art. 4(2).

to seek rapid economic growth regardless of political and social considerations. In other words, many developing countries consider the right to development as granting the right to pollute as an unavoidable evil in the process of achieving pressing developmental goals. In fact, many developing countries justify the construction of large dams, which are often accompanied by a wealth of human rights violations, on the grounds of rapid economic growth. It is estimated that 40–80 million people have been displaced worldwide as a result of the construction of large dams. In India and China alone, large dams were responsible for the displacement of 26 to 58 million people between 1950 and 1990.[114] Although China and India are among the top five dam-building countries in the world,[115] a report released by the World Commission on Dams (2000) showed that large dam projects fall short of producing their alleged benefits. In fact, human and ecological catastrophes often accompany the construction of large dams. One might question the need for huge dams in light of the growing evidence of their devastating effects on ecosystems and populations, especially in the developing world. Physical displacement, pollution and biodiversity loss are just some examples of the devastating effects of these mega-projects on vulnerable people such as tribal and Indigenous communities.[116]

The partnership between international financial institutions and dictatorial regimes in the Third World is a deadly combination for local and vulnerable communities. To illustrate, the construction of the Chixoy hydroelectric project, undertaken by the National Institute for Electrification (INDE), a Guatemalan public agency, and financed by the World Bank and the Inter-American Development Bank (IDB) caused the Maya-Achi Indigenous communities to be forcibly displaced from their fertile land to an infertile region.[117] The Guatemalan government considered Mayan communities little more than an impediment to the dam construction and consequently to the flow of international funds to governmental agencies. In a retaliatory move, Guatemalan armed forces killed hundreds of people mostly, women and children, under

---

[114] World Commission on Dams, *Dams and Development: A New Framework for Decision-Making* (London: Earthscan, 2000), 104.

[115] Ibid., 9.

[116] Simultaneously, large dam projects wreak havoc on riverine ecosystems. No environmental impact assessment is able to predict or counter the scale of damage caused by these 'monster' projects. Entire geographic areas were disfigured and permanently altered. Estimates reveal that "dams, interbasin transfers, and water withdrawals for irrigation have fragmented 60% of the world's rivers." See World Commission on Dams, *Dams and Development: A New Framework for Decision-Making*, 72.

[117] See generally COHRE Americas Programme and COHRE ESC Rights Litigation Programme, *Mission Report-Continuing the Struggle for Justice and Accountability in Guatemala: Making Reparations a Reality in the Chixoy Dam Case* (Geneva, Switzerland: Centre on Housing Rights and Evictions (COHRE), 2004).

the banner of 'counterinsurgency'.[118] Despite the Guatemalan authorities' horrendous act, the World Bank kept financing the project and took steps to investigate the issue only under the pressure from human rights groups.[119] In the end, the Chixoy dam project was a striking example of the myths of pure economic development. Apart from its inefficiency in meeting Guatemala's energy needs, the project proved to be detrimental to the livelihoods of dam-affected communities.[120]

The emergence of sustainable development has gradually rendered obsolete the notion of economic development that does not consider social and ecological factors. In the *Gabčikovo-Nagymaros* case, Judge Weeramantry denied the absolute nature of the right to development and stressed the necessity of linking it to environmental provisions. According to Weeramantry, the right to development is 'compendiously referred to as sustainable development.'[121] However, sustainable development is a more revolutionary concept than Weeramantry's view because it takes into consideration the need to reconcile environmental concerns with both developmental and social goals. The right to development has also been re-conceptualised in the context of sustainable development, as Principle 3 of the Rio Declaration provides that "[t]he right to development must be fulfilled so as to equitably meet developmental and environmental needs of present and future generations",[122] and Principle 2 of the ILA Declaration echoes the wordings of the Rio Declaration.[123] Both principles reiterate the definition of sustainable development as conceived in the Brundtland Report. In the same vein, the IUCN Draft Covenant positions the right to development in the context of sustainable development, stating in Article 8 that "[t]he exercise of the right to development entails the obligation to meet the developmental and environmental needs of humanity in a sustainable and equitable manner."[124]

Couching development in human rights terms highlights the necessity of respecting the individual person while pursuing economic development. The right to development is necessary because it recognises the right of a sovereign state to reach its development goals as well as the right of the individual to development.[125] Whether we accept the concept of solidarity rights or not,

[118] Monti Aguirre, "The Chixoy Dam Destroyed Our Lives," *Human Rights Dialogue* 2, no. 11 (Spring 2004): 20.
[119] Ibid.
[120] Ibid.
[121] *Hungary v. Slovakia (Separate Opinion of Judge Weeramantry)*, 92.
[122] *Rio Declaration on Environment and Development*, Principle 3.
[123] *New Delhi Declaration of Principles of International Law Relating to Sustainable Development*, Principle 2(3).
[124] *Draft International Covenant on Environment and Development*, 3.
[125] Rich, "Right to development," 327.

by adding the human dimension to development laws and policies, the right to development, like all new types of rights, is conceived in a way as to hold a wide range of stakeholders accountable for achieving a decent social and economic environment conducive to the development of the human person. This conception is well articulated in the DRTD, which proclaims that the "human person is the central subject of the development process and that development policy should therefore make the human being the main participant and beneficiary of development."[126]

3. *A Right to Environment or Environmental Rights?*

The 1994 Draft Declaration of Principles on Human Rights and the Environment (1994 Draft Declaration), examined in Chapter 3, offers an extensive interpretation of 'the right to a secure, healthy and ecologically balanced environment' but the exhaustive list of principles and rights provided by the Draft adds more confusion to the ongoing debate over the content and scope of environmental rights.[127] In addition to procedural rights, the Draft presents well-established rights, such as the right to adequate housing and the right to health, in an environmental context, without explicitly considering these rights as part of the right to environment.

In contrast to the 1994 Draft Declaration, I limit the list of substantive environmental rights to emerging rights only, such as the right to a clean environment, the right to natural resources, the right to water and the right to food. All other rights, including procedural rights that are prone to being interpreted or expanded in an environmental context are considered derivative rights. Despite their probable role in furthering the human rights-based approach to environmental issues, derivative rights do not justify the recognition of a distinct human right to environment. Moreover, by affixing the term 'environment' to every relevant human right, we risk an inflation of rights. Similarly, the proliferation of environmentally related rights like the right to water, the right to food—and probably the 'right to be cold'—[128] may open the door to a wealth of environmental human rights. To manage this proliferation, I propose a two-level conceptualisation of environmental rights. The first level of conceptualisation, represented by the 'Right to Environment' and likened to the right to development, is a solidarity right that provides a broad legal

[126] *Declaration on the Right to Development*, Preamble.

[127] *The 1994 Draft Declaration of Principles on Human Rights and the Environment*, Part I (2).

[128] The 'right to be cold' has been invoked in relation to climate change. See Martin Wagner, "The Right to Be Cold: Global Warming and Human Rights," in *Human Rights 2007, the Year in Review*, ed. Marius Smith and Erica Contini (Castan Centre for Human Rights Law, Monash University 2008).

and policy framework for international cooperation in matters involving the human rights implications of ecological degradation. The second level of conceptualisation conforms to the genesis theory discussed above and offers a set of specific rights that could be included in a new international covenant on environmental rights similar to the 1966 Covenants.

D. *Towards a New Covenant on Environmental Rights*

Based on the developments of emerging rights and regional and national environmental provisions, I categorise substantive environmental rights into six sub-rights: the rights of nature, the right to a clean environment, the rights to natural resources, the right to water, the right to food and Indigenous land rights. The dividing lines between these sub-rights are not clear-cut; for instance, the right to natural resources includes water and food as essential means of subsistence, while the right to water includes the right to water free from toxic pollution. Moreover, this list is by no means exhaustive or unique, since there could be many ways of classifying these rights. However, the taxonomy used in this book implies that what are commonly referred to—albeit ambiguously—as environmental human rights are intrinsically sub-rights that could be classified either under the broader scope of a single right like the 'Right to Environment' or under a separate covenant on environmental rights. This approach will clarify the content and scope of environmental rights and minimise the ambiguity arising from the proliferation of environment-related human rights.

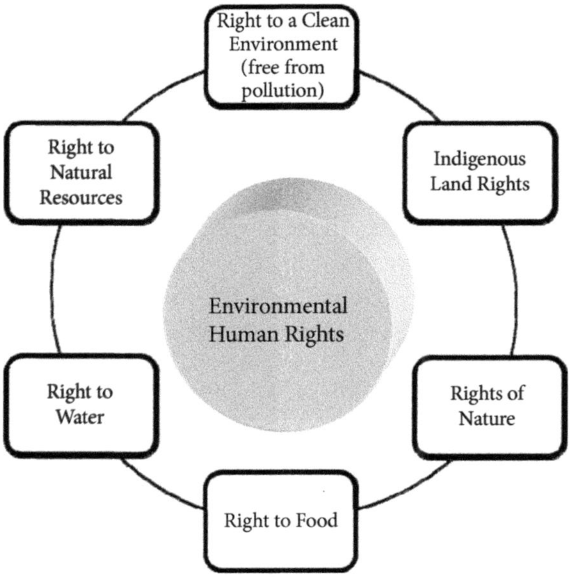

Fig. 4. Environmental Human Rights.

1. *The Rights of Nature*

One way to connect rights and the natural world is through the ascription of rights to nature and its biotic and non-biotic components. This formulation can be expressed in the form of the 'right of the environment' or the rights of nature, defined as the rights of 'non-human species, elements of the natural environment and … inanimate objects' to 'a continued existence unthreatened by human activities'.[129] Proponents of environmental rights such as Christopher Stone and Laurence Tribe have often argued that conferring rights to an entity guarantees its recognition for its own moral worth without necessarily tying it to human use or benefits.[130] In his landmark article "Should Trees Have Standing?",[131] Stone suggested that following the legal historical trend of expansion that stretched to new rights-holders such as blacks, women, children, minorities and corporations, the scope of rights should embrace natural objects.[132] Whenever new entities have been added to the realm of rights, it has always been considered an unexpected or 'unthinkable' move.[133] Stone advocated the attribution of legal rights to "forests, oceans, rivers and other so-called "natural objects"…indeed, to the natural environment as a whole."[134] Tribe went even further by suggesting an unconventional alternative to the mainstream legal, intellectual and religious heritage underpinning Western societies.[135] Tribe called this tradition of dichotomies— God/man, nature/culture and human/animal—the 'transcendence theory' against which he placed his 'theory of immanence', which stands for the sanctification of nature for its own intrinsic qualities independent of anthropocentric ends.[136] In order to reconcile humankind and the natural world, Tribe advocated the synthesis of the ideals of transcendence and immanence and posited that "conceptions like harmony, rootedness in history, connectedness with the future … seem more pertinent than the ultimately conventional concept of the "natural".[137]

Many scholars and philosophers have decried this rights-based approach to nature on many grounds. Elder argued that Stone's proposal to attribute legal rights to non-human entities is unjustified, and suggested instead the reliance

---

[129] Christopher Miller, "Environmental Rights: European Fact or English Fiction?" *Journal of Law and Society* 22, no. 3 (1995): 375.
[130] Cynthia Giagnocavo and Howard Goldstein, "Law Reform or World Re-Form: The Problem of Environmental Rights," *McGill Law Journal* 35(1990): 356.
[131] Christopher D. Stone, "Should Trees Have Standing? Toward Legal Rights for Natural Objects," *Southern California Law Review* 45(1972).
[132] Ibid., 450–56.
[133] Ibid., 453.
[134] Ibid., 456.
[135] Laurence H. Tribe, "Ways Not to Think About Plastic Trees: New Foundations for Environmental Law," *The Yale Law Journal* 83, no. 7 (1974): 1336.
[136] Ibid., 1333–36.
[137] Ibid., 1340.

on conventional law to approach environmental problems.[138] In the presence of more pressing environmental issues, such as deadly contaminants, nuclear threats and human famine, Elder contended that deep ecologists' move towards assigning rights to 'canyons, trees and mule deer' is insignificant, hence environmental political philosophy should not follow such a path.[139] Others have criticised the idea of granting rights to nature from very different perspectives. Livingston, a 'nature preservationist', argued that, in order to extend the rhetoric of rights to the whole of nature, as is already accepted for domesticated and caged animals that belong to human societies, humankind has to domesticate the whole planet.[140] Livingston did not welcome such an 'absurd' extension of rights to non-human nature because it relies on conventional legal and moral systems to deal with ecological issues rather than "systematically address[ing] … the pathological species-chauvinist belief structure itself."[141] This line of thought described as 'rightness' seeks to mend the distorted relationship between humankind and nature through a deeper approach to ecological disasters than mere environmental regulations and rights.

Drawing upon the concept of 'rightness', Giagnocavo and Goldstein advocated the promotion of 'planetary consciousness' to induce profound behavioural change towards nature and criticised the overemphasis on legal reform and remedies in addressing ecological disasters.[142] They rebutted the emphasis on the rights language as a common language, arguing that this language is restricted and limited to the legal community, rather than to the broader public. They also warned that the ultimate objective of the environmental movement, which is to bring on social change, could be potentially jeopardised if the movement becomes excessively immersed in the legal realm and confuses means with ends.[143] As for the argument positing that environmental rights may compel humans to value nature and its constituents as rights-holders, Giagnocavo and Goldstein contended that such a rationale is restrictive and overlooks the impact of cultural and social predispositions on the valuing process.[144] In their opinion, bestowing rights on the natural world does not appropriately serve the cause of ecological conservation and protection because of the law's inability to induce social reform; hence, moral entitlements (rightness) are better suited to dealing with environmental problems than are legal rights.[145]

---

[138] P. S. Elder, "Legal Rights for Nature: The Wrong Answer to the Right(S)," *Osgoode Hall Law Journal* 22, no. 2 (1984): 291.
[139] Ibid., 295.
[140] John Livingston, "Rightness or Rights?" *Osgoode Hall Law Journal* 22, no. 2 (1984).
[141] Ibid., 320–21.
[142] Giagnocavo and Goldstein, "Law Reform or World Re-Form," 351.
[143] Ibid., 365–66.
[144] Ibid., 366–67.
[145] Ibid., 372.

It might be easy to agree with deep ecologists like Stone and Tribe that non-human entities have inherent values, but it is still theoretically unclear why human beings should have a moral obligation to defend these values. For instance, in order to protect animals from being used in medical testing and vivisection, people in general tend to be driven by sentiment and subjective values such as sympathy or compassion, while scientists are driven by another set of values related to scientific progress and compassion about the suffering of humankind. Prioritising one value over another whether in moral or legal terms is a political choice, not a philosophical one. However, the need to protect and enhance ecosystems, regardless of evident human use or value (as such value is currently understood) is well accepted and provides some common ground. The essence of ecocentrism lies in the notion that human welfare and well-being should not be the ultimate goal that underpins the protection and conservation of the natural environment. In fact, people who defend the rights of the environment from an ecocentric position are, to an extent, fulfilling their own anthropocentric needs, such as spiritual connection with nature or self-satisfaction through the adoption of a specific philosophical approach to life. Non-human beings are the main beneficiaries of the ecocentric approach, while human beings benefit most from the anthropocentric attitude towards nature. It is a matter of prioritising one entity over another, but such altruism does not answer the puzzling question as to whether it is more ethical to protect animals than human beings. In both cases, we humans are the point of reference, and the centrism of the human rationale cannot be avoided. The choice concerns only which dimension of our beings is being fulfilled; it is about the interplay between two sets of values in environmental protection: values associated with spirituality and aestheticism and values associated with materialism and economic abundance.

Both physical integrity and psychological integrity are necessary to the well-being of human beings. For instance, tribal and traditional communities defend their sacred lands against ambitious developmental projects because land constitutes a vital cultural aspect of their existence. Economy is an arrogant and dominant concept in our modern societies, where the monetary value of anything and everything supersedes all other values. While economic interests, in the modern sense, are important to humankind's progress, the overemphasis on these interests may alienate other valuable meanings of human life. Similarly, elevating ecological interests above human interests creates a taxing ethical problem for the human conscience. For example, by prioritising the survival of protected species over the interests of local communities, conservationists often work to push people away from designated area in order to transform it into a national park.[146]

---

[146] See generally Peter G. Veit and Catherine Benson, "When Parks and People Collide," *Human Rights Dialogue* 2, no. 11 (Spring 2004).

The concept of human rights revolves around the preservation of human dignity, which goes beyond the physical and mental integrity of the individual human. This dignity can stretch to non-human entities such as animals, effigies, sacred places and natural entities. Human beings can bestow this privilege on anything they value, whether for its intrinsic worth or just for being an integral part of their well-being. In fact, the ascription of rights to nature and ecosystems is no longer a philosophical matter. In 2008, the Ecuador Constitutional Assembly, elected to rewrite the country's constitution, approved provisions that recognise rights for nature and ecosystems.[147] Article 1 of the draft constitution provides that "[n]ature or Pachamama, where life is reproduced and exists, has the right to exist, persist, maintain and regenerate its vital cycles, structure, functions and its processes in evolution. Every person, people, community or nationality, will be able to demand the recognitions of rights for nature before the public organisms."[148]

2. *The Right to a Healthy Environment (Free from Pollution)*

The right to a healthy or clean environment is the best-known form of environmental rights. Hancock drew a line between two types of environmental rights: the right to an environment free from toxic pollution and the right to natural resources.[149] The first is identified with the claim to the 'clean', 'healthy' or 'sound' environment often referred to in academic literature, as well as in legal texts such as constitutions and international declarations. As for the right to natural resources, it is associated with the right to cultural self-determination and the right to be free from hunger.[150] The right to a clean environment is related to the protection of the environment and its vital components—like water, air and soil—from toxins and pollutants. Industrial and developmental projects are the main sources of threat to natural ecosystems. In 1998, the results of a questionnaire sent to 196 environmental NGOs showed that many of these organisations recognised a right to an 'unpolluted', 'clean' and healthy environment while a few only identified a right to natural resources.[151]

3. *The Right to Natural Resources*

The right to natural resources constitutes, along with the right to a clean and healthy environment, the building blocks of environmental rights. Natural resources include renewable and non-renewable components of nature. The scarcity or depletion of such resources may jeopardise the life of human and

---

[147] Climate and Capitalism, "Ecuadorian Assembly Approves Constitutional Rights for Nature," http://climateandcapitalism.com/?p=479.
[148] Ibid.
[149] Hancock, *Environmental Human Rights*, 107–55.
[150] Ibid., 11–12.
[151] Ibid., 73.

non-human beings on earth. Renewable resources such as fauna and flora provide humans with food, traditional medicines and economic benefits, while non-renewable sources such as oil, gas, minerals, and gems are often exploited for economic and developmental purposes. Natural resources are also known as the 'communal ownership systems to natural resources' (CPR systems) where traditional moral authority controls the use of common resources.[152] These traditional systems of exploiting environmental resources with minimal effect on ecosystems are sometimes advanced from an ecological perspective as an alternative to the destructive effect of private property rights.[153] However, the collective management of natural resources is often disturbed by ecosystem degradation, population growth, erosion of customary and local legal systems and the introduction of modern economic concepts like profit maximisation. In this regard, many radical environmentalists believe that ecological sustainability is not compatible or achievable in a global capitalist economy.[154] Beyond the view of resources as commodities, Zimmerman defined resources as a matter of relationships that cannot be severed from the complex interplay among societies, technologies, cultures, economics and environments.[155]

The conceptualisation of resources as relationships is at the heart of the putative right to natural resources, which has great affinity with the well-established right to self-determination and the principle of permanent sovereignty over natural resources because the management or mismanagement of natural resources, whether renewable or not, has tremendous effect on people's livelihoods. Article 1 of the ICCPR stipulates that "[a]ll peoples may, for their own ends, freely dispose of their natural wealth and resources without prejudice to any obligations arising out of international economic co-operation, based upon the principle of mutual benefit, and international law. In no case may a people be deprived of its own means of subsistence."[156] Similarly, the UN Resolution on Permanent Sovereignty over Natural Resources ties the exercise of this principle to 'the well-being of the people of the state concerned.'[157] Drawing upon this limitation to the principle of sovereignty, local communities can claim their right to natural resources as part of the overall right to environment. The 1994 Draft Declaration recognises the right of everyone "to benefit equitably from the conservation and sustainable use of nature and natural resources for cultural, ecological, educational, health, livelihood,

---

152 See generally Hancock, *Environmental Human Rights*, 152–53.
153 Ibid.
154 Ibid., 155.
155 Richard Howitt, *Rethinking Resource Management: Justice, Sustainability and Indigenous Peoples* (London: Routledge, 2001), 4.
156 *International Covenant on Civil and Political Rights*, art.1.
157 *Resolution on Permanent Sovereignty over Natural Resources*, GA Res 1803(XVII), UN GAOR Supp No 17, UN Doc A/5217 (1962), par. 1.

recreational, spiritual or other purposes. This includes ecologically sound access to nature."[158]

This putative right can take different forms. The first form entails the collective accessibility of local communities to vital elements in their environment, such as forests, agricultural lands, fish stocks and other available resources.[159] The paucity or the overexploitation of these essential components of nature can affect deeply and perilously the livelihoods of millions of local, tribal and Indigenous communities around the world. In many instances, these communities are denied access to the income from renewable resources as well as that from non-renewable resources like minerals and fuel. The systemic violation of peoples' rights to natural resources exacerbates the problem of poverty in developing countries. For example, since the beginning of the last century, timber production has been responsible for destroying and exploiting most of the Philippines forests. This led to the terrible ecological loss of very valuable common heritage for Filipinos and the whole of humanity.[160] Apart from the environmental and social implications of such unsustainable activities, the tragedy lies in the fact that Filipinos did not benefit economically from the loss of their public resource. Present and future generations will inherit floods, arid lands, droughts, scarcity of food and water, pollution, and a chain of human rights abuses. Antonio Oposa, a passionate Filipino environmental lawyer and activist, noted that "the liquidation of more than 90% of the Philippines' primary forests from the mid 1960s made a few hundred families US $42 billion dollars richer; but it left 18 million upland dwellers economically, and the rest of the economy, ecologically, much poorer."[161]

Another form of the right to natural resources is predicated on the public trust doctrine, where the state is supposed to hold common natural resources for the benefits of its citizens. Accordingly, government authorities are restricted in their use of these public trusts on the grounds that public lands cannot be granted to private parties without the consent of the public.[162] The third form of environmental rights entails the global commons, like the atmosphere, the oceans, and even the outer space. For instance, global warming is believed to be the result of the burning of fossil fuels for industrial and personal purposes, which causes the release of greenhouse gases in the atmosphere—a vital global common. The Inuit Circumpolar Conference petition to the Inter-American Commission on Human Rights (IACHR) is a new trend in

---

[158] *The 1994 Draft Declaration of Principles on Human Rights and the Environment*, Part II (13).

[159] See especially Hancock, *Environmental Human Rights*, 137.

[160] See generally Oliver A. Houck, "Light from the Trees: The Stories of Minors Oposa and the Russian Forest Cases," *Georgetown International Environmental Law Review* 19, no. 3 (2007): 326–30.

[161] Quoted in Houck, 332.

[162] Joseph L. Sax, "The Public Trust Doctrine in Natural Resource Law: Effective Judicial Intervention," *Michigan Law Review* 68(1970): 556.

this direction as people of the Arctic claimed that greenhouse gases emitted over time by the United States have contributed to the massive thinning of the sea ice, a basic natural resource for Arctic livelihoods.[163] Even more futuristic is the idea of dumping toxic or radioactive waste in the space, which will one day be a controversial environmental issue for the international community if it is embraced by some industrialised countries.

On the other hand, the right to natural resources offers a new perspective when viewed through the prism of private property rights. For instance, some environmental laws and regulations can have a crippling effect on landholders' rights. To illustrate, under the *New South Wales (NSW) Native Vegetation Act* (2003), farmers are prohibited from clearing native vegetation on their lands without approval.[164] Peter Spencer, a NSW farmer, brought this issue to the fore when he went on a 52-day hunger strike to draw attention to the plight of farmers who had been stripped of vital means of subsistence without adequate compensation. The Act does not expropriate farming lands per se but causes depreciation of their economic value by restricting farmers' ability to generate income from growing crops and raising livestock. In this case, the right of farmers to use their land and its natural resources is inherently a 'subsistence right' because it captures the environmental and economic dimensions of property rights. Thus, the conceptualisation of natural resources as environmental rights should not be automatically pitted against property rights. On the contrary, the right to natural resources protects individual and group rights from stringent environmental laws that enable public authorities to expropriate lands without compensation in the name of the common good.

4. *The Right to Water*

Fresh water, an essential component of our natural environment, is undeniably a precondition, not only for a healthy environment, but also for life itself. In this regard, the provision of safe, potable water and adequate sanitation cannot be successfully achieved without the protection of ecosystems where water resources are located.[165] Therefore, a rights-based approach to water problems falls squarely within the broad scope of environmental rights.

---

[163] The Inuit Circumpolar Conference (ICC) is an international non-governmental organisation, founded in 1977, which represents approximately 150,000 Inuit living in the Arctic regions of Alaska, Canada, Greenland, and Chukotka (Russia). The ICC holds a Consultative Status at the UN. See Inuit Circumpolar Conference (Canada), "Inuit Circumpolar Conference (ICC)," http://inuitcircumpolar.com/index.php?auto_slide=&ID=16&Lang=En&Parent_ID=&current_slide_num=.; See ———, "Inuit Petition to the Inter-American Commission on Human Rights to Oppose Climate Change Caused by the United States of America," http://inuitcircumpolar.com/index.php?ID=316&Lang=En.

[164] *Native Vegetation Act 2003 (NSW)*, sec. 12. Available at http://www.austlii.edu.au/au/legis/nsw/consol_act/nva2003194/.

[165] John Scanlon, Angela Cassar, and Noémi Nemes, "Water as a Human Right?" (paper presented at the 7th International Conference on Environmental Law: Law for a Green Planet Institute, Sao Paulo, Brazil, 2–5 June 2003), 27.

The right to water is intrinsically an environmental right because the supply of safe and sufficient water requires healthy and balanced ecosystems: drought, desertification, climate change and pollution are important indicators of the global water crisis.

As with most environmental rights, the adoption of a distinct right to water is justified on the grounds that water is a prerequisite for the enjoyment of other human rights. It is estimated that 1.2 billion people have no access to safe water and 2.6 billion have no adequate sanitation.[166] Human dignity is tremendously degraded when people struggle to satisfy basic needs such as those for clean water and hygiene. According to the 2006 Human Development Report on the water crisis, "[u]pholding the human right to water is an end in itself and a means for giving substance to the wider rights in the Universal Declaration of Human Rights and other legally binding instruments—including the right to life, to education, to health and to adequate housing."[167]

In the absence of a human right to water in the Universal Bill of Rights,[168] the adoption of a broader interpretation of existing human rights by both the UN Human Rights Committee (UNHRC) and the UN Committee on Economic, Social and Cultural Rights (CESCR) has provided a suitable normative framework for the human right to water. General Comment 6 on the right to life extends the obligations of States Parties beyond the traditional protection of human life against arbitrary arrests and killings, to life-threatening issues like malnutrition and the spread of disease. Drawing upon this expansive interpretation, some legal scholars have concluded that a human rights approach to water is necessary on the basis that contaminated or scarce water resources directly jeopardise people's lives.[169] This point of view is emphasised in the 2006 UNDP Human Development Report, which states that "a human right to water is violated with impunity on a widespread and systematic basis—and it is the human rights of the poor that are subject to the gravest abuse."[170]

Because of the socio-economic nature of the right to water, the ICESCR is an appropriate avenue for linking between water and human rights. For instance, Article 12 of the ICESCR grants everyone the right to the enjoyment of the highest attainable standard of physical and mental health. Obviously,

---

[166] United Nations Development Programme (UNDP), "Human Development Report 2006: Beyond Scarcity: Power, Poverty and the Global Water Crisis," http://hdr.undp.org/en/reports/global/hdr2006/.

[167] Ibid., 4.

[168] It consists of the 1948 Universal Declaration of Human Rights and the 1966 International Covenants.

[169] See generally Scanlon, Cassar and Nemes, "Water as a Human Right?"; Salman M.A. Salman and Siobhán McInerney-Lankford, *The Human Right to Water: Legal and Policy Dimensions* (Washington, D.C.: The World Bank, 2004).

[170] United Nations Development Programme (UNDP), "Human Development Report 2006: Beyond Scarcity: Power, Poverty and the Global Water Crisis," 4.

this right cannot be attained without safe drinking water and appropriate sanitation. Similarly, the right of everyone to an adequate standard of living, as laid down in Article 11 of the ICESCR, includes adequate food, clothing and housing, and the continuous improvement of living conditions. In rural communities that depend directly on agricultural produce and livestock for livelihood, the supply of adequate food is inextricably tied to the availability of water. In its General Comment 15 on the Right to Water (Articles 11 and 12 of the ICESCR), the CESCR asserts that "[t]he human right to water is indispensable for leading a healthy life in human dignity. It is a prerequisite to the realisation of all other human rights."[171] The General Comment defines the human right to water as the right of "everyone to sufficient, safe, acceptable, physically accessible and affordable water for personal and domestic uses."[172] Despite this explicit recognition, the implementation of socio-economic rights is progressive and does not require an immediate response from states. Still, even though General Comments issued by the CESCR are non-legally binding, they provide States Parties and the international community with valuable explanations and interpretations on the scope and content of the rights embedded in the ICESCR. For example, General Comment 15 provides significant 'legal and moral support' to the realisation of the Millennium Development Goal related to water.[173]

In its decision on Human Rights and Access to Water in 2006, the UN Human Rights Council requested the OHCHR "to conduct, within existing resources, a detailed study on the scope and content of the relevant human rights obligations related to equitable access to safe drinking water and sanitation under international human rights instruments, which includes relevant conclusions and recommendations."[174] Pursuant to this decision, the OHCHR submitted its report to the UN Human Rights Council in August 2007 highlighting the growing recognition of access to safe drinking water and sanitation as a matter of human rights. This growing recognition is obvious from the numerous references to water in many international instruments, such as the *UN Convention on the Rights of the Child* and the Millennium Development Goals.[175] At the same time, the report pointed out that "[d]ebate is still needed ... on whether access to safe drinking water and sanitation is a self-standing right or is derived from other human rights."[176]

---

171 *General Comment 15: The right to Water*, par. I(1).

172 Ibid., par. I(2).

173 Salman and McInerney-Lankford, *Human Right to Water*, 88.

174 *Decision 2/104 on Human Rights and Access to Water*, UNHRC, 31st meeting, UN Doc A/HRC/2/L.3/Rev.3 (2006).

175 *Convention on the Rights of the Child*, art. 2(c); United Nations Development Programme (UNDP), "Goal 7: Ensure Environmental Sustainability," http://www.undp.org/mdg/goal7.shtml.

176 *Report of the United Nations High Commissioner for Human Rights on the Scope and Content of the Relevant Human Rights Obligations Related to Equitable Access to Safe Driving*

In addition to the international legal framework, some countries have already incorporated provisions related to water in their constitutions. These provisions are usually part of more general provisions on environmental rights and duties. For instance, Uganda's Constitution obligates the government to "protect important natural resources, including land, water, wetlands, minerals, oil, fauna and flora."[177] Similarly, under the Cambodian Constitution, the state is required "to protect the environment and ... establish a precise plan of management of land, water, air, wind geology ... wildlife, fish and aquatic resources."[178] A few constitutions have explicitly recognised a distinct right to water; for example, the 1996 South African Bill of Rights grants everyone the right to have access to sufficient food and water.[179]

The conceptualisation of water as an economic and environmental right goes against the tendency to transform this vital natural resource into a pure market commodity, which tremendously affects the poor and the disadvantaged in a given society. The protests that erupted in Cochabamba, Bolivia, as a result of the privatisation of water services illustrate the struggle of poor communities to guarantee their right to water as a public good. In addition to water price hikes, water privatisation affected the Bolivians' ability to access and use water in lakes and rivers.[180] Since access to water is a matter of survival, water should not be left to the whims of market supply and demand. By rebelling against government water policies and giant water corporations, Bolivians were essentially exercising their sovereignty over natural resources and their right to participate in decisions affecting their basic needs. It is in this context that the right to water acquires its substantive and inherent meaning. However, the legal and socio-political context in which privatisation is applied, not privatisation itself, is the real problem.[181] There is no one-size-fits-all solution to water accessibility. While water privatisation proved to be successful in Britain and Chile, it failed dramatically in other countries, notably Bolivia and Ghana. Fitzmaurice suggested partial privatisation of water supplies as a probable solution to problems plaguing the provision of water in developing countries.[182] Privatisation is not necessarily the antithesis of the right to water; Britain, which fully privatised its water system, recognised the

---

Water and Sanitation under International Human Rights Instruments, UNHRC, 6th sess, UN Doc A/HRC/6/3 (2007), pars. 66, 68.

[177] *The Constitution of the Republic Uganda* 1995 Preamble. Available at http://www.trybunal.gov.pl/constit/constitu/constit/uganda/uganda-e.htm.

[178] *The Constitution of the Kingdom of Cambodia* art. 59. Available at http://www.embassy.org/cambodia/cambodia/constitu.htm.

[179] *Constitution of the Republic of South Africa* 1996 sec. 27(1) (b). Available at http://www.info.gov.za/documents/constitution/1996/96cons2.htm#27.

[180] Malgosia Fitzmaurice, "The Human Right to Water," *Fordham Environmental Law Review* 18(2006–2007): 565.

[181] Ibid., 567–68.

[182] Ibid., 583.

right to water in 2006.[183] The 2006 Human Development Report clarified that declaring water as a human right will not end the crisis related to water and sanitation in the short-term, but will mark a useful starting point. The Report noted that "human rights represent a powerful moral claim. They can also act as a source of empowerment and mobilization, creating expectations and enabling poor people to expand their entitlements through legal and political channels and through claims on the resources of national governments and the international community."[184]

5. *The Right to Food*

Approximately 852 million people lack proper food and nutrition, and every five seconds a child dies from hunger.[185] Guaranteeing the right to food is an integral part of poverty eradication and food security. Unlike the right to water, the right to food is explicitly recognised on the international level; this right can be inferred from Article 25 of the UDHR and Article 11 of the ICESCR. While the former affirms the right of everyone "to a standard of living adequate for the health and well-being of himself and of his family, including food",[186] the latter recognises the right of everyone to an adequate standard of living, including adequate food and the right of everyone to be free from hunger and malnutrition.[187] According to General Comment 12 issued by the CESCR,

> the core content of the right to adequate food implies: The availability of food in a quantity and quality sufficient to satisfy the dietary needs of individuals, free from adverse substances, and acceptable within a given culture, [and] the accessibility of such food in ways that are sustainable and that do not interfere with the enjoyment of other human rights.[188]

This definition suggests that the right to food depends on four criteria: accessibility to food, its quality, its sustainability and its cultural suitability. The accessibility to food and its quality depend chiefly on environmental sustainability. In rural and agricultural societies, the direct reliance on environmental resources to guarantee proper and sufficient nutrition necessitates proper access to rural lands, wildlife, forests and rivers. According to the Millennium Project Task Force, half of the world's hungry live on 'marginal, dry and degraded lands.'[189] When environmental disasters such as desertification and drought hit a region, the production and availability of food is directly affected.

---

[183] Ibid., 584.
[184] United Nations Development Programme (UNDP), "Beyond Scarcity".
[185] *Report of the Special Rapporteur on the Right to Food*, Jean Ziegler, UN Doc A/61/306 (2006).
[186] *Universal Declaration of Human Rights*, art. 25.
[187] *International Covenant on Economic, Social and Cultural Rights*, art. 11.
[188] *General Comment 12: The Right to Self-Determination of Peoples (Art 1)*, par. 8.
[189] Ibid., par. 29.

The droughts that hit the Horn of Africa in 2006 are indicative of the negative consequences of environmental disasters on pastoralists' livelihoods and basic human rights: the United Nations estimated that 16 million people, including four million children, were affected by the severe drought.[190] Usually, the nomadic pastoral tribes in that region move from one area to another along the common borders of five countries, searching for water and food for their livestock, which represents their only economic assets. The drought made the search for water and pasture more difficult and, with the decimation of animals, the pastoralists lost their means of subsistence, and many malnourished children contracted diseases or died.[191]

In its 2006 Report, the Special Rapporteur on the Right to Food examined the close connection between land degradation and hunger in many regions of the world, especially Africa, where farmers and villagers rely solely on the land for their livelihoods.[192] The 2006 Report shows that, while poor people can be mistakenly accused of hastening desertification and land degradation by pursuing unsustainable activities like deforestation and overgrazing, much broader causes are to blame.[193] The main factors that affect arid regions and their inhabitants range from global climate change and economic globalisation to inadequate international and national policies.[194] The Report emphasises the sustainability of traditional practices such as pastoralism that matches the tough conditions of life in dry regions and suggests the adoption of small-scale irrigation and water management projects as remedies for drought and water shortages; fighting desertification and land degradation is central to preventing famine and food insecurity in rural areas.[195] According to the Report, environmental degradation leads to grievous human rights violations that must be addressed on national and international levels.[196]

The intimate connection with the environment is what makes the right to food a part of environmental human rights; it is insufficient to deal with the right to food as a mere socio-economic right when deep environmental problems are at the root of its violation.

6. *Indigenous Land Rights*

The right to environment acquires a special and deeper meaning when it applies to Indigenous peoples. With the spread of economic globalisation,

---

[190] UNICEF, "Child Alert: Crisis in the Horn of Africa: A Report on the Impact of Drought on Children," http://www.unicef.org/infobycountry/files/Child_Alert_HoA_FINAL.pdf.

[191] Ibid.

[192] *Report of the Special Rapporteur on the Right to Food*, Jean Ziegler, UN Doc A/61/306 (2006), par. 30.

[193] Ibid.

[194] Ibid.

[195] Ibid., par. 31.

[196] Ibid., par. 54.

tribal and Indigenous communities are witnessing the invasion of their ancestral lands, livelihoods and cultural lifestyles. There are nearly 370 million Indigenous Peoples living in over 70 countries around the world.[197] Despite the diversity of their ethnic origins, the seminal commonality among Indigenous peoples stems from their intimate and vital relationship with the land and its resources. Environmental degradation and land dispossession can threaten the very core of Indigenous livelihoods by disturbing their traditional ways of life and creating poverty and forced evictions. In this respect, Indigenous and Western legal cultures collide especially sharply in the field of land ownership.

In Indigenous societies, the conception of private land ownership is different from that of capitalist societies, where land is viewed as a commodity to be exploited for economic and individual purposes. However, in the Indigenous culture, land is viewed as a collective resource and is revered for its spiritual and cultural values.[198] When Indigenous communities claim land rights, they are usually seeking cultural integrity and collective management of local resources, rather than the acquisition of private property rights. The *ILO Convention (NO. 169) Concerning Indigenous and Tribal Peoples in Independent Countries* provides a remarkable international legal framework for Indigenous rights to land and natural resources.[199] It was the first international instrument to use the term 'peoples' when referring to Indigenous and tribal communities.[200] Because of fear of self-determination claims, the Convention included a clause restricting the interpretation of the term 'peoples' under international law.[201] Apart from this restriction, the term itself reinforces the collective aspect of Indigenous rights.[202] The non-western concept of collective ownership has a specific meaning when it applies to Indigenous lands and resources. Article 14 of the Convention explicitly recognizes 'the rights of ownership and possession of the peoples concerned' of their traditional lands. These rights also include the rights of nomadic peoples and shifting cultivators to access lands not exclusively occupied by them for subsistence and traditional activities.[203] For instance, the Sami, the Indigenous Peoples of Northern Europe and Russia, have been involved in several lawsuits related to their right

---

[197] United Nations Permanent Forum on Indigenous Issues UNPFII, "About UNPFII and a Brief History of Indigenous Peoples and the International System," http://www.un.org/esa/socdev/unpfii/en/history.html.

[198] Hancock, *Environmental Human Rights*, 141.

[199] *Convention (No. 169) Concerning Indigenous and Tribal Peoples in Independent Countries*, Opened for signature 27 June 1989, 28 ILM 1382 (Entered into force 5 Sept. 1991).

[200] Alexandra Xanthaki, *Indigenous Rights and United Nations Standards: Self-Determination, Culture and Land* (Cambridge: Cambridge University Press, 2007), 70.

[201] *ILO Convention (No. 169)*, art. 1(3). See Patrick Thornberry, *Indigenous Peoples and Human Rights* (New York: Juris Publishing, 2002), 343–44.

[202] Xanthaki, 73–74.

[203] *ILO Convention (No. 169)*, art. 14.

to reindeer-herding in privately owned lands.[204] In Sweden, many private forest owners brought legal suits against Sami reindeer herders, claiming that the Sami have no herding rights on their private lands. According to Swedish law, to retain their rights, the Sami have to prove that they have historical ties with the land, which is difficult to establish. Obviously, the Sami lost most cases, as reindeer herding cannot be traceable.[205] However, in the *Selbu* case, the Norwegian Supreme Court explained its ruling in favour of the Sami herders by arguing that the right to pasture can be justified by the Sami use of traditional lands since 'time immemorial'.[206]

This principle of communal ownership is also included in the newly adopted 2007 UN Declaration on the Rights of Indigenous Peoples (2007 Declaration), which expressly recognises the right of Indigenous peoples to environmental protection and conservation. Part VI of the 2007 Declaration details the right of Indigenous peoples to their environment and its resources: lands, territories, waters, coastal seas, flora, fauna and all other resources present on their traditional lands.[207] Article 29 of the 2007 Declaration made it clear that Indigenous peoples have 'full ownership, control and protection [over] their cultural and intellectual property' including human and other genetic resources, seeds, medicines, knowledge of properties of fauna and flora and the like.[208] In order to guarantee the right of Indigenous peoples to collective ownership, states are obligated to give legal recognition and protection to these lands and resources according to the customs, traditions and land tenure systems of the Indigenous peoples concerned.[209]

The collective ownership of lands is a cultural norm for Indigenous communities whose cultural rights emanate from their spiritual connection with nature. The UNHRC expanded the scope of Article 27 on the cultural rights of minorities by incorporating the right of Indigenous communities to the use of land resources. Article 27 of the ICCPR stipulates that persons belonging to minorities "shall not be denied the right, in community with the other members of their group, to enjoy their own culture, to profess and practice their own religion, or to use their own language."[210] This right, the UNHRC explains

---

[204] *Länsman et al. v. Finland*, Communication No. 511/1992, UNCHR, UN Doc CCPR/C/52/D/511/1992 (1994); *Handölsdalen Saami Village and Others v. Sweden*, App. No. 39013/04(2009); *Taxed Lapp Mountain Case*, Swedish Supreme Court NJA (1981).

[205] The International Work Group for Indigenous Affairs (IWGIA), *The Indigenous World 2007* (Copenhagen: IWGIA, 2007), 44–45.

[206] *Jon Inge Sirum et al. v. Essand Reindeer Pasturing District and Riast/Hylling Reindeer Pasturing District (Selbu Case)*, Norwegian Supreme Court serial number 4B/2001(2001). (Unlike Norway, Sweden has not yet ratified the *ILO Convention*).

[207] Ibid., arts. 25–26.

[208] Ibid., art. 29.

[209] *UN Declaration on the Rights of Indigenous Peoples*, GA Res, UN GAOR, 61st sess, UN Doc A/61/L.67 (2007), art. 26.

[210] *International Covenant on Civil and Political Rights*, art. 27.

in a General Comment, "may include such traditional activities as fishing or hunting and the right to live in reserves protected by law."[211] Similarly, the 2007 Declaration acknowledges the right of Indigenous peoples to "maintain and strengthen their distinctive spiritual relationship with their traditionally owned or otherwise occupied and used lands, territories, waters and coastal seas and other resources."[212]

The legal basis for Indigenous rights to land can also be inferred from the well-recognised right to self-determination. The 2007 Declaration clarifies that, by exercising their right to self-determination, Indigenous peoples "have the rights to autonomy or self-government in matters relating to their internal and local affairs, as well as ways and means for financing their autonomous functions."[213] Most provisions listed in the 2007 Declaration acknowledge the international right to self-determination of Indigenous nations in the form of self-governance and autonomy.[214] Both the *ILO Convention* and the 2007 Declaration require states to safeguard Indigenous rights to natural resources and to protect the environment of the territories where Indigenous communities live.[215] The 2007 Declaration urges states to take the necessary measures to inhibit the dumping of dangerous pollutants in Indigenous territories without Indigenous consent or knowledge.[216] In a 2007 report, the Special Rapporteur on the Situation of Human Rights and Fundamental Freedoms of Indigenous Peoples highlighted the destructive impacts of extractive industries on Indigenous populations.[217] According to the report, these highly polluting industries, such as gold-mining in San Miguel Ixtahuacán and Sipakapa in Guatemala, nickel extraction in the Goro and Prony deposits in New Caledonia, the Chad-Cameroon oil pipeline, and the gas pipeline in Camisea in the Peruvian Amazon, violate local communities' right to environment.[218] In addition, the report found that the "widespread practice of dumping toxic waste in Indigenous territories has been the cause of many abortions and cases of cancer and other diseases among Indigenous women."[219] In his visit to the Philippines, the Rapporteur emphasised the detrimental impacts of large-scale development projects such as mining, logging and dams on the livelihoods of Indigenous peoples, and especially on young girls. He concluded that the very

211 *General Comment 23: The Rights of Minorities (Art 27)*, par. 7.
212 *The 2007 Declaration*, art. 25.
213 Ibid., arts. 3, 4.
214 *General Comment 23: The Rights of Minorities (Art 27)*, United Nations Human Rights Committee, 50th sess, UN Doc CCPR/C/21/Rev.1/Add.5 (1994), art. 25.
215 *ILO Convention (No. 169)*, arts. 7(4), 15; *The 2007 Declaration* art. 29(2).
216 *The 2007 Declaration*, art. 29(2).
217 *Report of the Special Rapporteur on the Situation of Human Rights and Fundamental Freedoms of Indigenous People*, Rodolfo Stavenhagen, UN Doc A/HRC/4/32 (2007).
218 Ibid., 52.
219 Ibid.

life of these communities is jeopardised if appropriate measures are not taken to curb the effects of 'development aggression'.[220]

This evolving body of law on Indigenous rights will necessarily entail serious restrictions on the exploitation of Indigenous lands and resources, or will at least require states to establish procedural safeguards such as prior consultations with Indigenous and Tribal Peoples regarding any development projects that affect their livelihoods.[221] Many virgin lands, not yet touched by modern technology, are, based on tradition, owned by Indigenous and tribal peoples. However, because of this form of collective ownership of land, the government treats these Indigenous lands as if they are state-owned, so it is common for the governments of developing countries to grant permits to large corporations that allow them to operate in these traditionally owned lands without prior consultation with or proper compensation for Indigenous peoples. This practice is a typical example of power politics as conflicts arise between states' interests to pursue economic progress and their duties to protect Indigenous and Tribal livelihoods. However, the tendency to ignore or manipulate Indigenous rights reigns supreme when economic and political factors come into play.

In a seminal case, the *Mayagna (Sumo) Awas Tingni Community v. Nicaragua*,[222] the Inter-American Court of Human Rights (Inter-American Court) set precedent by laying out the obligations of Nicaragua and other American States regarding Indigenous rights to land.[223] The court found that land rights in the form of land titles or other legal forms are the collective version of individual property rights.[224] The absence of legal documents asserting the ownership of Indigenous peoples to their ancestral lands should not allow governmental authorities to view these lands as public property. In *Awas Tingni*, the Inter-American Court affirmed that "[a]s a result of customary practices, possession of the land should suffice for Indigenous communities lacking real title to property of the land to obtain official recognition of that property, and for consequent registration."[225]

Despite constitutional and statutory guarantees, Nicaragua did not formally recognise the rights of the Mayagna peoples to their ancestral lands. Moreover,

---

[220] *Report of the Special Rapporteur on the Situation of Human Rights and Fundamental Freedoms of Indigenous People: Addendum: Mission to the Philippines*, Rodolfo Stavenhagen, UN Doc E/CN.4/2003/90/Add.3 (2003), par. 63.

[221] *ILO Convention (No. 169)*, art. (6).

[222] *Mayagna (Sumo) Awas Tingni Community v. Nicaragua*, Inter-Am Comm HR, Case No. 11.140(2001).

[223] Jennifer A. Amiott, "Environment, Equality, and Indigenous Peoples' Land Rights in the Inter-American Human Rights System: Mayagna (Sumo) Indigenous Community of Awas Tingni v. Nicaragua," *Environmental Law* 32(2002).

[224] See *Maya Indigenous Communities v. Belize*, Inter-Am Comm HR, Case No 12.053, par. 113 (2004).

[225] *Mayagna (Sumo) Awas Tingni Community v. Nicaragua*, par. 151.

the Nicaraguan government granted a logging concession to the company SOLCARSA within the territories of Awas Tingni without notifying or consulting the community. As a result, the community lodged a petition with the IACHR accusing the Nicaraguan government of infringing on their land rights by consistently refusing to demarcate their territories. The IACHR found that Nicaragua had violated the property rights of the petitioners (Article 21 of the ACHR) and had failed to provide them with effective remedies (Article 25).[226] It issued recommendations urging the Nicaraguan government to suspend logging activities until the matter of Indigenous ownership was settled and to adopt appropriate legal procedures leading to "the rapid official recognition and demarcation of the Awas Tingni territory and the territories of other communities of the Atlantic coast."[227] Because Nicaragua denied the allegations, the IACHR transferred the case to the Inter-American Court on 4 June 1998. The Inter-American Court upheld the findings of the Commission and ordered the Nicaraguan government to grant financial compensation to Awas Tingni members, to undertake investment projects in order to improve their living conditions and to demarcate their traditional territories. In rendering this decision, the Inter-American Court expanded the right to property as provided in the ACHR to include "the right of Indigenous peoples to the protection of their customary land and resource tenure."[228]

Defending Indigenous rights to land is a key factor in protecting both their livelihoods and the environment. The right to property invoked by both the Commission and the Court implies the respect of Indigenous right to an environment suitable for life. As one commentator remarked, "the Awas Tingni decision ... sets a powerful precedent that is essential to acknowledging Indigenous rights and environmental protection on an international scale."[229] The *ILO Convention*, the 2007 Declaration and the various international human rights instruments play an important role in sensitizing the international community to the vulnerability of the environments of Indigenous peoples. Since lands and resources are integral parts of any environment, Indigenous land rights could easily fall within the ambit of emerging environmental rights.

7. *Beneficiaries and Duty-Bearers of Environmental Rights*

The beneficiaries of environmental rights can be individuals, group of individuals, or a whole community, depending on the formulation adopted in

---

[226] Ibid., pars. 142–43.
[227] Ibid., par. 143.
[228] S. James Anaya and Claudio Grossman, "The Case of Awas Tingni v. Nicaragua: A New Step in the International Law of Indigenous Peoples," *Arizona Journal of International and Comparative Law* 19, no. 1 (2002): 1.
[229] Amiott, "Land Rights," 903.

international instruments, regional treaties and national constitutions.[230] For instance, while Principle 1 of the Stockholm Declaration recognises an individual right to environment, the *African Charter on Human and Peoples' Rights (Banjul Charter)* guarantees a collective right to environment.[231] In progressive formulations, such as the rights of nature discussed above, species and ecosystems can be potential candidates for environmental protection.

According to many formulations, the beneficiaries of the emerging rights are individuals who are entitled to a 'clean', 'healthy' and 'safe' environment necessary to their health and well-being. Rights-holders are also entitled to an economic right to local natural resources and to economic benefits from developmental projects. The importance of this right is most obvious in developing countries where local and Indigenous communities have strong connections with their natural environment and wish to maintain sustainable livelihoods based on natural resource use and management. Environmental rights can also extend to protect present and even future generations, where short-term economic benefits are sacrificed for long-term ethical commitments to children and future generations, known as the right of future generations. However, this right leads to questions concerning what will compel present generations to preserve the environment and sacrifice their economic welfare for the sake of unborn human beings and what will drive people to safeguard nature for its own worth or intrinsic value. In this regard, environmental rights are useful because they offer a potential solution to this philosophical dilemma. The strength of human rights is that they are not contingent upon the benevolence of states or the moral commitments of people; they are strong entitlements that allow their beneficiaries to escape the unfavourable will of the majority, even if the majority chooses to elevate their own interests above those of the environment or future generations.

As for obligations, public authorities are the main duty-bearers in fulfilling the 'Right to Environment', although responsibility should also be stretched to include private actors like transnational corporations and individuals. The obligations imposed on state actors are much more sophisticated than the positive/negative dichotomy, in particular, states must address the complexities of environmental problems through both passive and proactive approaches. The tripartite obligations—*to respect, to protect* and *to fulfil*—discussed in Chapter 2 provide a sound legal basis for dealing with multifaceted issues such as environmental rights. The obligations and corollary international environmental standards related to environmental rights can be inferred from the various global environmental treaties and protocols. The IUCN Draft International Covenant on Environment and Development (IUCN Draft

---

[230] Birnie and Boyle, *International Law and the Environment*, 254.
[231] Ibid.

Covenant) puts forward a comprehensive list of obligations, reiterating general obligations of states and individuals regarding the protection of the environment.[232] Then it fleshes out these obligations in relation to natural systems and resources, such as stratospheric ozone, global climate, soil and biological diversity and in relation to processes and activities like pollution and waste.[233] These obligations conform to existing international environmental norms. Article 17 of the IUCN Draft Covenant requires States Parties "to prevent dangerous anthropogenic interference with the climate system by, inter alia, reducing concentrations of greenhouse gases within an internationally-agreed time frame."[234] This provision is predicated upon standards and obligations enshrined in the UNFCCC and the *Kyoto Protocol*. The connections between these obligations and emerging environmental rights are particularly important because they imply that the violations of legally binding environmental norms and standards constitute a violation of human rights.[235] This implication is indicative of possible complementarities, rather than overlaps, between environmental rights and international environmental law.

Conclusion

Instead of the generational approach to human rights, I proposed the generalist-specialist approach. In this approach, the umbrella rights identified above—the right to democracy, the right to development and the 'Right to Environment'—are considered generalist rights. Each generalist right offers a broad framework that binds together the corresponding specialist rights and allows, when necessary, the integration of these rights with other generalist rights. For example, victims of environmental pollution caused by an extractive industry operating in a developing country will have to invoke their rights to health, life or privacy to seek injunctive relief or compensation, while environmental advocates will probably seek to protect the whole ecosystem for the sake of present and future generations, and company workers will be much more concerned about the effects of environmental litigation on their rights to work. This environmental issue may also involve a governance problem in which public authorities provide legal and logistical protection to the company's harmful activities on the grounds that the economic profits generated by the extractive industry are necessary to achieve the state's economic goals.

This amalgam of rights violated by a polluting activity illustrates the complexity of environmental issues that often involve different concepts and

[232] *Draft International Covenant on Environment and Development*, 4–9.
[233] Ibid., 6–9.
[234] Ibid., 68.
[235] See especially Lee, "Underlying Legal Theory," 300.

interests, e.g., development, ecocentrism, anthropocentrism, human rights and governance. The generalist-specialist model, along with the sustainable development concept, provides the judiciary, decision-makers and other stakeholders with a relatively satisfactory conceptual and normative framework on which to deal with these multifaceted matters. Instead of analysing whether certain specialised rights are violated as a result of an environmental hazard, the judiciary will find it easier to review the content of generalist rights which offer broad guidelines and parameters, along with the interpretive tools necessary to assess the level of harm inflicted on human beings, the environment and the economy. In addition, generalist rights conform to the general and supervisory nature of international human rights law.

CONCLUSION

The Declaration on Human Rights Defenders, albeit a non-binding instrument, shows that the mood of the international community is open to the idea of new human rights. The Declaration provides that "[e]veryone has the right, individually and in association with others, to develop and discuss new human rights ideas and principles and to advocate their acceptance."[1] In spite of the innate resistance of states and intergovernmental institutions to recognising new rights, there is a growing trend towards adopting diverse aspects of environmental human rights on global, regional and national levels. I have examined this trend in order to identify and develop some of the philosophical, theoretical and legal foundations of these emerging rights and to offer a re-conceptualisation of the human rights system.

Viewed from a philosophical perspective, a human rights-based approach to environmental issues brings nature and its components into the exclusive field of human rights. Throughout history, the concept of human rights has expanded to accommodate a broad spectrum of interests and a wide array of beneficiaries, so it is feasible that it could stretch further to non-humans. Human beings tend to extend rights and privileges to anything they value or cherish, such as pets, trees and even wild animals. In the same way, the rights of nature, which reflect the ecocentric dimension of the 'Right to Environment', fall into this rights-based rhetoric. However, contradictory as it may seem, ecocentrism as a concept is not inherently immune from anthropocentric interests. Deep ecologists, who believe that non-human beings and ecosystems have to be protected for their own worth, view nature and animal protection as part of what they call 'self-realisation' or 'self-identification' with nature. The idea of self-fulfilment in terms of higher ecological values is anthropocentric in itself; whether we protect the environment for our biological/economic survival or for our spiritual/psychological well-being, the human factor cannot be logically separated from the rights-based analysis.

The distinction between shallow ecology and deep ecology, coined by Naess, corresponds to our biological/economic needs as well as to our spiritual/psychological needs. In some respects, ecocentrism is no more than the spiritual, cultural and psychological aspect of anthropocentrism. From this perspective, the rights of nature and its components are compatible with the concept of human rights because they accommodate our human interests, albeit at a

---

[1] *Declaration on the Right and Responsibility of Individuals, Groups and Organs of Society to Promote and Protect Universally Recognized Human Rights and Fundamental Freedoms*, GA Res 53/144, UN GAOR, 53rd sess, Agenda Item 110(b), UN Doc A/Res/53/144 (1999), art.7.

higher and nobler level. In this context, the concept of human dignity seems to be compatible with the deep ecologists' call for more respect for and awe of nature. In contrast, the ethical perspectives examined in Chapter 1 stretch the boundaries of our human dignity beyond narrow human interests in an attempt to mend the human/nature relationship by transferring the intrinsic worth of non-human beings into the sphere of human rights. If the rights of nature are recognised as human rights, a single individual could argue that the abuse of nature or the ferocious killing of animals disturbs his or her spiritual or psychological well-being, while another might claim that a stringent law prohibiting the killing of animals violates his or her economic rights. While this conflict of rights is an integral part of human rights doctrines and litigation, the intensity of the conflict increases when non-human agents are assigned rights. Therefore, the recognition of a distinct 'Right to Environment' in international law could bring human rights interests into environmental laws and policies in a more consistent and systematic fashion. Similarly, the elaboration of a third international covenant on environmental rights would be useful in addressing the piecemeal proliferation of various environment-related rights.

Three theories—the expansion theory, the environmental democracy theory and the genesis theory—encapsulate the recent academic debates and controversies around the various human rights approaches to environmental issues. The expansion theory makes use of existing substantive rights to defend environmental interests. While several global, regional and national courts have adopted this approach in adjudicating environmental cases, the expansion theory is of limited use for three reasons. First, it is particularly difficult for plaintiffs to show a causal connection between environmental harm and human life, health or an adequate standard of living. Second, existing human rights cannot easily be invoked to defend the rights of future generations, or even more problematically, the non-anthropocentric interests such as the preservation of species and ecosystems. Third, reliance on existing rights lacks the consistency necessary to the recognition of new rights, which impedes the transformation of this practice into a principle of customary international law.[2]

The environmental democracy theory, an innovative way of mobilising procedural and democratic rights around ecological matters, is essential to the conceptual link between environmental protection and democratic values and practices. Although both the expansion theory and the environmental democracy theory claim to protect the environment without the need for a substantive right to environment, they prepare the legal and philosophical ground for

2 See Lee, "Underlying Legal Theory," 291.

the future recognition of environmental rights by greening the concept of human rights and reshaping our beliefs and attitudes towards nature.

The genesis theory builds the case for a new human right in international law based on the indispensability of environmental rights to the realisation of all human rights. From a legal perspective, the importance of environmental rights lies in facilitating injunctive relief, rather than in merely providing compensatory damages to victims. In many environmental cases, harmful activities must be suspended immediately in order to halt irreparable environmental damage and save the costs of future restoration of ecosystems. However, compensatory damages can play a key role in deterring future environmental abuses, similar to the deterrent effect that litigation had on the asbestos and tobacco industries. Such litigation eventually led to a ban on the use of asbestos in many countries and the adoption of stringent laws regarding tobacco advertising.

An examination of the universality, justiciability, scope and nature of environmental rights is necessary in order to construct the theoretical and legal underpinnings of those rights. The criterion of universality is vital to building a case for a new human right and the notion of subsistence rights, as elaborated by Shue, is helpful in this regard because it prioritises basic rights over all other rights. The case for universality is established when environmental rights are seen as subsistence rights equally indispensable for all human beings. The justiciability of environmental rights is intimately related to the concept of three generations of rights and the way we classify the emerging rights. First-generation rights, despite their strong legal status, cannot be a sufficient framework for the new rights because they are often negative rights. Second-generation rights traditionally lack the legal status of political and civil rights, so it is not useful to place the new rights in this category. Classifying them into a new set of rights called 'third-generation' or 'solidarity' rights is even more complicated because of the debate over whether human rights can be addressed on a collective basis, rather than using the traditional individual approach. Some authors have advocated the incorporation of environmental rights into all three generations of rights because "environmental protection is perhaps the clearest example of the merging of three classes of human rights into a workable entity."[3] Actually, a puzzling ambiguity surrounds the concept of third-generation rights because they "somehow belong to humankind without being held by anyone or any group in particular."[4]

In order to transcend the ambiguity of third-generation rights and to address the complexities of ecological problems, I put forward two complementary conceptualisations of environmental rights and linked them to

[3] Gormley, "Legal Obligation," 110.
[4] Edmundson, *Introduction to Rights*, 177.

existing international human rights. First, by emulating the more advanced right to development and the less developed right to democracy, an international 'Right to Environment' can be conceived as a generalist or umbrella right. The need for a 'Right to Environment' that mimics the right to development on the international level is necessary to create a balance between developmental and environmental interests, a balance essential to the concept of sustainable development. If development is couched in human rights terms, there is no compelling reason to leave the environment outside the human rights realm. This rationale draws upon the interconnectedness between the human rights discourse and the sustainable development discourse: human rights are the common denominator in the two otherwise divergent concepts of development and environment.

Development and economic growth, the arteries of modern civilisations, are of paramount importance to our societies, but no state can survive without appropriate economic and developmental policies and legislation. In this context, the concept of sustainable development presents itself as a revolutionary and integrative approach to resolving the dilemma of how to preserve the environment while continuing development. The Hungary-Slovakia Danube River dispute is a perfect illustration of the tension that often arises between developmental projects and environmental protection. In his separate opinion, Judge Weeramantry presented the concept of sustainable development as a practical solution to the collision between the right to development and the right to environment, stating that "[t]he Court must hold the balance even between the environmental considerations and the developmental considerations raised by the respective Parties. The principle that enables the Court to do so is the principle of sustainable development."[5] Initially, the concept of sustainable development seemed to undermine the fervour about the adoption of an environmental right as conceived by Principle 1 of the Stockholm Declaration. However, the evolution of this concept into an integrative framework for developmental, social and ecological issues is potentially useful for a future recognition of a distinct 'Right to Environment' and/or corollary substantive environmental rights.

The second of the two complementary conceptualisations of environmental rights concerns a third covenant on environmental rights that is necessary to overcome the definitional ambiguity often cited as an argument against the adoption of a distinct right to environment. Regardless of the multitude of formulations used to describe a desirable environment e.g., the right to a healthy, clean, safe, or ecologically balanced environmental quality cannot be assessed by courts and administrative bodies based solely on qualitative features; eventually, quantitative measures and standards will be needed to

[5] *Hungary v. Slovakia(Separate Opinion of Judge Weeramantry)*, 88.

overcome the vagueness of the formulation. Broad formulations of environmental rights are better suited to accommodating the dynamic, complex and technical nature of ecological problems. Although environmental rights are not yet recognised in international law, the environmental law system and the human rights system have demonstrated to varying degrees their awareness of the human rights approaches to environmental issues.

Because of the role of soft law in the development of international environmental law, environmental rights are in their embryonic stage in international law. Principle 1 of the Stockholm Declaration, the Draft Principles on Human Rights and the Environment, the Hague Declaration on the Environment and the Declaration of Bizkaia all contain strong statements in favour of environmental rights, while other soft law instruments, such as the Brundtland Report and the Rio Declaration, contain less ambitious provisions. Of special importance is the role of UN special rapporteurs in addressing and developing the synergies between environment-related issues and specific human rights. An analysis of their reports and other UN documents reveals that the right to water, the right to food and Indigenous rights to land and its resources should be considered environmental rights and hence be included in a separate covenant on environmental rights. This wider conceptualisation of environmental rights also entails the protection of the environment, regardless of its direct connection to human interests, and the preservation of natural wealth for present and future generations. This refutes the argument that environmental rights are unnecessary in the presence of expressly recognised human rights, which can be invoked in relation to the environment. In short, substantive environmental rights, or 'specialist' rights, may include the rights of nature, the right to an environment (air, soil, and water) free from pollution, the right to water, the right to food, the right to natural resources (including preservation of ecosystems and species), and the right of Indigenous peoples to land.

Based on this analysis, I propose a new reconfiguration of the human rights system through the re-conceptualisation of rights into 'generalist' rights and 'specialist' rights. 'Generalist' rights belong to a new category of rights, similar to 'third-generation' rights, which are universal and collective in nature. In this case, the main rights-holders are people living within each state, although NGOs, government authorities and local communities can represent and act on people's behalf on the international stage regarding collective interests. The international community as a whole, represented by the UN and its agencies, are the duty-bearers responsible for the realisation of these rights. Generalist rights are designed to provide guidelines and benchmarks to state and non-state actors regarding the implementation of broad goals, such as development, environmental protection and good governance, and to connect all corollary human rights with one another.

As a broad and multifaceted type of rights in international law, generalist rights should not be regarded as predominantly justiciable because the judicial enforceability of human rights is not the only determinant of their legal worth. Given the notion of synthetic rights, the right to democracy, the right to development and the proposed 'Right to Environment' may be associated with the corollary rights embedded in the *International Covenant on Civil and Political Rights* (ICCPR), the *International Covenant on Economic, Social and Cultural Rights* (ICESCR), and the proposed third covenant on environmental rights. The rights enshrined in the Covenants are considered 'specialist' rights because they provide rights-holders, individuals and groups with specific entitlements and are justiciable and enforceable in international, regional and national jurisdictions. Of special importance to the enforcement of 'specialist' rights is the notion of the tripartite obligations (*to respect, to protect* and *to fulfil*) that transcend the rigid dichotomy of negative and positive duties. In its adjudication of the *SERAC* case, the African Commission drew upon this notion to identify the duties of the state to respect, protect, promote and fulfil the right to a satisfactory environment. The interconnection and solidarity among the three 'generalist' rights mentioned above, although they are at different stages of their development, constitute a holistic approach to the implementation of all human rights, whether enshrined in the 1966 Covenants, other international human rights treaties or the proposed covenant on environmental rights. As a new type of rights, generalist rights would bring together complex concepts like development, environment and democracy in order to provide a more integrative approach to international laws and policies. Indeed, development, democracy and environment constitute the foundations of peace—the ultimate objective of international law.

BIBLIOGRAPHY

Acevedo, Mariana T. "The Intersection of Human Rights and Environmental Protection in the European Court of Human Rights." *New York University Environmental Law Journal* 8 (2000): 437–96.

Adams, W.M. *Green Development: Environment and Sustainability in the Third World*. 2nd ed. London/New york: Routledge, 1990.

Additional Protocol to the American Convention on Human Rights in the Area of Economic, Social, and Cultural Rights (Protocol of San Salvador). Opened for signature 17 Nov. 1988, OAS Treaty Series No. 69 (Entered into force 29 Nov. 1999).

African Charter on Human and Peoples' Rights (Banjul Charter). Opened for signature 27 June 1981, OAU Doc CAB/LEG/67/3 rev 5, 21 ILM 58 (Entered into force 21 Oct. 1986).

Aguirre, Daniel. "Multinational Corporations and the Realisation of Economic, Social and Cultural Rights." *California Western International Law Journal* 35 (2004): 53–82.

Aguirre, Monti. "The Chixoy Dam Destroyed Our Lives." *Human Rights Dialogue* 2, no. 11 (Spring 2004): 20.

Alston, Philip. "Conjuring up New Human Rights: A Proposal for Quality Control." *American Journal of International Law* 78 (1984): 607–21.

——. "Making Space for New Human Rights: The Case of the Right to Development." *Harvard Human Rights Year Book* 1 (1988): 3–40.

——. "Peace as a Human Right." *Security Dialogue* 11 (1980): 319–29.

——. "A Third Generation of Solidarity Rights: Progressive Development or Obfuscation of International Human Rights Law?" *Netherlands International Law Review* 29 (1982): 307–22.

American Convention on Human Rights. Opened for signature 20 Nov. 1969, 1144 UNTS 123 (Entered into force 18 July 1978).

American Declaration of the Rights and Duties of Man. OAS Res XXX, Opened for signature in Apr. 1948, OEA/Ser.L.V/II.82 doc.6 rev.1 (1992) (Entered into force in Apr. 1948).

Amiott, Jennifer A. "Environment, Equality, and Indigenous Peoples' Land Rights in the Inter-American Human Rights System: Mayagna (Sumo) Indigenous Community of Awas Tingni v. Nicaragua." *Environmental Law* 32 (2002): 873–903.

Amnesty International. *Clouds of Injustice: Bhopal Disaster 20 Years On*. London: Amnesty International Publications, 2004.

Anaya, S. James, and Claudio Grossman. "The Case of Awas Tingni v. Nicaragua: A New Step in the International Law of Indigenous Peoples." *Arizona Journal of International and Comparative Law* 19, no. 1 (2002): 1–15.

Anderson, Michael R. "Individual Rights to Environmental Protection in India." In *Human Rights Approaches to Environmental Protection*, edited by Alan E. Boyle and Michael R. Anderson. Oxford: Clarendon Press, 1996.

Answers.com. "George Perkins Marsh: Biography." http://www.answers.com/topic/george-perkins-marsh.

Appiah, K. Anthony. "Grounding Human Rights." In *Human Rights as Politics and Idolatry*, edited by Amy Gutmann. Princeton: Princeton University Press, 2001.

Armstrong, Susan J., and Richard G. Botzler, eds. *Environmental Ethics: Divergence and Convergence*. 3rd ed. New York: McGraw-Hill 2003.

Arnold, Ron. "Overcoming Ideology." In *A Wolf in the Garden: The Land Rights Movement and the New Environmental Debate*, edited by Philip D. Brick and R. McGreggor Cawley. Lanham, Maryland: Rowman & Littlefield Publishers, 1996.

Asbjørn, Eide. "Economic, Social and Cultural Rights as Human Rights." In *Economic, Social and Cultural Rights*, edited by Allan Rosas, Eide Asbjørn and Catarina Krause. Dordrecht/Boston/London: Martinus Nijhoff Publishers, 1995.

Atapattu, Sumudu. "The Right to a Healthy Life or the Right to Die Polluted? : The Emergence of a Human Right to a Healthy Environment under International Law." *Tulane Environmental Law Journal* 16 (2002–2003): 65–126.

Atik, Jeffery. "Commentary." *Human Rights Dialogue* 2, no. 11 (Spring 2004): 26.

Attfield, Robert. *Environmental Philosophy: Principles and Prospects*. Aldershot: Ashgate 1994.

Barrett v. State, 220 NY 423 (1917).

Beder, Sharon. *The Nature of Sustainable Development*. Newham, Australia: Scribe Publications, 1993.

Bentham, Jeremy. "Critique of the Doctrine of Inalienable, Natural Rights." *Anarchical Fallacies* 2 (1843).

Birnie, Patricia, and Alan E. Boyle. *International Law and the Environment*. 2nd ed. New York: Oxford University Press, 2002.

Birnie, Patricia, Alan E. Boyle, and Catherine Redgwell. *International Law and the Environment*. 3nd ed. New York: Oxford University Press, 2009.

Bonine, John E. "The Construction of Participatory Democracy in Central and Eastern Europe." In *Human Rights in Natural Resource Development*, edited by Donald N. Zillman, Alistair Lucas and George Pring. New York: Oxford University Press, 2002.

Bookchin, Murray. "Social Ecology versus Deep Ecology: A Challenge for the Ecology Movement." *Green Perspectives*, no. 4–5 (Summer 1987).

——. *The Ecology of Freedom: The Emergence and Dissolution of Freedom*. California: Cheshire books, 1982.

Bosselmann, Klaus. *The Principle of Sustainability: Transforming Law and Governance*. Aldershot: Ashgate, 2008.

——. *When Two Worlds Collide: Society and Ecology*. Auckland: RSVP Publishing, 1995.

Boyle, Alan E. "Human Rights or Environmental Rights? A Reassessment." *Fordham Environmental Law Review* 18 (2006–2007): 471–511.

——. "The Role of International Human Rights Law in the Protection of the Environment." In *Human Rights Approaches to Environmental Protection*, edited by Alan E. Boyle and Michael R. Anderson. Oxford: Clarendon Press, 1996.

Brandl, Ernst, and Hartwin Bungert. "Constitutional Entrenchment of Environmental Protection: A Comparative Analysis of Experiences Abroad." *Harvard Environmental Law Review* 16, no. 1 (1992): 1–100.

Brauch, Jeffrey A. "The Margin of Appreciation and the Jurisprudence of the European Court of Human Rights: Threat to the Rule of Law." *Columbia Journal of European Law* 11 (2004–2005): 113–50.

Brennan, Andrew. "Ethics, Ecology and Economics." In *Ecologists and Ethical Judgements*, edited by N.S. Cooper and R.C.J. Carling. London: Chapman & Hall, 1996.

Buergenthal, Thomas. "Centennial Essay: The Evolving International Human Rights System." *American Journal of International Law* 100 (2006): 783–807.

Callicott, J. Baird. "The Pragmatic Power and Promise of Theoretical Environmental Ethics: Forging a New Discourse." *Environmental Values* 11 (2002): 3–25.

Callicott, J. Baird, and William Grove-Fanning. "Should Endangered Species Have Standing? Toward Legal Rights for Listed Species." *Social Philosophy and Policy* 26, no. 2 (2009): 317–52.

Cameron, James, and Ruth Mackenzie. "Access to Environmental Justice and Procedural Rights in International Institutions." In *Human Rights Approaches to Environmental Protection*, edited by Alan E. Boyle and Michael R. Anderson. Oxford: Clarendon Press, 1996.

Carson, Rachel. *Silent Spring*. Boston: Houghton Mifflin, 1962.

Cha, J. Mijin. "A Critical Examination of the Environmental Jurisprudence of the Courts of India." *Albany Law Environmental Outlook Journal* 10, no. 2 (2005): 197–228.

Chirwa, Danwood Mzikenge. "Toward Revitalizing Economic, Social, and Cultural Rights in Africa: Social and Economic Rights Action Centre and the Center for Economic and Social Rights v. Nigeria." *Human Rights Brief* 10, no. 1 (2002): 14–25.

Churchill, Robin. "Environmental Rights in Existing Human Rights Treaties." In *Human Rights Approaches to Environmental Protection*, edited by Alan E. Boyle and Michael R. Anderson. Oxford: Clarendon Press, 1996.

Climate and Capitalism. "Ecuadorian Assembly Approves Constitutional Rights for Nature." http://climateandcapitalism.com/?p=479.

COHRE Americas Programme, and COHRE ESC Rights Litigation Programme. *Mission Report-Continuing the Struggle for Justice and Accountability in Guatemala:Making Reparations a Reality in the Chixoy Dam Case*. Geneva, Switzerland: Centre on Housing Rights and Evictions (COHRE), 2004.

Collins, Paul. *God's Earth: Religion as If Matter Really Mattered*. North Blackburn, Vic: Dove, 1995.

Connelly, James, and Graham Smith. *Politics and the Environment: From Theory to Practice*. 2nd ed. London/New York: Routledge, 2003.

Convention (No. 169) Concerning Indigenous and Tribal Peoples in Independent Countries. Opened for signature 27 June 1989, 28 ILM 1382 (Entered into force 5 Sept. 1991).

Convention against Torture and Other Cruel, Inhuman or Degrading Treatment or Punishment. Opened for signature 10 Dec. 1984, 1465 UNTS 85 (entered into force 26 June 1987).

Convention for the Protection of Human Rights and Fundamental Freedoms (European Convention on Human Rights). Opened for signature 4 Nov. 1950, 213 UNTS 222 (Entered into force 3 Sept. 1953, as amended by Protocols Nos. 3, 5, 8 and 11, Entered into force 21 Sept. 1970, 20 Dec. 1971, 1 Jan. 1990, and 1 Nov. 1998 respectively).

Convention on Access to Information, Public Participation in Decision-Making and Access to Justice in Environmental Matters (Aarhus Convention). Opened for signature 25 June 1998, UNECE, 2161 UNTS 447 (Entered into force 30 Oct. 2001).

Convention on Biological Diversity. Opened for signature 5 June 1992, 1760 UNTS 79 (Entered into force 29 Dec. 1993).

Convention on the Elimination of All Forms of Discrimination against Women. Opened for signature 18 Dec. 1979, 1249 UNTS 13 (Entered into force 3 Sept. 1981).

Convention on the Rights of the Child. Opened for signature 20 Nov. 1989, UN Doc A/44/49 (Entered into force 2 Sept. 1990).

Cranston, Maurice. *What Are Human Rights?* London: The Bodley Head, 1973.

Dam, Shubhankar, and Vivek Tewary. "Polluting Environment, Polluting Constitution: Is a 'Polluted' Constitution Worse Than a Polluted Environment?" *Journal of Environmental Law* 17 (2005): 383–93.

De Steiguer, J. E. *The Age of Environmentalism*. New York: McGraw-Hill, 1997.

Debeljak, Julie. "Rights Protection without Judicial Supremacy: A Review of the Canadian and British Models of Bills of Rights." *Melbourne University Law Review* 26 (2002): 285–324.

Decision 2/104 on Human Rights and Access to Water. UNHRC, 31st meeting, UN Doc A/HRC/2/L.3/Rev.3 (2006).

Declaration of Bizkaia on the Right to the Environment. UNESCO, 30th sess, UN Doc C/INF.11 (1999).

Declaration on the Establishment of a New International Economic Order. GA Res 3201, UN GAOR, 6th special sess, 2229th plen mtg, Agenda item 7, A/RES/S-6/3201(1974).

Declaration on the Right and Responsibility of Individuals, Groups and Organs of Society to Promote and Protect Universally Recognized Human Rights and Fundamental Freedoms. GA Res 53/144, UN GAOR, 53rd sess, Agenda Item 110(b), UN Doc A/Res/53/144 (1999).

Declaration on the Right to Development. GA Res 41/128, UN GAOR, 41st, 97th plen mtg, UN Doc A/Res/41/128 (1986).

De Jonge, Eccy. *Spinoza and Deep Ecology: Challenging Traditional Approaches to Environmentalism*. Aldershot: Ashgate, 2004.

Dershowitz, Alan. *Rights from Wrongs: A Secular Theory of the Origins of Rights*. New York: Basic Books, 2004.

Desai, Nitin. "Johannesburg: Achievements and Challenges." Carnegie Council Podcast, http://www.cceia.org/resources/transcripts/622.html#1.

Deshaney v. Winnebago County Department of Social Services, 489 U.S. 189 (1989).

Devall, Bill. "Deep Ecology and Radical Environmentalism." In *American Environmentalism: The US Environmental Movement 1970–1990*, edited by Riley E. Dunlap and Angela G. Mertig. New York: Taylor and Francis, 1992.

Devall, Bill, and George Sessions. *Deep Ecology: Living as If Nature Mattered*. Salt Lake City, Utah: Gibbs Smith, 1985.

Dewitt, Calvin B. "Ecology and Ethics: Relation of Religious Belief to Ecological Practice in the Biblical Tradition." In *Ecologists and Ethical Judgements*, edited by N.S. Cooper and and R.C.J. Carling. London: Chapman & Hall, 1996.

Diamond, Jared. "The Worst Mistake in the History of the Human Race." *Discover Magazine* (1987): 64–66.

Dias, Ayesha. "Human Rights, Environment and Development: With Special Emphasis on Corporate Accountability." UNDP, http://hdr.undp.org/en/media/hdr_2000_ch0.pdf.

Dictionary of the History of Ideas. "Chain of Being." http://etext.virginia.edu/cgi-local/DHI/dhi.cgi?id=dv1-45.

Dommen, Caroline. "Claiming Environmental Rights: Some Possibilities Offered by the United Nations Human Rights Mechanisms." *Georgetown International Environmental Law Review* 11 (1998): 1–48.

Donnelly, Jack. *Universal Human Rights in Theory and Practice.* 2nd ed. Ithaca, NY: Cornell University Press, 2003.

Douglas-Scott, S. "Environmental Rights in the European Union-Participatory Democracy or Democratic Deficit." In *Human Rights Approaches to Environmental Protection*, edited by Alan E. Boyle and Michael R. Anderson. Oxford: Clarendon Press, 1996.

Draft Optional Protocol to the International Covenant on Economic, Social and Cultural Rights: Note by the Secretary-General. UN CHR, 53rd sess, E/CN.4/1997/105(1996).

Draft Resolution on Human Rights and Climate Change. UNHRC, 7th sess, UN Doc A/HRC/7/L.21/Rev.1(2008).

Dupuy, Pierre-Marie. "Soft Law and the International Law of the Environment." *Michigan Journal of International Law* 12 (1991–1992): 420–35.

Eacott, Erin. "A Clean and Healthy Environment: The Barriers & Limitations of This Emerging Human Right." *Dalhousie Journal of Legal Studies* 10, no. 1 (2001): 74–103.

Earthjustice. "Environmental Rights Report 2005: Human Rights and the Environment." http://www.earthjustice.org/library/references/2005_ENVIRONMENTAL_RIGHTS_REPORTrev.pdf.

EarthRights International. "Bhopal Survivors Win 2004 Goldman Prize." http://www.earthrights.org/index2.php?option=com_content&do_pdf=1&id=80.

Eaton, Joshua P. "The Nigerian Tragedy: Environmental Regulation of Transnational Corporations and the Human Right to a Healthy Environment." *Boston University International Law Journal* 15 (1997): 261–307.

Edmundson, William A. *An Introduction to Rights*, Introductions to Philosophy and Law Series. Cambridge: Cambridge University Press, 2004.

Edwards, Andres R. *The Sustainability Revolution: Portrait of a Paradigm Shift* New Society Publishers, 2005.

Ehrlich, Paul R. *The Population Bomb.* New York: Ballantine Books, 1968.

Ekbom, Anders, and Jan Bojo. "Poverty and Environment: Evidence of Links and Integration into the Country Assistance Strategy Process, Discussion Paper, No 4.", 1999.

Elder, P. S. "Legal Rights for Nature: The Wrong Answer to the Right(S)." *Osgoode Hall Law Journal* 22, no. 2 (1984): 285–95.

ESCR-Net. "Optional Protocol to the ICESCR Initiative." http://www.escr-net.org/actions_more/actions_more_show.htm?doc_id=433788.

Fabra, Adriana. "The Intersection of Human Rights and Environmental Issues: A Review of Institutional Developments at the International Level." Paper presented at the Joint UNEP_OHCHR Expert Seminar on Human Rights and the Environment, Geneva, 14–16 Jan. 2002.

Fadeyeva v. Russia, App. No. 55723/00, 45 Eur. H. R. Rep. 10 (2005).

Final Report Prepared by the Special Rapporteur on Human Rights and the Environment. Fatma Zohra Ksentini, Commission on Human Rights, UN Doc E/CN.4/Sub.2/1994/9.

Final Working Paper Prepared by the Special Rapporteur on Indigenous Peoples and Their Relationship to Land. Erica-Irene A. Daes, UN Doc E/CN.4/Sub.2/2001/21 (2001).

Fitzmaurice, Malgosia. "The Human Right to Water." *Fordham Environmental Law Review* 18 (2006–2007): 537–85.

Fitzmaurice, Malgosia, and Jill Marshall. "The Human Right to a Clean Environment-Phantom or Reality? The European Court of Human Rights and English Courts Perspective on Balancing Rights in Environmental Cases." *Nordic Journal of International Law* 76 (2007): 103–51.

Fleiner, Thomas. *What Are Human Rights?* Sydney: The Federation Press, 1999.

Forsythe, David P. *Human Rights in International Relations.* Cambridge: Cambridge University Press, 2000.

Fox, Warwick. *Toward a Transpersonal Ecology: Developing New Foundations for Environmentalism*. 2nd ed. New York: State University of New York Press, 1995.
Franck, Thomas M. "The Emerging Right to Democratic Governance." *American Journal of International Law* 86, no. 1 (1992): 46–91.
Freeman, Mark, and Gibran Van Ert. *International Human Rights Law*. Toronto: Irwin Law, 2004.
Freeman, Michael. *Human Rights: An Interdisciplinary Approach*. Cambridge: Polity Press, 2002.
Fuentes, Ximena. "International Law-Making in the Field of Sustainable Development: The Unequal Competition between Development and the Environment." *International Environmental Agreements: Politics, Law and Economics* 2 (2002): 109–33.
Fuyane, Bukhosi, and Ferenc Madai. "The Hungary-Slovakia Danube River Dispute: Implications for Sustainable Development and Equitable Utilization of Natural Resources in International Law." *International Journal of Global Environmental Issues* 1, no. 3 (2001): 329–44.
Gabčikovo-Nagymaros Project (Hungary v. Slovakia), ICJ Rep 7 (1997).
Gabčikovo-Nagymaros Project (Hungary v. Slovakia)(Separate Opinion of Judge Weeramantry), ICJ Rep 7 (1997).
Gamlund, Espen. "Who Has Moral Status in the Environment? A Spinozistic Answer." *The Trumpeter* 23, no. 1 (2007): 3–27.
Gearty, Conor. *Can Human Rights Survive?* Cambridge: Cambridge University Press, 2006.
General Agreement on Tariffs and Trade (GATT). 1867 UNTS 187, 33 ILM 1153 (1994).
General Comment 3: Implementation at the National Level. United Nations Human Rights Committee, UN Doc HRI/GEN/1/Rev.7 (1981).
General Comment 3: The Nature of States Parties Obligations. Committee on Economic, Social and Cultural Rights, UN Doc E/1991/23 (1990).
General Comment 6: The Right to Life. United Nations Human Rights Committee, 16th sess, UN Doc HRIGEN1Rev.7 (1982).
General Comment 12: The Right to Self-Determination of Peoples (Art 1). United Nations Human Rights Committee, 21st sess, UN Doc HRI/GEN/Rev.1 (1984).
General Comment 14: The Right to the Highest Attainable Standard of Health. Committee on Economic, Social and Cultural Rights, UN Doc E/C.12/2000/4 (2000).
General Comment 23: The Rights of Minorities (Art 27). United Nations Human Rights Committee, 50th sess, UN Doc CCPR/C/21/Rev.1/Add.5 (1994).
Giagnocavo, Cynthia, and Howard Goldstein. "Law Reform or World Re-Form: The Problem of Environmental Rights." *McGill Law Journal* 35 (1990): 345–86.
Gordon, Joy. "The Concept of Human Rights: The History and Meaning of Its Politicization." *Brooklyn Journal of International Law* 23 (1997–1998): 689–791.
Gormley, W. Paul. "The Legal Obligation of the International Community to Guarantee a Pure and Decent Environment: The Expansion of Human Rights Norms." *Georgetown International Environmental Law Review* 3 (1990): 85–116.
Government of Republic of South Africa and Others v. Grootboom, 11 BCLR 1169 (2000).
Gravelle, Ryan K. "Enforcing the Elusive: Environmental Rights in East European Constitutions." *Virginia Environmental Law Journal* 16, no. 4 (1997): 633–60.
Gregg, Samuel. "The Tragedy of Democracy: 'Rights', Tolerance and Moral 'Neutrality'." *Comment* (Winter 2000): 39–43.
Grootboom v. Oostenberg Municipality and Others, 3 BCLR 277 (2000).
Guerra and Others v. Italy, App. No. 14967/89, 26 Eur. H.R. Rep. 357 (1998).
Guha, Ramachandra. "Radical American Environmentalism and Wilderness Preservation: A Third World Critique." *Environmental Ethics* 11 (1989): 71–83.
Hague Declaration on the Environment. 28 ILM 1308 (1989).
Hamilton, Patrick Ryan. "Human Rights at the Doubling Point: Human Rights, the Environment and Climate Change in International Law." LLM diss., University of Toronto, 2006.
Hancock, Jan. *Environmental Human Rights: Power, Ethics and Law*. Aldershot: Ashgate, 2003.
Handl, Günther. "Human Rights and Protection of the Environment." In *Economic, Social, and Cultural Rights*, edited by Asbjørn Eide, Catarina Krause and Allan Rosas. Dordrecht/Boston/London: Martinus Nijhoff Publishers, 2001.
Handölsdalen Saami Village and Others v. Sweden, App. No. 39013/04 (2009).

Hardin, Garrett. "The Tragedy of the Commons." *Science* 162, no. 3859 (1968): 1243–48.
Hart, Vivien. "The Contagion of Rights: Constitutions as Carriers." In *Identity, Rights and Constitutional Transformation*, edited by Patrick J. Hanafin and Melissa S. Williams. Aldershot: Ashgate, 1999.
Hay, Peter. *Main Currents in Western Environmental Thought*. Sydney: UNSW Press, 2002.
Hayward, Tim. *Constitutional Environmental Rights*. New York: Oxford University Press, 2005.
Heffern, Rich. "The Fate of Nature Is Our Own." *National Catholic Reporter*, Oct. 8, 2004.
Henkin, Louis. *The Age of Rights*. New York: Columbia University Press, 1990.
Hillgenberg, Hartmut. "A Fresh Look at Soft Law." *EJIL* 10, no. 3 (1999): 499–515.
Hobbes, Thomas. "Leviathan." In *Oxford World's Classics Series*. New York: Oxford University Press, 1998.
Houck, Oliver A. "Light from the Trees: The Stories of Minors Oposa and the Russian Forest Cases." *Georgetown International Environmental Law Review* 19, no. 3 (2007): 321–73.
Howarth, Jane M. "Ecology: Modern Hero or Post-Modern Villain? From Scientific Trees to Phenomenological Wood." In *Ecologists and Ethical Judgements*, edited by N.S. Cooper and R.C.J. Carling. London: Chapman & Hall, 1996.
Howitt, Richard. *Rethinking Resource Management: Justice, Sustainability and Indigenous Peoples*. London: Routledge, 2001.
Ignatieff, Michael. "Human Rights as Politics and Idolatry." In *Human Rights as Politics and Idolatry*, edited by Amy Gutmann. Princeton: Princeton University Press, 2001.
International Covenant on Civil and Political Rights. Opened for signature 16 Dec. 1966, 999 UNTS 171 (Entered into force 23 Mar. 1976).
International Covenant on Economic, Social and Cultural Rights. Opened for signature 16 Dec. 1966, 933 UNTS 3 (Entered into force 3 Jan. 1976).
Inuit Circumpolar Conference (Canada). "Inuit Circumpolar Conference (ICC)." http://inuitcircumpolar.com/index.php?auto_slide=&ID=16&Lang=En&Parent_ID=&current_slide_num=.
——. "Inuit Petition to the Inter-American Commission on Human Rights to Oppose Climate Change Caused by the United States of America." http://inuitcircumpolar.com/index.php?ID=316&Lang=En.
IPCC Intergovernmental Panel on Climate Change. "IPCC Fourth Assessment Report: Climate Change 2007." http://www.ipcc.ch/ipccreports/assessments-reports.htm.
Ishay, Micheline R. *The History of Human Rights: From Ancient Times to the Globalization Era*. Berkeley: University of California Press, 2004.
IUCN Commission on Human Rights. *Draft International Covenant on Environment and Development*. 3rd ed. Gland and Cambridge: IUCN, 2004.
Johannesburg Declaration on Sustainable Development. UN Doc A/CONF.199/20 (2002).
Jon Inge Sirum et al. v. Essand Reindeer Pasturing District and Riast/Hylling Reindeer Pasturing District (Selbu Case), Norwegian Supreme Court serial number 4B/2001 (2001).
K.M. Chinnappa and T.N. Godavarman Thirumalpad v. Union of India and Others, 10 SCC 606 (2002).
Kennedy, David. *The International Human Rights Movement: Part of the Problem?* Sydney: The Federation Press, 2001.
Kent, George. *Freedom from Want: The Human Right to Adequate Food*. Washington, D.C.: GeorgeTown University Press, 2005.
Kirby, Justice Michael. "Human Rights: An Agenda for the Future." In *Rethinking Human Rights*, edited by Brian Galligan and Charles Sampford. Sydney: The Federation Press, 1997.
Klabbers, Jan. "The Redundancy of Soft Law." *Nordic Journal of International Law* 65 (1996): 167–82.
Koch, Ida Elisabeth. "Dichotomies, Trichotomies or Waves of Duties?" *Human Rights Law Review* 5, no. 1 (2005): 81–103.
Kravchenko, Svitlana. "The Aarhus Convention and Innovations in Compliance with Multilateral Environmental Agreements." *Colorado Journal of International Environmental Law and Policy* 18, no. 1 (2007): 1–50.
Kyrtatos v. Greece, App. No. 41666/98, 40 Eur. H. R. Rep. 16 (2003).
L.K.Koolwal v. State of Rajasthan and Others, AIR 1988 Raj.2 (1998).

Länsman et al. v. Finland, Communication No. 511/1992, UNCHR, UN Doc CCPR/C/52/D/511/1992 (1994).
Lauren, Paul Gordon. *The Evolution of International Human Rights: Visions Seen*. Philadelphia: University of Pennsylvania Press, 2003.
Ledewitz, Bruce. "Establishing a Federal Constitutional Right to a Healthy Environment in US and in Our Posterity." *Mississippi Law Journal* 68, no. 2 (1998–1999): 565–674.
Lee, John. "The Underlying Legal Theory to Support a Well-Defined Human Right to a Healthy Environment as a Principle of Customary International Law." *Columbia Journal of Environmental Law* 25 (2000): 283–339.
Leopold, Aldo. "The Land Ethic." In *An Environmental Law Anthology*, edited by Robert L. Fishman, Maxine I. Lipeles and Mark S. Squillace. Cincinnati, Ohio: Anderson Publishing Co., 1996.
Livingston, John. "Rightness or Rights?" *Osgoode Hall Law Journal* 22, no. 2 (1984): 309–21.
Lomborg, Bjørn. *The Skeptical Environmentalist: Measuring the Real State of the World*. Cambridge: Cambridge University Press, 2001.
Lopez Ostra v. Spain, App. No. 16798/90, 20 Eur. H. R. Rep. 277 (1994).
Lovejoy, Arthur O. *The Great Chain of Being: A Study of the History of an Idea*. Cambridge, MA: Harvard University Press, 1936.
M.C. Mehta v. Union of India and Others, 1991 SCC (2) 353 (1992).
Macrory, Richard. "Environmental Citizenship and the Law: Repairing the European Road." *Journal of Environmental Law* 8, no. 2 (1996): 219–35.
Malhotra, Rajeev. "Right to Development: Where Are We Today?" In *Reflections on the Right to Development*, edited by Arjun Sengupta, Archna Negi and Moushumi Basu. New Delhi: Sage Publications, 2005.
Marks, Stephen P. "Emerging Human Rights: A New Generation for the 1980s?" *Rutgers Law Review* 33, no. 2 (1980–1981): 435–53.
Mason, Michael. *Environmental Democracy: A Contextual Approach*. London: Earthscan, 1999.
Mathews, Freya. "Beyond a Materialist Environmentalism." *Nanjing Forestry University* (2005), http://www.freyamathews.com/default.asp?p=CR&id=4.
Maya Indigenous Communities v. Belize, Inter-Am Comm HR, Case No 12.053 (2004).
Mayagna (Sumo) Awas Tingni Community v. Nicaragua, Inter-Am Comm HR, Case No. 11.140 (2001).
McCormick, John. *The Global Environmental Movement: Reclaiming Paradise*. London: Belhaven Press, 1989.
Miller, Christopher. "Environmental Rights: European Fact or English Fiction?" *Journal of Law and Society* 22, no. 3 (1995): 374–97.
Miller, Jon. "Spinoza and the Concept of a Law of Nature." *History of Philosophy Quarterly* 20, no. 2 (2003): 257–76.
Minors Oposa et al. v. Secretary of the Environment and Natural Resources Fulgencio Factoran, 33 ILM 173 (1994).
Mizzoni, John. "St. Francis, Paul Taylor and Franciscan Biocentrism." *Environmental Ethics* 26 (2004): 41–56.
Morsink, Johannes. *The Universal Declaration of Human Rights: Origins, Drafting, and Intent*. Philadelphia: University of Pennsylvania, 2000.
Moser, Caroline, and Andy Norton. *To Claim Our Rights: Livelihood Security, Human Rights and Sustainable Development*. London: Overseas Development Institute, 2001.
Motala, Ziyad. "Socio-Economic Rights, Federalism and the Courts: Comparative Lessons for South Africa." *South African Law Journal* 112 (1995): 61–87.
Murphy, W. H. "Anthropocentrism: A Modern View." In *Environmental Ethics: Divergence and Convergence*, edited by Susan J. Armstrong and Richard G. Botzler. London: McGraw-Hill, 1993.
Naess, Arne. "Self-Realization: An Ecological Approach to Being in the World." *The Trumpeter* 4 (1987): 35–42.
——. "The Shallow and the Deep, Long-Range Ecology Movement." *Inquiry* 16 (1973): 95–100.
Nash, Roderick Frazier. *The Rights of Nature: A History of Environmental Ethics*. Wisconsin: University of Wisconsin Press, 1989.
Nash, Ronald. "The Case against Radical Environmentalism." Christian Research Institute, http://www.equip.org/free/DE403.htm.

Native Vegetation Act 2003 (NSW).

New Delhi Declaration of Principles of International Law Relating to Sustainable Development. Res 3/2002, 70th Conference of the International Law Association, New Delhi, 2–6 Apr. 2002.

Newman, Frank C., and Karel Vasak. "Civil and Political Rights." In *The International Dimensions of Human Rights*, edited by Karel Vasak. Paris: Greenwood Press, 1982.

Nickel, James W. "The Human Right to a Safe Environment: Philosophical Perspectives on Its Scope and Justification." *Yale Journal of international Law* 18 (1993): 281–95.

Norms on the Responsibilities of Transnational Corporations and Other Business Enterprises with Regard to Human Rights. UN Doc E/CN.4/Sub.2/2003/12/Rev.2 (2003).

Northcott, Michael S. *The Environment and Christian Ethics.* Cambridge: Cambridge University Press, 1996.

Nwobike, Justice C. "The African Commission on Human and Peoples' Rights and the Demystification of Second and Third Generation Rights under the African Charter: *Social and Economic Rights Action Center (SERAC) and the Center for Economic and Social Rights (CESR) v. Nigeria.*" *African Journal of Legal studies* 1 (2004–2005): 129–46.

Office of the High commissioner for Human Rights. "Human Rights Bodies." http://www.ohchr.org/EN/HRBodies/Pages/HumanRightsBodies.aspx.

Office of the United Nations High Commissioner for Human Rights. "Commission on Human Rights and General Assembly Resolutions Relating to Democracy and Governance 1998 – 2003." http://www.unhchr.ch/democracy/resolutions.htm.

Optional Protocol to the Convention on the Elimination of All Forms of Discrimination against Women. Opened for signature 10 Dec. 1999, UN Doc A/54/L4 (Entered into force 22 Dec. 2000).

Optional Protocol to the International Covenant on Civil and Political Rights. GA Res 2200A (XXI), UN GAOR Supp, UN Doc A/6316 (1966), 999 UNTS 302 (Entered into force Mar. 23, 1976).

Osmani, Siddiqur Rahman. "An Essay on the Human Rights Approach to Development." In *Reflections on the Right to Development*, edited by Arjun Sengupta, Archna Negi and Moushumi Basu. New Delhi: Sage Publications 2005.

Pallemaerts, Marc. "Introduction: Human Rights and Environmental Protection." In *Human Rights and the Environment*, edited by Dejeant-Pons Maguelonne and Marc Pallemaerts. Strasbourg: Council of Europe Publishing, 2002.

Pathak, R.S. "The Human Rights System as a Conceptual Framework for Environmental Law." In *Environmental Change and International Law: New Challenges and Dimensions*, edited by Edith Brown Weiss. Tokyo, Japan: United Nations University Press, 1992.

Pepper, David. *Modern Environmentalism.* New York: Routledge, 1996.

Percival, Robert V. ""Greening" The Constitution-Harmonizing Environmental and Constitutional Values." *Environmental Law* 32 (2002): 809–63.

Pevato, Paula M. "International Law and the Right to Environment: Encouraging Environmental Cooperation Via the International Protection of Human Rights." PhD diss., London School Economics and Political Science, 1998.

Plan of Implementation of the World Summit on Sustainable Development. UN Doc A/CONF.199/20 (2002).

Popovic, Neil A. F. "In Pursuit of Environmental Human Rights: Commentary on the Draft Declaration of Principles of Human Rights and the Environment." *Columbia Human Rights Law Review* 27 (1996): 487–620.

Popovski, Vesselin. "Sovereignty as Duty to Protect Human Rights." *UN Chronicle* 41, no. 4 (2004): 16–18.

Proclamation of Teheran. Final Act of the International Conference on Human Rights, Teheran, UN Doc A/CONF. 32/41 (1968).

Pulp Mills on the River Uruguay (Argentine v. Uruguay), ICJ Rep 135 (2006).

Quicho, Rodolfo Ferdinand N. *Watching the Trees Grow: New Perspectives on the Standing to Sue.* Manila: IUCN-CEL Philippine Group, 1995.

Rajagopal, Balakrishnan. "Counter-Hegemonic International Law: Rethinking Human Rights and Development as a Third World Strategy" In *International Law and the Third World: Reshaping Justice* edited by Richard Falk, Balakrishnan Rajagopal and Jacqueline Stevens. London/New York: Routledge-Cavendish, 2008.

Ramlogan, Rajendra. "The Environment and International Law: Rethinking the Traditional Approach." *Vermont Journal of Environmental Law* (2001–2002), http://www.vjel.org/journal/VJEL10008.html.

Register of International Treaties and Other Agreements in the Field of the Environment. UN Doc UNEP/Env.Law/2005/3 (2005).

Report of the Expert Group Meeting on Identification of Principles of International Law for Sustainable Development. United Nations Commission on Sustainable Development, UN CSD 4th Session (1996).

Report of the Joint OHCHR-UNEP Seminar on Human Rights and the Environment 16 Jan. 2002. UN Doc E/CN.4/2002/WP.7 (2002).

Report of the Special Rapporteur on the Right to Food. Jean Ziegler, UN Doc A/61/306 (2006).

Report of the Special Rapporteur on the Situation of Human Rights and Fundamental Freedoms of Indigenous People. Rodolfo Stavenhagen, UN Doc A/HRC/4/32 (2007).

Report of the Special Rapporteur on the Situation of Human Rights and Fundamental Freedoms of Indigenous People: Addendum: Mission to the Philippines. Rodolfo Stavenhagen, UN Doc E/CN.4/2003/90/Add.3 (2003).

Report of the Special Rapporteur: Mission to Mozambique. Paul Hunt, UN Doc E/CN.4/2005/51/Add.2 (2005).

Report of the Special Rapporteur: Mission to Peru. Paul Hunt, E/CN.4/2005/51/Add.3 (2005).

Report of the Special Rapporteur: The Right of Everyone to the Enjoyment of the Highest Attainable Standard of Physical and Mental Health. Paul Hunt, UN Doc E/CN.4/2003/58 (2003).

Report of the United Nations High Commissioner for Human Rights on the Scope and Content of the Relevant Human Rights Obligations Related to Equitable Access to Safe Driving Water and Sanitation under International Human Rights Instruments. UNHRC, 6th sess, UN Doc A/HRC/6/3 (2007).

Resolution on Draft International Covenant on Human Rights and Measures of Implementation: Future Work of the Commission on Human Rights. GA Res 421, UN GAOR, 5th sess, 317th plen mtg, UN Doc A/Res/421 (1950).

Resolution on Permanent Sovereignty over Natural Resources. GA Res 1803(XVII), UN GAOR Supp No 17, UN Doc A/5217 (1962).

Resolution on the Preparation of Two Draft International Covenants on Human Rights. GA Res 543, UN GAOR, 6th sess, 375th plen mtg, UN doc A/Res/543 (1952).

Resolution on the Right to Development. CHR Res 1998/24, UN ESCOR Supp No 3, 58th mtg, UN Doc E/CN.4/1998/24 (1998).

Revista Inter-Forum. "*Final Declaration on Defeating Corruption through Integrity, Transparency and Accountability* (the Second Global Forum on Fighting Corruption, Hosted by the Dutch Government and Co-Sponsored by the United States, Held in May 2001 at the Hague, Netherlands)." http://www.revistainterforum.com/english/articles/121701artprin_en.html.

Rich, Ronald. "The Right to Development as an Emerging Human Right." *Virginia Journal of International Law* 23 (1982–1983): 287–328.

Robinson, Mary. "Civil Society Workshop on Human Rights, Sustainable Development and Environmental Protection (Speech Delivered at the World Summit on Sustainable Development, Johannesburg, South Africa, 1 Sept. 2002)." http://www.unhchr.ch/huricane/huricane.nsf/0/A551686D4B5905D0C1256C28002BF3D6?opendocument.

Rodriguez-Rivera, Luis E. "Is the Human Right to Environment Recognized under International Law? It Depends on the Source." *Colorado Journal of International Environmental Law and Policy* 12 (2001): 1–48.

Rogers, Peter P., Kazi F. Jalal, and John A. Boyd. *An Introduction to Sustainable Development*. London: Earthscan, 2008.

Rolston, Holmes. *Environmental Ethics: Duties to and Values in the Natural World*. Philadelphia: Temple University Press, 1988.

Rosas, Allan. "So-Called Rights of the Third Generation." In *Economic, Social, and Cultural Rights*, edited by Asbjørn Eide, Catarina Krause and Allan Rosas. Dordrecht/Boston/London: Martinus Nijhoff Publishers, 1995.

Rosas, Allan, and Martin Scheinin. "Implementation Mechanisms and Remedies." In *Economic, Social and Cultural Rights*, edited by Allan Rosas, Eide Asbjørn and Catarina Krause. Dordrecht/Boston/London: Martinus Nijhoff Publishers, 1995.

Rowe, J. Stan. "What on Earth Is Environment?" *The Trumpeter* 6, no. 4 (1989): 123–26.

Rowe, Stan. "From Shallow to Deep Ecological Philosophy." *The Trumpeter* 13, no. 1 (1996): 26–31.
Sachs, Hon. Mr. Justice Albie. "Enforcing Socio-Economic Rights." In *Sustainable Justice: Reconciling Economic, Social and Environmental Law*, edited by Marie-Claire Cordonier Segger and C.G. Weeramantry. Dordrecht/Boston/London: Martinus Nijhoff Publishers, 2005.
Sachs, Wolfgang. *Planet Dialectics*. London: Zed Books, 1999.
Sadeleer, Nicholas de. *Environmental Principles: From Political Slogans to Legal Rules*. New York: Oxford University Press, 2002.
Salman, Salman M.A., and Siobhán McInerney-Lankford. *The Human Right to Water: Legal and Policy Dimensions*. Washington, D.C.: The World Bank, 2004.
Sampford, Charles. "The Four Dimensions of Rights." In *Rethinking Human Rights*, edited by Brian Galligan and Charles Sampford. Sydney: The Federation Press, 1997.
Sands, Philippe. "International Courts and the Application of the Concept of "Sustainable Development"." In *Law and Development: Facing Complexity in the 21st Century: Essays in Honour of Peter Slinn*, edited by John Hatchard and Amanda Perry-Kessaris. Newport, Australia: Cavendish Publishing, 2003.
Sathe, S. P. "Judicial Activism: The Indian Experience." *Washington University Journal of Law and Policy* 6 (2001): 29–107.
Sawhoyamaxa Indigenous Community v. Paraguay, 146 Inter-Am Ct HR (ser c) (2006).
Sax, Joseph L. "The Public Trust Doctrine in Natural Resource Law: Effective Judicial Intervention." *Michigan Law Review* 68 (1970): 471–566.
Scanlon, John, Angela Cassar, and Noémi Nemes. "Water as a Human Right?" Paper presented at the 7th International Conference on Environmental Law: Law for a Green Planet Institute, Sao Paulo, Brazil, 2–5 June 2003.
Schlosser, Stephen. "Only a God Can Save Us: Disabling the Rational Subject in Heidegger's Reactionary Modernism." *Heythrop Journal* 36, no. 2 (1995): 190–201.
Scott, Craig. "The Interdependence and Permeability of Human Rights Norms: Towards a Partial Fusion of the International Conventions on Human Rights." *Osgoode Hall Law Journal* 27 (1989): 769–878.
Segger, Marie-Claire Cordonier, and Ashfaq Khalfan. *Sustainable Development Law: Principles, Practices and Prospects*. New York: Oxford University Press, 2004.
Sen, Amartya. *Development as Freedom*. New York: Oxford University Press, 2001.
——. "Human Rights and Development." In *Development as a Human Right: Legal, Political, and Economic Dimensions*, edited by Bård A. Andreassen and Stephen P. Marks. London: Harvard School of Public Health, 2006.
Sengupta, Arjun. "On the Theory and Practice of the Right to Development." In *Development as a Human Right: Legal, Political, and Economic Dimensions*, edited by Bård A. Andreassen and Stephen P. Marks. Boston: Harvard School of Public Health, 2006.
Shelton, Dinah. "Human Rights and the Environment: Jurisprudence of Human Rights Bodies." Paper presented at the Joint UNEP-OHCHR Expert Seminar on Human Rights and the Environment, Geneva, 14–16 Jan. 2002.
——. "Normative Hierarchy in International Law." *American Journal of International Law* 100 (2006): 291–323.
——. "The Environmental Jurisprudence of International Human Rights Tribunals." In *Linking Human Rights and the Environment*, edited by Romina Picolotti and Jorge Daniel Taillant. Tucson, Arizona: The University of Arizona Press, 2003.
——. "What Happened in Rio to Human Rights?" *Yearbook of International Environmental Law* 3 (1992): 75–93.
Shiva, Vandana. *Earth Democracy*. Cambridge: South End Press, 2005.
Shue, Henry. *Basic Rights: Subsistence, Affluence, and US Foreign Policy*. Princeton: Princeton University Press, 1980.
Sierra Club v. Morton, 405 U.S. 727 (1972).
Singer, Peter. *Animal Liberation*. 2nd ed. London: Pimlico, 1995.
Sirchin-The Free Encyclopaedia. "Environment: Definition." http://www.science.sirchin.com/?topic:environment.
Soveroski, Marie. "Environment Rights versus Environmental Wrongs: Forum over Substance?" *RECIEL* 16, no. 3 (2007): 261–73.

Stanford Encyclopaedia of Philosophy. "Human Rights." http://plato.stanford.edu/entries/rights-human/.
Statute of the International Court of Justice. 3 Bevans 1179; 59 Stat. 1031; T.S. 993; 39 AJIL Supp. 215 (1945).
Stone, Christopher D. "Should Trees Have Standing? Toward Legal Rights for Natural Objects." *Southern California Law Review* 45 (1972): 450–501.
Subhash Kumar v. State of Bihar, AIR 1991 SC 420 (1991).
Symonides, Janusz. "The Human Right to a Clean, Balanced and Protected Environment." *International Journal of Legal Information* 20 (1992): 24–39.
Szabo, Imre. "Historical Foundations of Human Rights and Subsequent Developments." In *The International Dimensions of Human Rights*, edited by Karel Vasak. Paris: Greenwood Press, 1982.
Tauira and 18 Others v. France, App. No. 28204/95, 83-B Eur Comm HR 112 (1995).
Taxed Lapp Mountain Case, Swedish Supreme Court NJA (1981).
Tay, Alice Erh-Soon. "Human Rights Problems: Moral, Political, Philosophical." In *Rethinking Human Rights*, edited by Brian Galligan and Charles Sampford. Sydney: The Federation Press, 1997.
Taylor, Prudence E. "From Environmental to Ecological Human Rights: A New Dynamic in International Law?" *Georgetown International Environmental Law Review* 10 (1998): 278–325.
Thamilmaran, V. T. *Human Rights in Third World Perspective*. New Delhi: Har-Anand Publications, 1992.
The 1994 Draft Declaration of Principles on Human Rights and the Environment. UN Doc E/CN.4/Sub.2/1994/9, Annex I (1994).
The Case Against Shell. "Wiwa v. Shell: Victory Settlement!" http://wiwavshell.org/wiwa-v-shell-victory-settlement/.
The Ecologically Sustainable Development Steering Committee. "National Strategy for Ecologically Sustainable Development." Australian Government, Department of the Environment and Heritage, http://www.deh.gov.au/esd/national/nsesd/strategy/intro.html#WIESD.
The International Work Group for Indigenous Affairs (IWGIA). *The Indigenous World 2007*. Copenhagen: IWGIA, 2007.
The Limburg Principles on the Implementation of the International Covenant on Economic, Social and Cultural Rights. UN ESCOR, 4th Comm, 43rd sess, Annex, UN Doc. E/CN.4/1987/17(1987).
The Report on Human Rights Situation in Ecuador. Inter-American Commission on Human Rights, OEA/Ser.L/V/II.96, Doc.10 rev.1(1997).
The Social and Economic Rights Action Center and the Center for Economic and Social Rights v. Nigeria (SERAC Case), Communication 155/96, ACHPR/COMM/A044/1 (2002).
The UN Framework Convention on Climate Change. Opened for signature 4 June 1992, 31 ILM 849 (Entered into force 21 Mar. 1994).
The World Commission on Environment and Development. *Our Common Future*. Oxford: Oxford University Press, 1987.
Thinkexist.com. "George Perkins Quotes." http://en.thinkexist.com/quotes/george_perkins/.
Thomas, Caroline. "Poverty, Development, and Hunger." In *The Globalization of World Politics*, edited by John Baylis, Steve Smith and Patricia Owens. New York: Oxford University Press, 2008.
Thorme, Melissa. "Establishing Environment as a Human Right." *Denver Journal of International Law & Policy* 19 (1990–1991): 301–42.
Thornberry, Patrick. *Indigenous Peoples and Human Rights*. New York: Juris Publishing, 2002.
Tomalin, Emma. "The Limitations of Religious Environmentalism for India." *Worldviews: Global Religions, Culture, and Ecology* 6, no. 1 (2002): 12–30.
Transparency International. "2007 Transparency International Corruption Perceptions Index." http://www.transparency.org/policy_research/surveys_indices/cpi/2007.
Tribe, Laurence H. "Ways Not to Think About Plastic Trees: New Foundations for Environmental Law." *The Yale Law Journal* 83, no. 7 (1974): 1315–48.
UN Conference on Environment and Development: Rio Declaration on Environment and Development. UN Doc A/CONF.151/26 (Vol. I) (1992).

UN Department of Economic and Social Affairs: Division for Sustainable Development. "Agenda 21." http://www.un.org/esa/dsd/agenda21/res_agenda21_23.shtml.

——. "Commission on Sustainable Development (CSD)." http://www.un.org/esa/sustdev/csd/aboutCsd.htm.

UN World Charter for Nature. GA Res 37/7, UN GAOR, 37th sess, 48th plen mtg, UN Doc A/Res/37/7 (1982).

UNECE. "Aarhus Convention: Convention on Access to Information, Public Participation in Decision-Making and Access to Justice in Environmental Matters." http://www.unece.org/env/pp/.

UNICEF. "Child Alert: Crisis in the Horn of Africa: A Report on the Impact of Drought on Children." http://www.unicef.org/infobycountry/files/Child_Alert_HoA_FINAL.pdf.

United Nations. "Africa and the Millennium Development Goals: 2007 Update." http://www.un.org/millenniumgoals/docs/MDGafrica07.pdf.

United Nations Convention against Corruption. GA Res 58/4, UN GAOR, 58th sess, UN Doc A/RES/58/4 (2003) (Entered into force 14 Dec. 2005).

United Nations Declaration on the Rights of Indigenous Peoples. GA Res, UN GAOR, 61st sess, UN Doc A/61/L.67 (2007).

United Nations Development Programme (UNDP). "Goal 7: Ensure Environmental Sustainability." http://www.undp.org/mdg/goal7.shtml.

——. "Human Development Report 2000: Human Rights and Human Development." http://hdr.undp.org/en/reports/global/hdr2006/.

——. "Human Development Report 2005: International Cooperation at a Crossroads: Aid, Trade and Security in an Unequal World." http://hdr.undp.org/en/reports/global/hdr2005/.

——. "Human Development Report 2006: Beyond Scarcity: Power, Poverty and the Global Water Crisis." http://hdr.undp.org/en/reports/global/hdr2006/.

United Nations Millennium Declaration. GA Res 55/2, UN GAOR, 55th sess, 8th plen mtg, UN Doc A/55/L.2 (2000).

United Nations Permanent Forum on Indigenous Issues UNPFII. "About UNPFII and a Brief History of Indigenous Peoples and the International System." http://www.un.org/esa/socdev/unpfii/en/history.html.

United States-Import Prohibition of Certain Shrimp and Shrimp Products, WTO Doc WT/DS58/AB/R, AB-1998-4 (1998) (Report of the Appellate Body).

Universal Declaration of Human Rights. GA Res 217A (III), UN GAOR, UN Doc A/810 (1948).

University of Minnesota: Human Rights Resource Center. "Justiciability of ESC Rights-the Indian Experience." http://www1.umn.edu/humanrts/edumat/IHRIP/circle/justiciability.htm.

Van der Linde, Morné, and Lirette Louw. "Considering the Interpretation and Implementation of Article 24 of the African Charter on Human and Peoples' Rights in Light of the SERAC Communication." *African Human Rights Law Journal* 3, no. 1 (2003): 167–87.

Vasak, Karel. "Pour Une Troisième Génération Des Droits De L'homme." In *ÉTudes Et Essais Sur Le Droit International Humanitaire Et Sur Les Principes De La Croix-Rouge En L'honneur De Jean Pictet* (Comité International de la Croix-Rouge 1984).

Veit, Peter G., and Catherine Benson. "When Parks and People Collide." *Human Rights Dialogue* 2, no. 11 (Spring 2004): 13.

Vienna Declaration and Programme of Action: Report of the World Conference on Human Rights. UN Doc A/CONF.157/23 (1993).

Wagner, Martin. "The Right to Be Cold: Global Warming and Human Rights." In *Human Rights 2007, the Year in Review*, edited by Marius Smith and Erica Contini: Castan Centre for Human Rights Law, Monash University, 2008.

Wang, Jiangyu. "China and the Universal Human Rights Standards." *Syracuse Journal of International Law and Commerce* 29 (2001–2002): 135–58.

Warren, Mary Anne. "The Rights of the Nonhuman World." In *Environmental Philosophy: A Collection of Readings*, edited by Robert Elliott and Arran Gare. St. Lucia, Brisbane: University of Queensland Press, 1983.

Webster v. Reproductive Health Services, 492 U.S. 490 (1989).

Weeramantry, H.E. Judge Christopher G. "Sustainable Development: An Ancient Concept Recently Revived (Speech Delivered at the Global Judges Symposium on Sustainable Development and the Role of Law, Colombo, 4–5 July 1997)." United Nations Environment Programme (UNEP), http://www.unep.org/law/symposium/Speeches.htm.

Wellman, Carl. "Solidarity, the Individual and Human Rights." *Human Rights Quarterly* 22, no. 3 (2000): 639–57.
Weston, Anthony. "Multicentrism: A Manifesto." *Environmental Ethics* 26 (2004): 25–39.
White, Lynn, Jr. "The Historical Roots of Our Ecologic Crisis." In *An Environmental Law Anthology*, edited by Robert L. Fishman, Maxine I. Lipeles and Mark S. Squillace. Cincinnati, Ohio: Anderson Publishing Co., 1996.
Wikiquote. "Ingrid Newkirk." http://en.wikiquote.org/wiki/Ingrid_Newkirk.
WLP Women's Learning Partnership. "Shadow Reports: Holding Governments Accountable for Women's Human Rights." http://www.learningpartnership.org/news/enews/2003/iss4/shadow.
Wolfe, Karrie A. "Greening the International Human Rights Sphere? An Examination of Environmental Rights and the Draft Declaration of Principles on Human Rights and the Environment." *Journal of Environmental Law and Practice* 13 (2003): 109.
World Commission on Dams. *Dams and Development: A New Framework for Decision-Making*. London: Earthscan, 2000.
World Rainforest Movement. "The Future of Tropical Forests." http://www.flonnet.com/fl2012/stories/20030620000207100.htm.
World Resources Institute. "Partnership for Principle 10." http://www.wri.org/governance/project_description2.cfm?pid=133.
World Trade Organization. "India etc versus US: 'Shrimp-Turtle'." http://www.wto.org/english/tratop_e/envir_e/edis08_e.htm.
World Wildlife Fund International (WWF), and Global Footprint Network. "Living Planet Report 2006." http://assets.panda.org/downloads/living_planet_report.pdf.
Wright, Shelley. *International Human Rights, Decolonization and Globalization*. London: Routledge, 2001.
X and Y v. Federal Republic of Germany, 15 Eur Comm HR 161 (1976).
Xanthaki, Alexandra. *Indigenous Rights and United Nations Standards: Self-Determination, Culture and Land*. Cambridge: Cambridge University Press, 2007.
Yanomami Community v. Brazil, Inter-Am Comm HR, Brazil, Resolution No. 12/85, Case No. 7615 (1985).
Yourow, Howard Charles. "The Margin of Appreciation Doctrine in the Dynamics of European Human Rights Jurisprudence." *Connecticut Journal of International Law* 3 (1987–1988): 111–59.
Zaharchenko, Tatiana R., and Gretta Goldenman. "Accountability in Governance: The Challenge of Implementing the Aarhus Convention in Eastern Europe and Central Asia." *International Environmental Agreements: Politics, Law and Economics* 4, no. 3 (2004): 229–51.

INDEX

www.ingramcontent.com/pod-product-compliance
Ingram Content Group UK Ltd.
Pitfield, Milton Keynes, MK11 3LW, UK
UKHW021031041026
15470UKWH00013B/1308

9 789004 188648